Street Sex Workers' Discourse

Incorporating the voices and insights of street sex workers through personal interviews, this monograph argues that the material conditions of people involved in street economies—the physical environments they live in and their effects on their bodies, identities, and spirits—are represented, reproduced, and entrenched in the language surrounding their work. As an ethnographic case study of a local system that can be extrapolated to other subcultures and the construction of identities, this book disrupts some of the more prevalent academic and lay understandings about street prostitution by providing a thorough analysis of the material conditions surrounding street work and their connection to discourse. McCracken offers an explanation of how constructions can be made differently in order to achieve representations that are generated by the marginalized populations themselves, while examining more closely society's role in this marginalization.

Jill McCracken is an Assistant Professor at the University of South Florida St. Petersburg where she researches and teaches the rhetoric of marginalized communities, in particular that of sex work/trafficking; public policy; gender studies; civic engagement; and communication across the curriculum. Her research appears in *Wagadu* (2011) and the *Community Literacy Journal* (2010).

Routledge Research in Gender and Society

For a full list of titles in this series please visit www.routledge.com.

2 **Women's Work and Wages**
 Edited by Inga Persson and Christina Jonung

3 **Rethinking Households**
 An Atomistic Perspective on European Living Arrangements
 Michel Verdon

4 **Gender, Welfare State and the Market**
 Thomas P. Boje and Arnlaug Leira

5 **Gender, Economy and Culture in the European Union**
 Simon Duncan and Birgit Pfau Effinger

6 **Body, Femininity and Nationalism**
 Girls in the German Youth Movement 1900-1934
 Marion E. P. de Ras

7 **Women and the Labour-Market**
 Self-employment as a Route to Economic Independence
 Vani Borooah and Mark Hart

8 **Victoria's Daughters**
 The Schooling of Girls in Britain and Ireland 1850–1914
 Jane McDermid and Paula Coonerty

9 **Homosexuality, Law and Resistance**
 Derek McGhee

10 **Sex Differences in Labor Markets**
 David Neumark

11 **Women, Activism and Social Change**
 Edited by Maja Mikula

12 **The Gender of Democracy**
 Citizenship and Gendered Subjectivity
 Maro Pantelidou Maloutas

13 **Female Homosexuality in the Middle East**
 Histories and Representations
 Samar Habib

14 **Global Empowerment of Women**
 Responses to Globalization and Politicized Religions
 Edited by Carolyn M. Elliott

15 **Child Abuse, Gender and Society**
 Jackie Turton

16 **Gendering Global Transformations**
 Gender, Culture, Race, and Identity
 Edited by Chima J Korieh and Philomina Ihejirika-Okeke

17 **Gender, Race and National Identity**
 Nations of Flesh and Blood
 Jackie Hogan

18 **Intimate Citizenships**
Gender, Sexualities, Politics
Elżbieta H. Oleksy

19 **A Philosophical Investigation of Rape**
The Making and Unmaking of the Feminine Self
Louise du Toit

20 **Migrant Men**
Critical Studies of Masculinities and the Migration Experience
Edited by Mike Donaldson, Raymond Hibbins, Richard Howson and Bob Pease

21 **Theorizing Sexual Violence**
Edited by Renée J. Heberle and Victoria Grace

22 **Inclusive Masculinity**
The Changing Nature of Masculinities
Eric Anderson

23 **Understanding Non-Monogamies**
Edited by Meg Barker and Darren Langdridge

24 **Transgender Identities**
Towards a Social Analysis of Gender Diversity
Edited by Sally Hines and Tam Sanger

25 **The Cultural Politics of Female Sexuality in South Africa**
Henriette Gunkel

26 **Migration, Domestic Work and Affect**
A Decolonial Approach on Value and the Feminization of Labor
Encarnación Gutiérrez-Rodríguez

27 **Overcoming Objectification**
A Carnal Ethics
Ann J. Cahill

28 **Intimate Partner Violence in LGBTQ Lives**
Edited by Janice L. Ristock

29 **Contesting the Politics of Genocidal Rape**
Affirming the Dignity of the Vulnerable Body
Debra B. Bergoffen

30 **Transnational Migration, Media and Identity of Asian Women**
Diasporic Daughters
Youna Kim

31 **Feminist Solidarity at the Crossroads**
Intersectional Women's Studies for Transracial Alliance
Edited by Kim Marie Vaz and Gary L. Lemons

32 **Victims, Gender and Jouissance**
Victoria Grace

33 **Gender, Development and Environmental Governance**
Theorizing Connections
Seema Arora-Jonsson

34 **Street Sex Workers' Discourse**
Realizing Material Change Through Agential Choice
Jill McCracken

Street Sex Workers' Discourse
Realizing Material Change
Through Agential Choice

Jill McCracken

LONDON AND NEW YORK

First published 2013
by Routledge
711 Third Avenue, New York, NY 10017

Simultaneously published in the UK
by Routledge
2 Park Square, Milton Park, Abingdon, Oxfordshire OX14 4RN

Routledge is an imprint of the Taylor and Francis Group, an informa business

First issued in paperback 2015

© 2013 Taylor & Francis

The right of Jill McCracken to be identified as author of this work has been asserted in accordance with sections 77 and 78 of the Copyright, Designs and Patents Act 1988.

All rights reserved. No part of this book may be reprinted or reproduced or utilised in any form or by any electronic, mechanical, or other means, now known or hereafter invented, including photocopying and recording, or in any information storage or retrieval system, without permission in writing from the publishers.

Trademark Notice: Product or corporate names may be trademarks or registered trademarks, and are used only for identification and explanation without intent to infringe.

Library of Congress Cataloging-in-Publication Data
McCracken, Jill.
 Street sex workers' discourse : realizing material change through agential choice / by Jill McCracken. — 1st Edition.
   pages cm. — (Routledge research in gender and society ; 34)
 Includes bibliographical references and index.
 1. Language and culture. 2. Rhetoric—Social aspects. 3. Semantics—Social aspects. I. Title.
 P35.M33 2013
 306.74—dc23
 2012040733

ISBN 978-0-415-88707-6 (hbk)
ISBN 978-1-138-95251-5 (pbk)
ISBN 978-0-203-38499-2 (ebk)

Typeset in Sabon
by IBT Global.

In memory of T . . . thank you for sharing yourself with us. I will never forget you.

And for all my participants . . . thank you for trusting me and sharing your stories.

Contents

List of Figures		xi
Note on the Transcriptions		xiii
Preface: Telling Our Stories about Street-Based Sex Work		xv
Acknowledgments		xxxv
1	Quotidian Rhetoric Creates Meaning through Collage	1
2	Who is the Victim: The Neighborhood or the Woman?	14
3	Is She a Criminal, a Victim, or a Victim of the Criminal Justice System?	55
4	"An Opportunity to Change": Responsibility and Choice	83
5	Systemic Violence Perpetuates Victim Status	98
6	Creating Agential Choice from Cages of Oppression	132
Appendix A: Participants		167
Appendix B: Research Process and Layers of Data		191
Appendix C: Number of Times Terms Included in Newspaper and Participant Interviews Corpora		209
Appendix D: Interview Materials		211
Notes		217
References		227
Index		237

Figures

P.1	Body.	xxx
P.2	Problems and solutions thematically represented.	xxxi
1.1	Influential and fixed material.	4
1.2	Duck-Rabbit ambiguous image.	6
2.1	Who is the victim?	24
2.2	Problems and solutions related to woman as victim.	26
2.3	Problems and solutions surrounding substance use and abuse.	41
3.1	Criminalization of prostitution impacts safety.	69
3.2	Problems and solutions related to criminalization of prostitution.	81
4.1	Trajectory from victim status to taking responsibility.	94
5.1	Control = Safety.	113
5.2	Language as a problem and solution.	117
5.3	Problems related to stigma.	119
5.4	Victim status versus agential choice.	129
6.1	Victim status reinforces problems.	138
6.2	Profiles.	160
A.1	Recruitment flier.	211

Note on the Transcriptions

The following conventions are used in the transcripts presented throughout this book:

... Indicates either a short pause (when occurring within utterances) or a lengthened sound (when occurring at the end of a turn)

[ ] Author's explanatory comments, contextual notes, and nonverbal actions

( ) Material not audible on the tape

[...] A break in or material omitted from the transcript

Preface
Telling Our Stories: Street-Based Sex Work

> My story is only told when it's needed to be told, because of people looking down on me. [. . .] I want to help somebody. And if one of my words, one thing that I share with somebody will be planted in their brain or their memory, then maybe they'll always remember it and they'll always come back, then what I've done is okay, by sharing my story.
> —Sandy[1]

> [W]e need to develop the capacity to listen to these stories without reducing them to competitors for the status of Truth. We need to listen for meaning rather than just "fact," to ask why a story is told in this way, how the location of the speaker shapes the tale, how the position of the audience affects what is heard, and to carefully consider what is at stake politically, personally, and strategically in invoking this particular version at this moment in this context.
>
> —Wendy Chapkis, *Live Sex Acts*, 1997

> So when you are listening to somebody, completely, attentively, then you are listening not only to the words, but also to the feeling of what is being conveyed, to the whole of it, not part of it.
> —Jiddu Krishnamurti, Theosophist Philosopher

We all tell stories in order to make sense of our lives. They are often comprised of problems created by antagonists, or villains, and solved by protagonists, or heroes. The way a problem is conceptualized directly impacts what solutions become available and how they are implemented. The storyteller may even find herself shaping reality into these preconceived categories because they make "sense" to the reader. My participants—women who participate in exchanges of sex for money on or near the street—told me their stories. Most mentioned they enjoyed sharing their lives with me, even though it was, at times, painful and difficult. Many hoped if, by telling their stories, more information about street-based sex work were made available, specifically about individual women's lives, then circumstances could be different for others. Their stories create the framework for this book, manifesting its depth and direction.

From 2005 through 2007, I researched street-based sex work in an undisclosed city in the southwest United States, referred to as Nemez in this text.[2] In order to examine a broad range of language use related to street-based sex work and its influence on surrounding material conditions, I focused on three distinct sites of analysis: (1) The language used by women who exchange sex for money in heterosexual work environments; (2) The language used by people in leadership roles, or public figures, who work with women participating in these exchanges; and (3) Newspaper articles about street-based sex work over a ten-year period.[3] Material conditions include the physical environments in which women who exchange sex for money or drugs live and the potential effects on their bodies, identities, and spirits. Current perceptions contribute to the constructions of problems and solutions surrounding street-based sex work and therefore influence the material conditions surrounding people who participate in these exchanges. Therefore, when the "problem" of street-based sex work is understood differently, different material conditions can and do emerge.

Drawing on the three primary newspapers in the Nemez community—*The Nemez Daily*, *The Nemez Weekly*, and *The State's Daily News*—I analyzed a decade of newspaper articles (1997–2006, the time period immediately preceding and during my ethnographic research) in order to offer the most comprehensive viewpoint of how sex work is framed and represented. My initial library search for terms commonly associated with sex work—sex work, sex worker(s), prostitute(s), and prostitution—led me to scan/read approximately thirteen hundred (1,300) articles. Because my goal was to examine how local sex work, specifically street-based sex work, is represented and discussed in the community, throughout my searches and subsequent analysis I included only the articles that specifically mentioned local sex work and issues related to sex work in the community. Within my corpus there were a total of 490 articles that mentioned or were specifically about local sex work. The newspaper articles related specifically to sex work include articles, news stories, commentaries, and letters to the editor.

The second site of my analysis includes interviews with twenty people in leadership roles, what I term *public figures*, who are directly involved with street-based sex work in Nemez. These participants include police officers, social service agents, sex worker rights activists, neighborhood association leaders, medical professionals, and academics.

I then incorporated this information into my interviews with seventeen women who identified as current or recent participants in exchanging sex for money or drugs. I intentionally waited to interview the women until I had completed the analysis of the newspaper articles and interviews with public figures in order to triangulate my analysis of these two sites with my participants. By triangulation, I mean I made this information central to my conversations and interviews with the women in order to better understand how they identify themselves and understand and explain the material conditions of their lives. This triangulation allowed for an analysis of "outsider" discourse about street-based sex work, i.e., the public figure and newspaper discourse, from the perspectives of those most closely associated with it. I chose this progression in order to create a proximal analysis whereby I focused on the layer furthest from the women who exchange sex for money or drugs (presented in the newspapers) and then moved toward the center by analyzing the language used to talk about street-based sex work by the people with the most intimate knowledge of this work.[4] As Sociologist Stéphanie Wahab (2004) emphasizes in "Tricks of the Trade," "Because sex workers have so frequently been denied the validity of their statements by researchers and service providers, the intention is for the narratives to speak by themselves, for themselves" (p. 145). I include the women's stories as well as extensive excerpts of the interviews to contextualize their lives and perspectives.[5]

In addition to the newspaper analysis and interviews with public figures and women who exchange sex, my multi-sited ethnography also consisted of participant observation in a variety of sex industry environments. I spent substantial time with the people I interviewed, integrating myself into their discursive circles and communities in order to understand the language used to describe their lives.

As I present information about the women's positionality in society throughout my analysis, let me first offer my own "situated knowledge" (Haraway 1988) as a white, feminist, middle-class, single mother in her early forties. When I began this research, I was a single, graduate student in her mid-thirties, and although well versed in theory, I knew much less about the practical realities of sex work at any level. I do not pretend I was not viewed as an outsider, at least initially, by most of my participants. It was through working and spending time with these women, some more than others, I created an environment that contributed to my understanding of the language they and others use to describe their lives. My volunteer and paid work at *Casa Segura*[6] and other social service agencies in Nemez allowed me opportunities to develop a rich understanding of street-based sex work and related institutions on a daily basis. Throughout my research, I also became involved in many sex worker rights organizations as a member and a leader, and now also identify as a sex worker rights advocate. I agree fully with Laura Agustín (2005b) when she argues: "researchers need to be prepared to confront their own preconceived ideas, their own "outsider" status and the structures of power they inevitably participate in. Reflexivity on the part of the researcher will be an essential element of the work, a continual questioning of where moral reactions come from and a humble attempt to leave them aside" (p. 627). I document my own attempts at this reflexivity and what I have learned about commercial sex , as well as myself, throughout.

This book's framework emerged from my participants' explanations of the problems and solutions surrounding street-based sex work. Challenged with the complexity of separating qualitative data into discrete, fixed categories of chapters, subtitles, and even the definitions of problems and solutions, my analyses offers a picture of the material conditions surrounding street-based sex work and how they influence an individual's power and agency as well as the culture that concurrently creates, supports, and works to dismantle street-based sex work.

Sex work, the industry surrounding the exchange of sexual services for money or other gain, is complex and riddled with contradictions. Patience and a skeptical suspension of preconceived beliefs therefore proves helpful. My research and analysis confronts the tensions between dichotomies: good/bad, moral/immoral, right/wrong, member/outsider, lawful/criminal, agent/victim, and many others. Being mindful of these tensions reveals the parts of stories that merely fulfill one's expectations based on what one has been conditioned to "hear," as well as possible disruptions in the categories and tensions themselves. The categories are always in flux, if even minutely. Therefore, in order to participate fully in this analysis, I ask the reader to become aware of and then blend, or shift, the dichotomies/dualities that perpetually inform discussions of sex work and allow for the tensions existing between and among these categories to emerge.

AN ETHNOGRAPHY OF STREET-BASED SEX WORK

This study is grounded in rhetorical analysis, or the study of how language shapes and is shaped by cultures, institutions, and the individuals within them. I then look at this language from an ideological perspective, or the identification and examination of the underlying assumptions of communicative interactions. Not only is my participants' language examined, but also the underlying belief systems of language. Situating sex work and the industry as rhetorical constructions, I offer an example of how signs and symbols that comprise material conditions (i.e., resources, criminal laws, punishment, avenues for entering and leaving these street economies), can be analyzed to better understand how goals, agendas, interests, and ideologies are represented and implemented through language. My analysis reveals the constructed nature of these problems and solutions, while offering insights into the rhetoric of the everyday and how language and ideologies shape the material conditions of street-based sex work.

Because language shapes our understanding of the world (McCracken 2010), one's language awareness and choices influence an individual's perception of herself as well as her available opportunities. These language choices are embedded in belief systems about one's worth, body, sexuality, race, class, and abilities even prior to one's birth, and therefore dissembling these constructs is, in fact, impossible. And yet it *is* possible to take an action or an identity like "prostitute" and pull at the threads that create and dismantle the construct in order to provide insights into restructuring the problems and issues surrounding street-based sex work. Existing research, policies, laws, and participants' spoken words transcribed allow for moments to be frozen in time in order to better understand the language in varied contexts. It is through this examination of the language and underlying belief systems that these beliefs become clear.[7]

My record of this language allows for an examination of the underlying ideologies surrounding street-based sex work; in particular, I show the way the problems of street-based sex work and their corresponding solutions are defined impact the material conditions surrounding people who participate in street economies. Examining these problems and solutions based on how people who exchange sex understand them reveals how language and its subsequent effects on belief systems and actions ultimately influence what choices, options, and paths are and are not available to an individual, which can then further constrain or create opportunities for action and change.

Because discourse is central to this analysis, the language used to talk about these transactions and the people who participate in them is also closely examined and deconstructed. Like the material conditions surrounding people who participate in street economies, these terms have histories and contexts. Embedded within systems of race, class, gender, citizen status, and other power structures, they reflect and co-create values and belief systems. And yet, notably, they are fluid, meaning they can and do change. The terminology and ideologies are central to this analysis because they co-create material reality.

My research is an ethnographic case study of a local system that can be extrapolated to other subcultures and the construction of identities based on the language of the individuals who are directly involved in this work. Because my study investigates the language of policy-making and the people who forge it, it has implications for ethics and policy in addition to gender studies, cultural studies, and ethnographic research.

THE SEX INDUSTRY

Sex work is defined as any commercial sexual service performed in exchange for material compensation. Rather than refer to the act of exchanging sex for money that in some countries is illegal, as the term *prostitution* usually does, *sex work* is a term that includes activities both legal (exotic dancing, phone sex operators, burlesque performers, adult pornography) and illegal (activities that involve face-to-face direct exchange of sexual stimulation for commercial gain).[8] In the United States, street-based sex work is illegal and involves those persons who solicit or exchange sex on or near the street, in cars, hotels, truck stops, or outdoors, as opposed to using telephones, the Internet, or other referral systems (McCracken, Thukral, and Savino 2006).

Men, women, and transgender/transsexual individuals all exchange sex for money or other gain. My study focused on women who exchange sex for drugs or money, what is commonly referred to as prostitution or street/survival sex work. Analyzing issues surrounding male and transgender sex workers in non-heterosexual environments was beyond the scope of this project. Although these issues are extremely important to consider in an analysis of sex work, trying to include them in this analysis would complicate the study by introducing those ideologies and discriminations that arise when concepts of gender and sexuality beyond heterosexual practices are involved. In my discussion of sex work in general, I strive to be gender-neutral, meaning men, women, and transgender individuals all sell sex. When I speak of my participants in particular, I refer to them as women. Although I was open to interviewing anyone who identified as a "woman" whether cisgendered[9] female or not, none of my participants identified as transgender,[10] and therefore my analysis focuses entirely on interviews with cisgendered female women.[11]

Issues surrounding sex work are convoluted and complicated. Policy makers, activists, academics, among others, wrestle with them to write laws and policies, design social services, and analyze existing policies, services, and circumstances of individuals. Discourse is always at the center of these struggles to frame an issue and reach specific goals based on various political and moral agendas. To complicate matters further, sex workers are the focus of public opinion and policy, and yet historically have not been direct contributors to the conversations surrounding sex work and policy. Research in the past twenty years has drastically changed this scenario.[12] Without sex workers' expert and lived understanding, external policy makers, researchers, and practitioners risk creating policies that exacerbate problems and perpetuate the material conditions that harm individuals, rather than co-creating solutions that emerge from lived experience.

The language used to discuss the exchange of sex for money or other gain, as well as those who participate in these activities, is fraught with difficulty. Naming is powerful, as I argue in this monograph, because it simultaneously creates and constrains those individuals it struggles to define. And yet, naming is also convenient and even necessary because it allows the speaker to discuss an agreed upon set of practices, actions, or identities. Take street-based sex work for example. As I explore more fully in Chapter 5, the terms *prostitute* and *sex worker* identify the person who participates in these transactions as primarily a victim or an agent. Integrated throughout my argument and analysis, I show that neither term accurately describes the participants in my study. Because I am a rhetorician and language is a central focus of this book, locating my own language has been a challenge. In order to simplify the varieties of language and to reflect my own values, I use the phrase *women who exchange sex for money or drugs* or the identities chosen by my participants. The title of this book, *Street Sex Workers' Discourse*, directly contradicts this statement, and in so doing reflects my own learning and growth as a researcher and scholar of language. I proposed this title to the publisher prior to completing my analysis, and it was included in publicity for the book. I have and continue to wrestle with this "terminology" issue, and it was only in the later stages of my analysis and completion of this project that I came to understand that although the terms *street sex workers* or *street-based sex workers* are commonly used in academic research, my participants, as well as many others involved in street-based economies, do not identify as sex workers.[13] *I use the term* street-based sex work *to refer to an* entity, *not an* identity, *because none of my participants identified themselves in this way.*[14] Because it was too late to change the title when I came to this understanding, it is a reminder to me that language evolves, reflects, and impacts our understanding of the world. The practices, identifications, actions, and positions of choice and power from which these exchanges are made cannot be neatly identified because they are attributed to an incredible range of individuals in varied sets of circumstances.

Because names and identities are so important and intrinsic to understanding the people participating in these activities, individuals must be able to identify themselves, using the terms most accurate for them. Sexual commerce occurs on myriad levels for everyone. I am not referred to as a "house-based flirter" because I can, with a wink and a smile, persuade the postal delivery man to bring a heavy package into my son's bedroom. The term *street-based sex work* reflects the location of the interactions, the vague positionality revealed about the people who participate in these interactions, as well as the belief these actions are sexual commerce, meaning they are a form of work provided in exchange for money. Although the term is similar to *sex work*, I differentiate it to emphasize the participants are often not approaching this work from the same position of power and choice as many self-identified sex workers do. As a point of clarification, the phrase, *women who exchange sex for money or drugs*, could be applied to any sex worker, but within this context, I refer to women in a street-based environment. I include the words *for money or drugs* in this phrase because the use of drugs is so prevalent in my study and was often provided directly in exchange for sex or purchased from the money earned in these exchanges.

THE MATERIAL CONDITIONS OF STREET-BASED SEX WORK IN NEMEZ

The material conditions surrounding street-based sex work cannot be mapped out in their entirety, as they differ substantially based on location and personal circumstances, but some of the primary considerations include social status, control and power over and within working conditions, experiences of and adjustment to the work, arrests, drug use, risk of HIV/AIDS, and resident issues with and responses to prostitution.[15] These conditions often interact to exacerbate oppression of and difficulty in the lives of women and men who exchange sex for drugs or money.

People who participate in exchanging sex for money or drugs are some of the most marginalized and victimized people in the sex industry and society.[16] They work near the street, in the park, and out of cars and hotels. Their exchanges of sex involve real time and proximal contact with their clients, which implies varying levels of danger and risk. Woven through the documented material conditions of street-based sex work in Nemez are the women's stories. Avery Gordon's (2008) "complex personhood" provides a framework from which to read them:

> It has always baffled me why those most interested in understanding and changing the barbaric domination that characterizes our modernity often—not always—withhold from the very people they are most concerned with the right to complex personhood. [. . .] Complex personhood means that all people (albeit in specific forms whose specificity is sometimes everything) remember and forget, are beset by contradiction, and recognize and misrecognize themselves and others. Complex personhood means that people suffer graciously and selfishly too, get stuck in the symptoms of their troubles, and also transform themselves. Complex personhood means that even those called "Other" are never never that. [. . .] At the very least, complex personhood is about conferring the respect on others that comes from presuming that life and people's lives are simultaneously straightforward and full of enormously subtle meaning. (p. 4–5)

One's "complex personhood" requires the reader to listen, as I included in J. Krisnamurti's epigram at the beginning of the Preface, "not only to the words, but also to the feeling of what is being conveyed, to the whole of it, not part of it." And it is grounded in respect for that individual as a human—just like the listener.

In the following section, I outline the material conditions related to street-based sex work in Nemez, specifically focusing on criminalization and arrests, neighborhood and community responses, drug use and risk of sexually transmitted infections, and violence.

Criminalization and Arrests

Prostitution was legal in Nemez at the end of the nineteenth century and into the early twentieth. In addition to receiving regular medical examinations, prostitutes also took out business licenses. Although primarily American, the women were also French, German, Belgian, and Dutch. Prostitution was permitted but not welcomed in Nemez, and as the city grew, the women were pushed to the edge of town. The Temperance Movement, which created the national prohibition on alcohol and gambling, chased away prostitution by the 1920s, at least as a legal business enterprise. Prostitution was forced underground, where it has remained since.

Nemez has a metropolitan population of approximately 1,000,000 and was identified as a High Intensity Drug Trafficking Area by the Office of the National Drug Control and Policy. Located at the crossroads of major interstates and being close to the Mexican border, Nemez is a hub for incoming drugs from Mexico and Central America. Some communities within Nemez serve as conduits for drug traffickers, generating a marketplace for gang members, men and women exchanging sex for drugs or money, and injection and other drug users.

Officer Tom Hixson, a white 52-year-old heterosexual male and a former supervisor of the vice unit,[17] described the penalties for prostitution arrests in Nemez: "If you're arrested for prostitution on the streets, the first offense, you're going to spend 15 days in jail, you're gonna get about a five-hundred and something dollar fine and you're going to be area restricted 1,000 feet from where you were arrested."

Between January 2003 and December 2006[18] there were approximately 1395 commercialized sex crimes[19] according to the Nemez Police Department. Of those arrests, approximately 1,370 were for prostitution, ten were for commercialized sex/pandering, and ten were for commercialized sex/other.[20] These statistics do not account for those individuals arrested for loitering, violating zone restrictions, and other crimes for which people involved in street commerce are often arrested. Discerning precise data about prostitution is difficult because it is illegal and the women, men, and transgender individuals who participate in prostitution are difficult to track. These figures only help to clarify the significant numbers of people arrested for prostitution.

Neighborhood Residents

In 2002, the Nemez Police Department created a unit that focused resources on problems affecting the community at large. One outcome was the Dover Project (made up of the Nemez Police Department, Building Safety, The City Council Ward Office, and six neighborhood associations) to curb violent crime in the area. In early 2003 (with pressure from the Dover Project), the Westwood Adult Hotel and Bookstore was closed. One police commander described this hotel as a "den for narcotics and prostitution." This closure encouraged the six neighborhood associations to believe their area's reputation as a place to find drugs and prostitutes might be changing.

In April 2004, the Nemez Police Department initiated a deterrence program that targeted the clients of prostitutes. The program required the "john," or client, be photographed by police and then given a booklet on prostitution that includes letters from the neighborhood associations explaining the negative impact prostitution and drug activity has on businesses and families. Within the first five weeks of the program, approximately 200 men were attracted to the undercover agents disguised as prostitutes. The john was not arrested unless he ran or fought, but his information was recorded, and if he were to be stopped again for the same offense, he would be arrested. The goal of this program was to reach out to as many johns as possible "and let them know what they're doing is wrong on so many levels" said Eric Roman, commander of the agency's North Side division.

The people interviewed from the neighborhood associations believed this project was a positive step and much needed because "prostitution affects everyone who lives or works nearby," and the neighborhoods and businesses were trying to get rid of the "stigma of being a red-light district." An article written by presidents of nearby neighborhood associations argues prostitution is not a victimless crime because prostitution brings on other crimes including drug dealing, burglary, robbery, assault, and homicide. The neighborhood association presidents argued prostitution is a symptom of a more serious situation, and the crime had harmed their neighborhoods for too long.

Nemez does not foster a liberal attitude toward the sex industry, and yet pockets of sex worker rights activism exist. Building on the popularity of similar festivals that have occurred in larger cities such as New York and San Francisco, during the late 1990s, activists and sex workers in Nemez brought performers to the local community for its first Sex Worker Festival in order to "celebrate, educate, and create awareness" about sex work. The organizers worked to create an "art as activism" event that would build a pro-sex coalition from a diverse group of people (sex workers; gay, lesbian, bisexual, and transsexual individuals; political organizations; sex-positive groups, etc.), and therefore, the above groups and their interests were at the forefront. One purpose of these events was to draw attention to sex work in general and simultaneously educate the community about street-based sex work. Initially, the festivals began as middle-class showings, but the organizers hoped if the festivals continued, more people participating in street-based sex work would be involved. And yet it is noteworthy that people participating in street economies were not a primary audience or focus of these events.

During an interview with a key organizer, Joan, a 43-year-old, white, bisexual woman said the organizers care very much about "street-based sex workers" and wanted to bring them into the community, but found they did not identify as sex workers and were not necessarily trying to make a political statement. Based on this knowledge, and because sex workers in general have consistently been spoken for by those who are outside their own community, the organizers did not want to make this same mistake and attempt to speak for those who were not participating. Films were included in the festivals that dealt with street-based sex work, and volunteers who had formerly worked on the street were involved. The organizers also chose a popular location for a protest site in order to draw attention to issues related to street-based sex work. Their goal was to improve public opinion because they were keenly aware people participating in street commerce bear the brunt of law enforcement activity and negative attention from the media and neighborhood associations. This situation is telling in two ways: one, similar to my findings, the people participating in these exchanges do not identify as sex workers and do not necessarily want to organize for political or labor purposes; and secondly, even the groups most concerned with sex worker rights had difficulty integrating street-based sex work into their festival because they did not want to speak for these individuals without their participation.

Drug Use and Sexually Transmitted Infections

People who participate in street-based sex work also have an increased risk of contracting drug and sexually transmitted illnesses.[21] Scholars and activists have extensively reported on the commonalities between prostitution, drug use, and an increased risk of HIV/AIDS. Many people involved in street-based sex work have high risk factors for HIV infection because of injection drug use. Based on a study of approximately 9,000 women who were addicted to drugs and who traded sex for drugs or money, Anthropologists Kail, Watson, and Ray (1995) found female injection drug users who trade sex for drugs or money are more likely to share needles and less likely to use new needles or to clean old ones compared to women who support themselves by other means (p. 241).

There is also an association between heavy crack cocaine use and HIV infection among women who exchange sex for drugs or money. A study that collected cumulative data from 1989 through 1995 in New York City surveyed clients about their drug use and sexual practices. The women who used crack rather than injecting drugs performed mostly oral sex and maintained inconsistent condom use. This combination exposed them to increased HIV infections in part because of the damage to the mouth (sores, cracked lips, etc.) from crack inhalation, which can lead to increased risk of contracting the HIV virus (Wallace, Porter, Weiner, Steinburg 1997, p. 470).

Sociologist Adele Weiner (1996) reports on the relationship among prostitution, drug use, ethnicity, and risk of HIV/AIDS. She found a greater percentage of Hispanic women were found to be HIV positive than white or black women (40.3 percent as opposed to 35.5 percent and 32.0 percent respectively) (p. 100). Her findings reveal the illegal drug most widely used was crack (68.3 percent). White women were more likely to use IV heroin (43.0 percent), whereas black women were more likely to use alcohol (67.5 percent) or smoke crack (74.5 percent). Hispanic women used nasal heroin more than other groups (37.1 percent) (p. 100). Weiner also reports the 653 women who were infected with HIV were more likely to be homeless, have a history of IV drug use, received a blood transfusion, and worked more years as a prostitute (p. 100). In addition to the high risk of contracting HIV due to shared needles and sexual interactions, the consumption of alcohol or other drugs can also lower a person's attention to safer sex practices, and dependency on these drugs can additionally impair judgment.

Nemez and its surrounding county is an area disproportionately affected by HIV. According to the State's Department of Health Services' Annual Report, Leagh County[22] has the highest estimated rate of people contracting HIV/AIDS in the state. The prevalence rate for Leagh County is estimated at 210 per 100,000 people, while the State Prevalence Rate is 183 per 100,000 people.[23] Leagh County, the state's second most populous urban county, has the highest prevalence rate of reported HIV Disease in the state (210 per 100,000).

Males comprise approximately 90 percent of all confirmed *emergent* HIV infections and 85 percent of current estimated prevalence—by far the majority.[24] And yet female cases are increasing. Comparing the three-year period from 1985 to 1987 to the three-year period from 2001 to 2003, the percentage of *emergent* cases of HIV infection in females doubled, rising from approximately 6 percent to 12 percent. And second to men who have sex with men, injection drug use is the next most frequently reported behavior associated with emergent HIV infection.

The race/ethnicity trends in the state are representative of the broader population trends except for Non-Hispanic blacks. According to the state's 2005 HIV/AIDS Annual Report, Non-Hispanic blacks were approximately three percent of the State's population in 2003, but accounted for almost thirteen percent of emergent HIV infection. This disproportionate impact is not seen among other minority groups. But in Leagh County specifically, women of color, particularly Hispanic women, are in great need of HIV prevention services. Of all those who tested positive in Leagh County, approximately 35 percent were Hispanic—a disproportionately higher percentage than the general Hispanic population in Leagh County (30%), the State as a whole (25%), or the United States (12.5%).

Violence

Because of its location, street-based sex work can contribute to one's lack of control over events because participants are vulnerable to arrests and assaults. Women often work by themselves or have boyfriends or partners who act as lookouts for police and potential assaults.[25] Of all sex workers, those working on or near the street have the fewest resources, work in the most dangerous circumstances, and face the most harassment from the police and other people who may assault or exploit them for monetary gain (Campbell and Kinnell 2000). They make less money than higher-end sex workers, and they are often beaten, victimized, robbed, and raped—crimes they have virtually no means to prosecute. Some women are under the protection of "pimps"[26] although the stereotypical pimp concept has evolved and is much more specific to individuals.[27] In some cases working "alone" or not having a pimp or protector is a strategy for reducing exposure to certain types of violence (Epele 2002). Women and men who exchange sex for money or other gain are often victims of exploitation, assault, rape, and even death.[28] Because violence within a street-based sex work context is often not reported, statistical information is not available about these crimes within Nemez. I explore violence from my participants' perspectives in Chapter 2.

Their low social status within the hierarchy of sex work and within their communities as a whole; lack of access to social and medical services; perhaps addiction to substances; and lack of housing, basic living requirements, and occupational skills makes it difficult for individuals to leave the street for work deemed more "legitimate" and less risky than their current practices.

Throughout this monograph, I explore how the material conditions are self-perpetuating and sustaining, as well as how they can be disrupted. Specific categories emerged from the interviews and literature surrounding street-based sex work including: criminalization, resident issues and responses, drug use, violence (both direct and indirect), health, victim status, stigma, poverty, abuse and neglect, as well as inequality and oppression. For each category, I ask how it sustains and/or disrupts the material conditions surrounding street-based sex work. Does poverty, for example, or abuse and neglect, further entrench one in exchanges of sex for money? And how might these conditions be improved?

Having few resources as well as the necessary access required to increase them, people who exchange sex for money or drugs often become even further marginalized in society. Marginalized communities—those on the margins, the sidelines—serve to reinforce the acceptable mores of the mainstream. Therefore, examining how marginalized communities are understood by those who do, as well as those who do not, occupy that status reveals the underlying beliefs that support and perpetuate these representations.

Placing the women's stories and lives at its center, this book offers an analysis of the central concepts that emerged from the data, namely, the "victim status" of women who exchange sex for money or drugs, an individual's responsibility to and for change, and systemic responsibility and power. Immersing myself in the language surrounding street-based sex work, I show how the identities and material conditions of my participants' lives are represented, reproduced, often entrenched, and at times, disrupted. In her work with African American essayists, English Professor Jacqueline Jones Royster (2000) reveals "a community's material conditions greatly define the range of what this group does with the written word, and to a significant degree, even how they do it" (p. 5). Although Royster focuses on the written word, her attention to contextual analysis is instructive here, as it "brings into focus the material conditions, forces, and circumstances that affect a writer's ability to perform and influence the shape and direction of the choices made in carrying out the performance" (p. 63). Royster argues taking "African American women into account as being not just redundant

xxviii *Preface*

but valuable—or as agents of change rather than simple victims of oppression and dominance" (p. 253) can "permit the emergence of alternative realities" (p. 254). Taking my participants into account as experts and valuable agents of change, my rhetorical analysis highlights the continuum through which systems and individuals co-create each other and reveals the systemic[29] influences on individuals' beliefs and ideologies. I show how material realities are both created and *dis*rupted by discourse and rhetoric, thereby providing a foundation for "the emergence of alternative realities" and material change.

Street-based sex work is largely considered to be a "problem" by society, which then necessitates a solution. The definition of the problem directly affects one's creation and implementation of solutions, which then impacts the material conditions of the lives of people who exchange sex for money or drugs. In other words, the way we conceptualize contemporary issues drives the approaches proposed to change the given situation or outcome. Based on this premise, how do current perceptions of street-based sex work contribute to how its problems and solutions are defined? What happens when the "problem" of street-based sex work is understood differently? And how does this reframing affect the material conditions and outcomes related to street-based sex work? These problems and their corresponding solutions directly impact the lives of people who exchange sex, as well as society's understanding of sexuality, race, bodies, labor, and myriad other constructions.

Street-based sex work was defined as a *problem* in primarily three ways: as the individuals who participate in these activities; the acts themselves of exchanging sex for money; and the various "street" practices commonly associated with street-based sex work, including homelessness, poverty, drug use and abuse, addiction, physical abuse, and violence. Resources granted through the state, private entities, or individuals to decrease or eliminate drug use, homelessness, violence, and abuse are necessarily tied to rhetoric. These issues are defined, researched, explained, and categorized through language. This same language is then used within and by larger political systems to distribute and make resources available. Therefore the agent of change, as well as the definition of the problem, directly impacts which solutions will be implemented and by what means. The language, in part, impacts the flow of resources, influencing an individual's access to them, and her corresponding material reality.

Within this monograph, I identify and illustrate the contradictions and complicated existence of street-based sex work guided by my participants' understanding and descriptions of its problems and solutions. I argue that the women who exchange sex, lay persons, and public figures' understanding of street-based sex work play a significant role in maintaining the focus on an individual's qualities (i.e. morality, homelessness, drug use, etc.) by focusing primarily on the rehabilitation of the participants rather than the systems that allow for, create, and perpetuate street-based sex work and other street economies, demonstrating the direct relationship between materiality and discourse in "everyday" rhetoric. When discovered and analyzed, this knowledge contributes to society's understanding of contemporary issues by revealing alternative understandings of, in this case, personal choice, responsibility, power, and agency, and their relationship to systemic change.

MAKING MEANING THROUGH COLLAGE

A collage is a composition of art created through the juxtaposition of diverse or unrelated elements in a way that can reveal new meaning. Emerging from both the intent of an artist as well as the materials gathered and combined, the collage reveals both the individual parts and the entire picture at once. Individually, the parts can not make up the message created without their assemblage in a specific format. And yet the assemblage is not the only agent, as the artist must take pre-existing pieces of information or art and combine them in a way that allows the viewer and the artist to see these elements differently, creating meaning beyond that which is contained in each individual piece.

Individuals create collages on a daily, even momentary, basis—assembling elements and combining them to create a whole. Systems can also be viewed as collages of individual needs, priorities, responsibilities, greed, and corruption. And the systems themselves can take on lives of their own to reinforce particular practices. The collage is fixed, and yet it can be pulled apart and remade to create different understandings and possibilities of meaning grounded in the same material elements.

I present two ideological collages that, when considered together, can begin to disrupt and change the material conditions surrounding street-based sex work: an individual's "responsibility to and for change" and the discourse and ideology of "agential choice." These frameworks emerged through my examination of the construction of problems and solutions attributed to street-based sex work. Five prominent themes capture these problems and solutions: Women who exchange sex for money or other gain are victims; Residents, neighborhoods, and the community are victims of prostitution; Criminalization of prostitution is both a solution and a problem; Women who exchange sex for money should take personal responsibility to "change"; and an individual's power, authentic choice, and agency create a foundation of agential choice, whereby material change can be realized. Figure P.2 illustrates how these themes overlap.

Women who Exchange Sex for Money are Victims flowed through every argument, and the others operated on gradations; all of which impact the material conditions of individuals' lives.

There is a demonstrable relationship between materiality and discourse that offers alternative perspectives on current realities of drug use and policy, homelessness, and the exchange of sex on or near the street for material

xxx *Preface*

Figure P.1   Body. Illustration by Kristine Richardson.

gain. This altered understanding reveals how individuals create and are co-created by the rhetoric of the everyday, whether they choose to exchange sex for money or not. I ask readers to participate in this presentation of data and analysis and then create their own collage of meaning. These findings contribute to conversations about the sex industry; poverty and

Preface xxxi

Problems and Solutions Thematically Represented

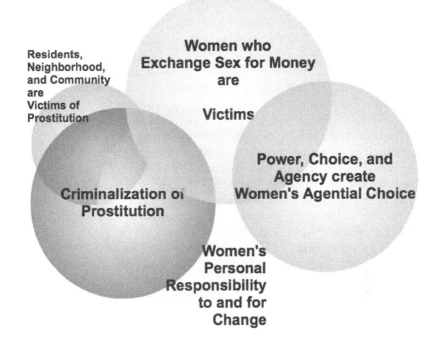

Figure P.2 Problems and solutions thematically represented.

homelessness; drug use, abuse and policy; the criminalization of prostitution; as well as the relationships between "everyday" moments and speech acts and their impact on material reality. The following chapters outline this theory, present the ethnography that informs it, and demonstrate its interpretive power.

TRAJECTORY OF THE TEXT

Drawing on Barry Brummett's "quotidian rhetoric" and its applications to street-based sex work, Chapter 1, "Quotidian Rhetoric Creates Meaning through Collage" presents the visual images of kaleidoscope and collage as a framework through which the viewer creates his or her own meaning. I present Judith Butler's (2011) argument that language is a condition under and through which materiality appears, and apply this theory to the idea, term, identity, and material reality of "the prostitute."

Street-based sex work is defined as a problem that victimizes the neighborhoods in which it occurs as well as the women who participate in it.

Chapter 2, "Who is the Victim: The Neighborhood or the Woman?" presents the evidence and analysis for how these problems and subsequent solutions emerge based on who occupies this victim status. I begin with an examination of the residents, neighborhoods, and the community as victims of prostitution and the central causes of this victimization; namely, drugs, violence, crime, and disease. I then present the "woman as victim of street-based sex work" arguments, which reveal an emphasis on the systemic conditions that often allow for and perpetuate this victim standing.

The historical intertwining of sex work and (im)morality complicates the power relations surrounding sex workers' victimization, legal status, and relationships with clients and others. Emerging from my participants' varied understandings of morality, sexuality, and the "wrongness" or "not wrongness" of exchanging sex for money, Chapter 3, "Is She a Criminal, a Victim, or a Victim of the Criminal Justice System?" explores the problem as both prostitution and the criminalization of prostitution. Defining the problem as prostitution leads to arrests; defining the problem as the criminalization of prostitution results in greater violence, individually and structurally, for individuals involved in street-based sex work.

Chapter 4, "'An Opportunity to Change': Responsibility and Choice" focuses on the woman and her need to change, or more precisely, the responsibility she has to "change," which resides in her choice to move from the "victim" status to one who takes responsibility for her life. This choice to "change" is grounded in an ideology of personal responsibility. I argue systemic violence and responsibility must be addressed as both a cause of the material conditions that require this "change" as well as an impediment to achieving it.

Chapter 5, "Systemic Violence Perpetuates Victim Status" presents an in-depth analysis of the language used to describe street-based sex work, which reveals the "victim" status at its foundation. Exploring this victim status in relationship to the overarching themes of violence, safety, health, and stigma reveals an emphasis on systemic violence and responsibility. Finally, I explore the role prostitution's criminal status plays in creating systemic conditions that allow for increased violence due to the women's marginal status, isolation, stigma, and lack of access to recourse when such violence does occur.

Chapter 6, "Creating Agential Choice from Cages of Oppression" presents suggestions for material change grounded in a framework of what I term *agential choice,* meaning an authentic choice one makes from her own internal and integral power. Drawing on Starhawk's (1990) concept of "power-with" as a framework for constructing agential choice, I argue the "victim" status be replaced with an ideology of agential choice, which is grounded in and facilitated through Marilyn Cooper's "responsible rhetorical agency." I then present an examination of agency and decriminalization and conclude with an exploration of agential choice grounded in respect for the agent who is an expert on her own life. I conclude by presenting examples of this agential choice, as well as systemic recommendations for street-based sex work and society.

The women's stories and perceptions challenge common understandings of the problems and solutions surrounding street-based sex work, and thereby offer a means through which individual perceptions and systemic policy can be influenced in order to co-create better material conditions with and for individuals participating in street economies.

Acknowledgments

First and foremost, I want to thank my participants for sharing their stories and lives with me.

I want to thank Max Novick, my editor at Routledge, who supported this project from the initial proposal to its completion. I also want to thank Jennifer Morrow at Routledge for her help in moving the manuscript through various stages, Ryan Kenney for patiently working with me to get the copyediting and formatting right, and George Pequignot for his help with the index.

Much gratitude goes to my graduate mentors who supported this work from the beginning: Melissa Ditmore, Amy Kimme Hea, and Sally Stevens. Ken McAllister, an academic and person I greatly admire and respect, has been an exceptional teacher, mentor, advocate, and friend. He asked insightful questions and respected both my research subject and my scholarship, giving me confidence from the start. I am incredibly grateful I was able to learn from his scholarship, teaching, and the way he lives his life.

I also want to thank my colleagues at my new academic home for their support of my work and vision: Morgan Gresham, Lisa Starks-Estes, Julie Armstrong, Jennifer Woroner, Mai Huynh, Harriett Fletcher, Frank Biafora, Tom Hallock, Trey Conner, Thomas Smith, and Mark Pezzo.

The librarians at the Nelson Poynter Memorial Library, especially Tina Neville and Cynthia Brown, were extremely helpful with locating sources. And David Brodosi saved my writing life when he helped to quickly replace my stolen laptop. Frank Biafora and Norine Noonan were also instrumental in making this replacement happen, and I am forever grateful.

A very special thank you to those students who have also been research assistants: Alisa Abreu, Eleanor Eichenbaum, Teresa Przetocki, Casey Shuniak, Michael Silva, and Mark Weber. Their energy and intellectual investment made this work much stronger. Jennifer Ingrassia Vogtner, in addition to her work as a research assistant, supported me intellectually and emotionally.

I want to thank the many sex worker rights organizations I have been privileged to be involved with: Sex Workers Outreach Project, Desiree Alliance, Sex Workers without Borders, and Human Rights for All.

So many friends contributed to this work by pushing my thinking, asking and answering questions, and educating me in such depth about sex

xxxvi *Acknowledgments*

work, including: Liz Coplen, Kym Cutter, Susan Lopez, Stacey Swimme, Juliana Piccillo, Carol Leigh, Penelope Saunders, Tara Birl, and Rowan Frost. Robyn Few has been such an inspiration, confidante, and model for living and fighting to the fullest. Susan Dewey read and commented on two full drafts of this manuscript and offered excellent suggestions for organization, sources, and content. Natalie Nguyen provided emotional, intellectual, and even co-parental support—from our initial conversations into our continually deepening relationship, she sustained and encouraged me. She also compelled me to take risks, ask difficult questions, work toward finding their answers, and have the patience to sit with the discontent as the answers and my own growth emerge.

I want to thank John Todd for helping me find my own body in the writing of this book.

I am also grateful for close friends who have listened to me for hours and provided a safe space to talk through ideas. Morgan Gresham has provided intellectual and emotional support since I first arrived at the University of South Florida St. Petersburg. One of my first colleagues and friends here, she has contributed in so many ways to my thinking about these issues through co-presentations, responding to drafts, as well as both laughing and crying in my office. Tiffany Chenneville provided co-parental and emotional support, but even more importantly—laughter. Sandy Thompson has been a close friend who always pushes my thinking. Sabrina Ruggiero has provided her special gifts of support, therapy, and laughter. All of these friends spent numerous hours (especially Sandy) caring for and playing with my son, Nathaniel, during many hours of writing. Reggie Craig and Karen Frank have also been a significant source of support and love for both Nathaniel and I.

My family has supported and sustained me throughout this journey. My dad read and commented on *every* complete draft of this manuscript—his questions, suggestions, and logic were invaluable. I especially appreciate his willingness and ability to listen, and when appropriate, alter his own opinions and beliefs. My mom also read and commented on the complete manuscript. As one of my first and closest models of feminism, I so appreciate her ability to speak and act on her beliefs. She was also always willing to listen to me vent and was a constant supporter of my work—emotionally and intellectually. My parents' loving dedication and support awe and sustain me.

Nathaniel, my son, has been with me through every step of this process—*in utero* during the planning, accompanying me on interviews and in field work, and dancing in our living room while I write. I am so grateful for his presence in my life, his questions, his teaching, and for his patience with me, our kitchen table, and the dining room, which were all consumed in the final months of writing. I know uncountable hours have been spent with this book rather than him, and I can only hope he values this work and my commitment to it.

1 Quotidian Rhetoric Creates Meaning through Collage

Language is fluid. It both shapes and reflects changes in society and local communities. Discourse is made up of ideologies and ethical systems held by the users of that language and their communities that create and continue to cultivate the language. As Norman Fairclough argues in *Discourse and Social Change*:

> Discourses do not just reflect or represent social entities and relations, they construct or "constitute" them; different discourses constitute key entities [. . .] in different ways, and position people in different ways as social subjects [. . .] and it is these social effects of discourse that are focused upon in discourse analysis. (p. 3–4)

These ideological belief systems affect people's lives. The language used to describe a person who exchanges sex for economic gain can embody different ideologies. For example, consider the words *whore, prostitute, sex worker, sacred prostitute,* or *new age priestess*. Each word conveys different values, and therefore interrogating the ideologies and ethical systems found in these concepts allows the reader to better understand how these identities are created and can perhaps be created differently.

My analysis draws on both rhetorical—the study of how language shapes and is shaped by cultures, institutions, and the individuals within them—and ideological—the identification and examination of the underlying belief systems contained within the language. Both language and the underlying belief systems contained within the language are examined. I draw on communication studies Professor Barry Brummett's concept of quotidian rhetoric as a foundation of my analysis of street-based sex work. Brummett (1991) defines quotidian rhetoric in *Rhetorical Dimensions of Popular Culture* as:

> the public and personal meanings that affect everyday, even minute-to-minute decisions. This level of rhetoric is where decisions are guided that do not take the form of peak crises [. . .] but do involve long-term concerns as well as the momentary choices that people must make to

get through the day. [. . .] People are constantly surrounded by signs that influence them, or signs that they use to influence others, in ongoing, mundane, and nonexigent yet important ways. (p. 41)

Brummett argues quotidian rhetoric is carried out through appropriational manifestations of rhetoric, or what is most appropriate in a given situation. Therefore people, in general, are relatively "less consciously aware that the management of shared meanings is underway," which means they are "*less likely* to take or assign responsibility for a rhetorical effort" (emphasis in original, p. 42). Because appropriational rhetoric is *participation in* as much as it is the *production of* the management of meaning, ultimately, individual responsibility for both is less defined. Ideologies as well as material reality are both fixed and continually changing based on both external and internal events. I use the terms *fixed material* and *influential material* to better understand the materiality of my participants' language and lives, as well as the material conditions that co-create their lives. After presenting this theory, I apply it to the constructions of problems and solutions surrounding street-based sex work as well as the material conditions of street-based sex work.

The concepts *fixed material* and *influential material* identify the malleability and changeability of material conditions. In other words, the level of embedded materiality in an object or concept influences how material can change. By *fixed material*, I mean this object, or material, is fixed for the moment and therefore has a momentary permanence, which does not imply that fixed material cannot be changed. For example, a house, a law, and even a person, would be considered fixed material—a concrete reality currently in existence. *Influential material* describes how conditions, objects, and circumstances impact fixed material—the thoughts, actions, words, and events that influence actions and fixed material conditions. The influential material is more fluid than the fixed material, and, in some cases, more pervasive.

An example is the wooden, kitchen table at which I sit. It is fixed material, although it is not permanent. Rather, I could, with influential material (my thoughts, ideas, conversations with others) and tools (fixed material), choose to chop it up into pieces, sand it down into dust, or burn it. I could also turn it upside down and make it into a piece of art. There are myriad options for fixed material based on the choices, options, perspectives, and influences available. And yet to illustrate the power of the influential material, the table is continuously defined by a culture that uses and understands tables. If this table were transported to a place where there is no word for table, or there are no objects used as tables, this fixed material would no longer be understood as a "table" and perhaps would take on a different purpose or be changed into something more usable and understandable within that culture. This fixed material would then embody other uses and purposes beyond that which was initially intended in its creation, allowing it to be a different fixed material subject to other influences, goals, uses, and perhaps changes.

Influential material is continually moving toward and away from "fixedness" and is less concrete than fixed material. It may be fixed in its own right, as a thought can have a momentary permanence and therefore be fixed, and yet it is less fixed than an action. Therefore, my stepping on a bug would be a fixed material action and would have very specific fixed material consequences for the bug's life, or lack thereof because of my action, as opposed to my influential material thought of thinking about stepping on the bug, which does not actually impact the bug's life (or mine as well) until I make a fixed action to step on the bug or walk away. A final example, the existence of a crack pipe is more fully embedded materially than, say, a participant who says she thinks about using crack. Both are products of material conditions and work to create other actions and realities, and yet one is more concrete than the other. Within a system of fixed and influential material, the influential is less tangible. In this example, the existence of a crack pipe on one's person could lead to arrest, whereas the thought of smoking crack would not.

The fixed materiality, likewise, impacts the influential material. For example, the law against exchanging sex for money in Nemez is a fixed material condition. It is subject to change, but at the time of the interviews and through the writing of this book, exchanging sex is illegal. An observer may feel pity, outrage, satisfaction, surprise, or fear upon viewing the arrest of someone for prostitution, and this response or description of their response would be considered an influential material condition. This response could, combined with multiple other actions and influences, create a fixed material condition of a petition to change the law, a petition to enforce more arrests, or the movement of a person from that location to avoid arrest. Because the movement from fixed to influential is not always easily defined, many material conditions can be defined according to both. For example, one's past could be considered both fixed and influential because it has occurred and can continue to influence the individual in different ways depending on present circumstances, intent, etc.

These categories do not clearly demarcate the concepts because nothing is ever entirely fixed or influential, and yet these terms offer a way of understanding the material conditions of street-based sex work and the ways these conditions might be disrupted. There are aspects more fixed and those more malleable and mutable. To complicate matters further, the level of material embeddedness does not progress respectively from influential to fixed. In other words, just because something is defined as influential, it is not necessarily more easily changed than that which is fixed. Take for example the material of a law and a belief—specifically, the law (fixed material) that makes prostitution illegal and the belief (influential material) "prostitutes are immoral". It may be far easier to change a law than a belief.

The above influential and fixed material conditions interact amongst and between each other to further entrench or concretize certain conditions.

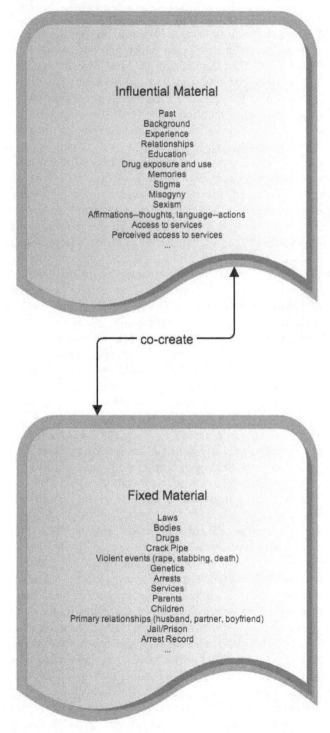

Figure 1.1 Influential and fixed material.

Most examples reside in both categories because although many incidents are fixed—like one's past, arrest record, or drug use, and therefore influence one's material reality in the present—these events or circumstances do not solely dictate one's future.

Through this analysis, I examine the discursive and material conditions understood and continually recreated that gain the density of fixed material or matter such that their constitution is no longer questioned. Take for instance the term *prostitute*, which has become fixed as an entity, construct, and identity in the past two hundred years (Karras 1996; Lerner 1986; Otis 1985). What is lost when this term becomes fixed material and is used to identify certain people in certain contexts? What can happen when the constitution of this term and action is questioned, as well as the related material conditions or commonly understood "problems" surrounding the exchange of sex for money? And finally, how do fixed and influential material influence and constrain each other? And what are the implications of these constraints for individuals who participate in these exchanges and the society in which they live?

The goal is not to discern whether something resides solely as fixed or influential material, but rather to use these terms as an heuristic that reveals how material conditions can stagnate, change, fluctuate, and be disrupted based on one's understanding of these fixed and influential materials as well as the influence they have on one's ability to act as an agent and influence material conditions and systems. English Professor Beverly Moss (2011) argues "we must expand the spaces and sites in which we examine these practices [literate activity and behavior]" (p. 2). Although Moss focuses on the written word, my goals align with hers in exploring how "the material, social, and cultural conditions in which they operate define the range of agency" (p. 5). Multiple discourses, ideologies, and perspectives influence the local media, the discourse used in social service and enforcement agencies, and in the language of the people I interviewed. Brummett (1991) refers to this blending of rhetorical transactions as "a complex of mosaics created within a certain time frame" (p. 70).[1] Brummett argues an individual orders her world by constructing patterns, or mosaics, that make their experience meaningful while at the same time creating herself as a subject who is positioned by the pattern (p. 84). Therefore, ideology, or the mosaic, is constructed by the individual in a way that makes her known experience meaningful, while it also constructs the individual as a subject who is recognizable within that same pattern. Examining and deconstructing these mosaics is a way of better understanding the underlying belief systems or patterns of experience that "make sense"—to an individual or individuals—while revealing how their own positions are created and reflected by that same belief system or pattern. This mosaic creation is a process of managing meaning.

I play with vision as a way to show how one's experiences, beliefs, history, and the available information influence one's perception of events, circumstances, and individuals.

6   Street Sex Workers' Discourse

Figure 1.2   Duck-Rabbit ambiguous image.

Like the duck and rabbit image in Figure 1.2, how one views the lines drawn influences the overall picture. It is possible to see both at once, or to switch back and forth between two entirely different images. The truth does not lie within the "lines" so to speak, nor the image of the duck or rabbit, but rather "truth" is created in the moment. Ultimately, one creates a collage of understanding.

Some collages create more dominant patterns than others. And a variety of collages make up an individual's and society's viewpoints about the exchange of sex for money or other gain based on one's experiences, history, and the patterns that emerge based on these contexts in media, events, and personal circumstances. As the mosaic is a fixed entity, the kaleidoscope image is a more malleable way of understanding how patterns are created and can shift and change based on external elements as well as the agency and perspective of the viewer. As a viewer reads the patterns, she can also change the theme with a slight shift. The kaleidoscope represents the mutable nature of our readings of texts and patterns of experience while simultaneously reflecting the fixed notions of terms and ideas. Although they can be altered, or may change, each picture bears some of the same ideas embedded in the previous scene. English Professor Jacquelyn Jones Royster introduces the "kaleidoscopic view" as a way

> rhetorical action becomes visible as a site of continuous struggle in response to an ongoing hermeneutic problem [. . . and] is designed to make the hidden and unrecognized visible. This view, by its very framing (that is, in being multi-lensed), encourages us, above all else, to complicate our thinking, rather than simplify it, in search of greater clarity and also greater interpretive power. (p. 73)

Using a "material kaleidoscope," so to speak, both the viewer and the view shifts: the viewer is an active participant in the process.

DO "PROSTITUTE" BODIES MATTER?

Drawing on Rhetoric and Comparative Literature Professor Judith Butler, I use the word *matter* as a noun (the material body) and a verb (the importance of certain bodies) in order to explore both in specific contexts. In *Bodies that Matter*, Judith Butler (2011) asks "Can language simply refer to materiality, or is language also the very condition under which materiality may be said to appear?" (p. 6). Drawing on Butler's argument that language is a condition under and through which materiality appears, within this study I apply this same question to the concept, construction, and reality of the *prostitute*. For example, Butler's "sex of materiality" is a site where she traces materiality as "the site at which a certain drama of sexual difference plays out" (p. 22). As Butler emphasizes, "to invoke matter is to invoke a sedimented history of sexual hierarchy and sexual erasures." The "prostitute" is also a site at which differences—morality, identification, belief systems, actions, and their implications—play out. What is gained and lost in the assumptions and beliefs embodied and materialized in the "prostitute" concept? Butler asks these questions about which bodies are said to "matter" in terms of importance and, I would add, as agents active in shaping their own lives. As Butler argues:

> It must be possible to concede and affirm an array of "materialities" that pertain to the body, that which is signified by the domains of biology, anatomy, physiology, hormonal and chemical composition, illness, age, weight, metabolism, life and death. None of this can be denied. [. . .] That each of those categories have a history and a historicity, that each of them is constituted through the boundary lines that distinguish them, and hence, by what they exclude, that relations of discourse and power produce hierarchies and overlappings among them and challenge those boundaries, implies that these are *both* persistent and contested regions. [. . .] We might want to claim that what persists within these contested domains is the "materiality" of the body. (2011, p. 36)

Butler clarifies this idea of repetition as enabling or constructing the subject: "for construction is neither a subject nor its act, but a process of reiteration by which both 'subjects' and 'acts' come to appear at all. There is no power that acts, but only a reiterated acting that is power in its persistence and instability" (p. xviii). She asks for a return to the idea of matter, "not as site or surface, but as *a process of materialization that stabilizes over time to produce the effect of boundary, fixity, and surface we call matter* (emphasis in original, p. xviii).

If materialities are "*both* persistent and contested regions," there is space through which the materialities can be and are made differently. Focusing on and integrating the voices of the women who inhabit these material bodies and their lived material conditions create opportunities not only for those who do not inhabit these bodies in the exact same way to understand, but also to change these materialities through altered perceptions and understandings. Simultaneously, I examine the "prostitute" concept based on Butler's exploration of what is represented and produced as "outside" oppositional discourse. Butler argues:

> The task is to refigure this necessary "outside" as a future horizon, one in which the violence of exclusion is perpetually in the process of being overcome. But of equal importance is the preservation of the outside, the site where discourse meets its limits, where the opacity of what is not included in a given regime of truth acts as a disruptive site of linguistic impropriety and unrepresentability, illuminating the violent and contingent boundaries of that normative regime precisely through the inability of that regime to represent that which might pose a fundamental threat to its continuity." (p. 25)

In other words, using this theory as a framework, I explore how the idea, term, identity, and material reality of "the prostitute" is constituted in the discourse surrounding women who exchange sex for money or other gain, and then, as the places for disruption are revealed, explore how materialities can be made differently.

What does the term *prostitute* constitute and label? How does the "outsider status," in terms of outside mainstream behaviors and identities, of the "prostitute" allow for an exploration of what is excluded in "non-prostitute" status? I do not argue the concept or term *prostitute* is "outside" oppositional discourse. The term co-constructs oppositional discourse (prostitute and non-prostitute) and thereby structures a "normative regime" (p. 25) or a given "regime of truth" simply in its application (or non-application) to describe a person or activity. When Butler talks about the preservation of the "outside" she is talking about that which cannot be linguistically named or represented, or "where discourse meets its limits." And it is through this examination of where discourse meets its limits that makes more precise the "violent and contingent boundaries" of those labels. My goal is to turn this definition inside out to examine not only the construct of the term and identity of "prostitute" but also that which remains outside of both the normative regimes of "non-prostitute" as well as "prostitute." If neither "prostitute" nor "non-prostitute" as normative regimes can capture the reality of individuals, how is the continuity between both disrupted? And what does that mean for the material realities and material bodies continually identified and co-constructed?

I draw on Butler because she pushes at what is outside and "unrepresentable" through discourse while simultaneously maintaining that "outside" as a threat to what is definitively known and therefore exclusionary. Because discourse is always partial, identifying what is "outside" specific terms illuminates the boundaries, questions the normative regimes, and *can* disrupt these categories of representation while allowing for the boundaries to be continually contested. This questioning and potential emergent disruptions open up space for the possibility of thinking, speaking, acting, and being constituted differently, which impacts the limits of what can and cannot be constituted. For example, if a human's gender is limited to only male or female and one pushes at the limits of these definitions and realities toward what is outside those norms, and the terms and physical bodies of "intersex" individuals are realized, this identity, knowledge of and about oneself, and even one's place in the world is constituted in a different way—much differently than had that discourse and material reality remained unknown and unrealized. The two concepts (and far beyond only two, for instance, spiritual, emotional, physiological, etc.) of discourse and material are mutually influential and intertwined—and it is through pushing at these limits of both that individuals can create space for themselves and their lived reality rather than relying on a norm or construction that may no longer fit.

What power is constituted, prohibited, and denied in the interpellation of the "prostitute" (Althusser 1971)? Who does that construction serve and how? And how are the boundaries of the "prostitute" crafted through sexual activities and sexual preferences? What is normalized in US society? Some answers include heteronormative power relations, consumer culture, capitalism, gender roles, bodily actions and roles. As Butler asks, "What has to be excluded for those economies to function as self-sustaining systems?"(2011, p. 10). What does the "exclusion" of the prostitute do for mainstream society? What does this exclusion maintain in society? Margo St. James (1987) in "The Reclamation of Whores" discusses the violence often perpetrated against prostitutes. The threat of this violence, which she argues is furthered by the criminalization of prostitution and other activities such as loitering, serves to endanger all women. She states:

> In Los Angeles recently the cops finally admitted that there had been a serial murderer on the loose for a year who had murdered ten women, ten prostitutes. The first eight prostitutes were Black women. Nothing was said. The last two were white prostitutes, so it got into the news. But usually it doesn't make the news until a non-prostitute is murdered. And may I say, murderers can't tell who's a prostitute and who's not any more than a customer can. It's their assumption. That kind of violence is generated when any single woman on the street is under suspicion and can be stopped and asked for an explaining of herself. That's what we're working against. We're just losing it if we don't stop these kinds of laws [loitering] from coming into play. (p. 85)

This regime keeps people, in particular women and other marginalized identities, in line—it guards a particular morality, action, and commerce that affects bodies, service, labor, and exchange.

INCITE! Women of Color Against Violence (2011) draws attention to criminalization and anti-trafficking legislation, arguing:

In fact, current ways of thinking about trafficking and the sex trade make LGBTQ [lesbian, gay, bisexual, transgender, transsexual, questioning] youth invisible. The 2007 study Lesbian, Gay, and Transgender Youth: An Epidemic of Homelessness found that, of the estimated 1.6 million homeless young people in the United States, between 20 and 40%, or approximately half a million, identify as LGB or T. Research also reveals that LGBTQ teens are more likely to remain homeless because they also experience homophobia and transphobia in foster care, shelters, and from service providers. A recent study, Hidden Injustice documented the systemic homophobia and transphobia LGBTQ youth experience in family and juvenile courts and in service provision, and the increased rates and lengths of detention they experience as a result. For these reasons, many LGBTQ homeless youth stay on the streets because they feel safer there. Once homeless, LGBTQ youth, and particularly LGBTQ youth of color are also at increased risk of profiling and police abuse in the context of "qualify of life" enforcement. They are also likely to become involved in the sex trades and street economies as a means of survival. Yet young men and transgender women, including those who are coerced into the sex trades, are denied access to programs such as GEMS [Girls Education and Mentoring Services], remain invisible as "victims" in the eyes of law enforcement, judges, and service providers. ("No Simple Solutions")

Not only is the marginalized status of transgender, transsexual, and people of color youth highlighted here, but the effects criminalization has on making them invisible.[2] These studies highlight the necessity of questioning the boundaries by which certain bodies are said to "matter." In addition to the violence criminalization is found to inflict on many individuals, whether involved in street economies or not, there is also the deadly violence that is enacted against those viewed as marginal—whether based on gender, race, or supposed "prostitute" status. As Kenna Quinet (2011) finds in her analysis of case studies done on victims of serial homicide from 1970–2009: "32% of all female victims of serial murder were known prostitutes suggests that female prostitutes are in fact a target for serial murder offenders in the United States, and the present analysis additionally indicates that this targeting has been increasing over time" (p. 93). She states that "because authorities are often unaware of crimes involving the 'missing missing,' investigations are delayed" (p. 81). These investigations may not be a high priority for investigators, and likewise, "The concept of the 'less dead' (S. Egger 2002)—marginal victim populations such as drug users, prostitutes, migrant workers, and other transients—suggest that some victims matter less than others" (qtd. in Quinet 93).[3] The "victim" status of women involved in street economies in concert with the combined material conditions increase the likelihood they are targets of violence.

Professor of Women's Studies, Lenore Kuo (2002) takes this question beyond that of the individual woman in her development of a prostitution policy feminists can support. She explores the conceptual construct of the prostitute and argues: "for some small number of activities an inextricable connection to the character and nature of the actor is presumed to exist. I can think of no instance where this is more obvious than in the case of prostitution" (p. 57). In her exploration of the whore-prostitute paradigm as a "significant weapon of patriarchy" she asks the following two questions: "(1) How does the conceptual construct of 'The prostitute' impact on the lives of both prostitute and nonprostitute women? (2) How will any proposed policy affect and alter this conceptual construct?" (p. 58). Like Kuo, I explore this construct as it is grounded in material reality. As "the prostitute" is constructed, what discursive and material options become more and less available? The discourse becomes the condition or occasion for further action, which necessarily constrains what actions are possible or can proceed. This always "partial" representation creates space for the integration and value of individual voices to inform what is and can be named.

RESPONSIBLE RHETORICAL AGENCY

As Butler states in her discussion of performativity, "if there is *agency*, it is to be found, paradoxically, in the possibilities opened up in and by that constrained appropriation of the regulatory law, by the materialization of that law, the compulsory appropriation and identification with those normative demands" (italics in original, p. xxi). Here, it appears agency is action taken within the "constrained appropriation" of a "normative regime". Butler explains "the account of agency conditioned by those very regimes of discourse/power cannot be conflated with voluntarism or individualism, much less with consumerism, and in no way presupposes a choosing subject" (xxiii). Humanities Professor Marilyn Cooper (2011) in "Rhetorical Agency as Emergent and Enacted" outlines the relationship between individual agency, rhetoric, and the possibilities for making meaningful change in the world. She critiques Butler's "performative notion of agency as repetition with a difference [as] unsatisfying, as the subject's actions are inevitably structured by the very norms that it attempts to resist" (p. 424). In *Bodies That Matter*, Butler (2011) points out her goal is not to "affirm the constraints under which sexed positions are assumed, but to ask how the fixity of such constraints is established, what sexual (im)possibilities have served as the constitutive constraints of sexed positionality, and what possibilities of reworking those constraints arise from within its own terms" (p. 61). I work to identify constraints that establish street-based sex work and explore the possibilities for reworking those constraints that both "make fixed" as well as "influence" the positionality of women who exchange sex for money or drugs. This process of identification and exploration reveals an opportunity for agency, or one's ability to act within and among these blending positionalities of prostitute, drug addict, impoverished person, or any other number of labels that could be applied. Cooper's definition of agency as "an emergent property of embodied individuals" is helpful in understanding "though the world changes in response to individual action, agents are very often not aware of their intentions, they do not directly cause changes, and the choices they make are not free from influence from their inheritance, past experiences, or their surround"[4] (p. 421). I draw on her concept of "embodied individual agency" and its application to all communicative interactions—in particular, those interactions with people who may be viewed as having or inhabiting less power. Cooper argues "responsible rhetorical agency is a matter of acknowledging and honoring the responsive nature of agency and that this is a kind of agency that supports deliberative democracy" (p. 422).

I place particular emphasis on the relationship created between the "rhetor" and "other" and where that responsibility lies. Cooper draws on Humberto R. Maturana: "if I invite someone to responsible action, I cannot tell him or her what to do. At most I can open the possibility for a reflection together so that we may join in bringing forth a world" (qtd. in Cooper, p. 442). Cooper goes on to say: "Responsible agency instead requires one to be aware that everyone acts out of their own space of meaning and that to affirm one's own meanings as absolute truth is to negate the other person" (p. 442). In much of the literature surrounding sex work, and street-based sex work in particular, not only have the people participating in these activities been excluded from the conversation, but those speaking have often affirmed their own meanings as "truth." I introduce the term *agential choice*, as a choice one makes for herself, according to her understanding of what is in her best interest, based on the power housed within her rather than in response to external pressure, expectations, or force. The responsibility lies in the listening and "reflection together" to create a space where agential choice can occur. In other words, it is imperative the listener places trust in the individual, or other, believing she or he is doing her or his best. Agential choice can be found in influential material and then becomes more "fixed" as it is exercised and trusted.

I remind the readers to keep in mind their own mosaics, or understandings, of street-based sex work, drug use and abuse, crime, etc., and then offer flexibility, a turn, if you will, can free the picture from a mosaic to a kaleidoscope shifting the meaning, and therefore one's perception of problems, solutions, responsibility, and their impact on the material reality of individual's lives. This examination of these material conditions and problems and solutions surrounding street-based sex work can create space for altered perspectives, perhaps shifts in ideological frameworks, leaving the viewer with a new kaleidoscopic image beyond what had previously been possible. The viewer is instrumental in this shift, as is explored more fully in the conclusion.

In line with examining the language and ideas from Butler's "normative regime", identifying what lies within fixed and influential material can help to discern what lies inside and outside the boundaries, the limits of discourse and its influence on fixed material, in order to better understand categories of representation as well as the material conditions that co-create and are co-created by the individuals participating in these exchanges. Although certainly not representative of all women who exchange sex for drugs or money throughout the United States, this analysis investigates how certain groups of people talk about sex work, sex workers, and the issues related to this work and how sex worker identities and the material conditions of their lives are represented, reproduced, and subverted in the language surrounding this work.

2 Who is the Victim
The Neighborhood or the Woman?

The "victim status" was prevalent in most public figure interviews. This chapter presents the evidence and analysis for how problems and subsequent solutions emerge based on who occupies this victim status. The neighborhoods were often considered to be victims, which included the residents and the community at large. I begin with an examination of these concepts as victims of prostitution and the central causes of this victimization; namely, drugs, violence, crime, and disease. In contrast to the neighborhoods and their residents, the women were also often viewed as "victims" of street-based sex work. The following section presents these arguments, which reveal an emphasis on the systemic conditions that often allow for and perpetuate this victim standing. Both arguments are complex and contain within them the underlying arguments and beliefs for the ideological kaleidoscopes that emerge in later chapters. I provide a brief overview to help guide the reader through the various tenets of each argument.

The "neighborhood as victim" stance is grounded in the argument that prostitution is not a "victimless crime," but rather the neighborhoods suffer directly from the presence of those participating in street economies. Emphasis is placed primarily on fear of drugs, violence, crime, and disease. Because prostitution is viewed as a crime that often leads to other more dangerous crimes, the argument follows that prostitution must be prosecuted or else the neighborhood sends the message their neighborhood is a location where these crimes can take place, which leads to an increase in all crime in that area. This argument results in an "us" versus "them" stance that positions the neighborhoods against the women who solicit exchanges of sex in their neighborhoods.

The "woman as victim" argument is rooted in the interrelated experiences of poverty, trauma, abuse, and neglect. I begin this section with several of the women's stories to provide a contextual framework that reveals their experiences of these conditions and how they often combine to create greater problems in their lives. Many of these stories culminate in drug use and abuse, which is a, if not the, central argument for the women's choice to exchange sex. The reasons both for and against using drugs are revealed most clearly, again, through the women's stories. Their reasons

Who is the Victim   15

for continued drug use range from wanting to hide their feelings, addiction itself, and the need to use drugs in order to participate in the exchanges of sex for money. I then present their reasons for choosing not to use drugs.

I conclude this chapter with an analysis of drug use and its correlation to prostitution as revealed through both stances of victimhood: the women and the neighborhoods.

"Prostitution Wrecks Neighborhood"
(Nemez newspaper article headline about street-based sex work)

Because of its presence and criminal status, prostitution and other crimes are often viewed as victimizing the residents and neighborhoods in which these crimes take place, as well as the community as a whole. Many of the public figures I interviewed attributed a "victim" status to the neighborhoods—the areas in which these exchanges occurred—making street-based sex work a problem that requires a solution. Although almost no public debate or protest occurs at the national level regarding prostitution, resident activism at the local level has grown during the 1980s and 1990s through neighborhood anti-prostitution groups (Weitzer 2000a, p. 166).[1] Street prostitution, as compared to indoor prostitution, affects the community in direct ways. In *Legalizing Prostitution*, Sociologist Ronald Weitzer (2012) refers to street prostitution as "an *ecological* problem insofar as it adversely affects the quality of life of host communities" (p. 57). As I write in the *Encyclopedia of Prostitution and Sex Work* (2006):

> As reasons for these activities to be criminalized, many neighborhood groups cite disorderly conduct, noise, declining property values, loss of business to local merchants, increase in crime, dangerous environments for children and women, and the public health risk of the spread of AIDS and other sexually transmitted infections that is evidenced by used condoms and drug paraphernalia that litter streets and sidewalks. Criminalization, in turn, allows for the removal of those who participate in these acts from the neighborhoods and society in general, at least for a short time. Rather than focusing on moral concerns, many studies find that people believe prostitution threatens their quality of life as well as a neighborhood's image and reputation. (399)

Street-based sex work is more visible, many consider it to be disruptive of the peace, and it is therefore the subject of public awareness in a way indoor sex work is not. This awareness leads people to actively work to remove street-based sex work from their neighborhoods (Clark 1993; Weitzer 2000a). Weitzer (1994) argues:

> It would be a mistake to simply dismiss these community groups as fanatics who are scapegoating prostitutes for problems not of their

making. These groups sometimes exaggerate the problem, but for the most part they appear to be reacting to real problems resulting from illegal street prostitution—problems that some prostitutes acknowledge as well. (p. 124)

Sociologist Wendy Chapkis (1997) argues "these negative social 'effects' of prostitution are used to justify criminalizing its participants in an effort to abolish the practice" (141). Police departments and neighborhood associations organize programs that try to curb prostitution in certain areas, whether by going after the women who exchange sex for money or drugs, going after their clients, or going after the owners of the property where prostitution occurs.

As revealed in the headlines above, the Nemez newspaper articles revealed this same emphasis on the neighborhoods. Using the word list feature in Antconc 3.2.0,[2] every word in the corpus is listed according to how many times it occurs. When I examined these words (aside from articles and words like *I*, *we*, and *they*) the words that appear most frequently occur as follows (from greatest to least): *police/cop* (1634); *neighborhood* (1226); *crime* (1212); *prostitute* (1135) and *drug*[3] (1061).[4] Because the words *police/cop*, *neighborhood*, and *crime* are read approximately as many times as the word *prostitute*, it becomes easy for the public to increasingly associate them[5]: Prostitution as a crime, as something the police need to respond to, and as something that exists within neighborhoods. These terms and their consistent use reiterate prostitution as a problem, and in particular a crime that can be solved through criminalization and police activities. The inclusion of the word *neighborhood* also works to construct the status of the neighborhood as a *victim* whereby the solution required to "help" the neighborhood is criminalization and arrests.

PROSTITUTION IS NOT A "VICTIMLESS CRIME"

A central concern of neighborhood association leaders and police officers were the crimes that "affected the quality of life in the neighborhood." As Sue, a white heterosexual woman in her 50s and a neighborhood association leader, stated in her interview, "I would come home from work and there would be as many as 40 prostitutes up and down the street. The 'victimless' crime was not victimless." And because the crime was commonly thought of as a "victimless one" by those who were not exposed to these activities daily, the neighborhood association members argued they had to work to educate people and city officials. Sue explains more fully:

> We had to change the judges' mindset to see that this was not a victimless crime, that this was what was happening to the residents of the neighborhoods and make them understand why this was so important

to us and why these people needed to be given appropriate jail time instead of slapping their hand and just sending them back out into the street again. It was a constant interaction and educational process between all involved.

A major concern of neighborhood association leaders and police officers is that the residents witness and are exposed to illegal activities. For example, Sue stated: "We were witnessing the acts of prostitution. We were witnessing the pimps beating the prostitutes. We witnessed shootings." And as Officer Eric Johnson, a white heterosexual man in his mid-40s and the supervisor of the Nemez Police Department vice unit, stated: "The problems that are basically the quality of life problems, obviously the prostitution problems are, some narcotic issues, things that people are seeing everyday that's in their face and they want it taken care of." Special emphasis was placed on children's exposure to these acts. As Officer Eric Johnson stated: "[Used drug paraphernalia on the street] become obviously a problem because you have children that could come in contact with these and they could spread diseases." Sue tells a story about her son's exposure:

> When my grade-school son [. . .] came home from school and said "Mom, what's a blow job?" Then I went ballistic and I said, "Where did you hear that?" and he said, "I was coming home from school and there was a woman and a man on the corner and she was telling him that she would do that for 20 dollars." And I said "That was it." [. . .] I just went off the deep end.

As the activities move closer, first within the neighborhood, and then within view of the residents, and finally, as children witness these conversations and are exposed to used needles and conversations about "blow jobs", the anxiety and agitation to solve the problem increases. The belief that children should be protected from these activities and people is clear. People who do not witness these activities may not understand their significance and therefore view prostitution as a victimless crime, but as the space between these activities and the residents decreases, the problems become more apparent.

The "victims" of this non-"victimless crime" are the residents and the neighborhoods. The education is initiated by the neighborhood association leaders and is intended to encourage the judges to increase penalties for prostitution, enforce laws against prostitution, remove the women from the street for a significant amount of time, and require jail time. The solution did not lie simply with the illegality of these activities, but rather, required the residents to educate the judges about these problems so extended sentences could be enforced. Although these activities were already illegal, they were enforced, or enforced more actively, based on the education and subsequent police activities encouraged by the neighborhood residents. And if a neighborhood or area is policed repetitively enough, the hope was the people involved in criminal activity would move to another area of town, which helps the specific neighborhood but does not solve the problem on a larger scale.

VICTIMIZED NEIGHBORHOODS: DRUGS, VIOLENCE, CRIME, AND DISEASE

> The most significant problem, especially with prostitution, obviously, is what it does to a particular neighborhood. [. . .] Everybody says prostitution is a victimless crime, which isn't correct if you've been out there, because what happens is you have prostitution in a particular neighborhood and if its allowed to continue, then you as an innocent person walking down the street will get approached by some guy wanting to know if you're dating [. . .] and you don't need that harassment. [. . .] Usually most of the prostitutes, a large percentage of them are drug addicts, and with the drug addicts you're going to get needles, syringes, whatever, cotton swabs, that are just going to be disposed on the street because the people live on the street. [. . .] Along with that you have drug activity because the prostitute is prostituting herself to get the money to pay for the next fix, so that particular drug person will be nearby so that they can get their money. Along with the drug usage, I mean what will happen is that the girls are out there prostituting themselves getting money for their habits, usually they have a security person, a male security person, not necessarily a pimp, but just somebody to provide protection for them and that person most likely is going to be a drug user also so that prostitute has to go out there and turn tricks, usually between 10 and 20 a day to cover her habit and his habit, plus they need a place to stay, they need food to eat, and so it comes into [where] we have economic issues and usually its into a lower area of town because that's the only place that they can afford the housing.
> —Officer Eric Johnson, a white heterosexual man in his mid-40s and the supervisor of the Nemez Police Department vice unit

First and foremost, exposure to criminal behaviors victimizes the residents in the neighborhood and the neighborhood itself. In addition to the arguments made about prostitution and its status as a victimless crime, multiple associations are made between prostitution, drug use, violence, and crime in general.

In response to my question about the public perception of these women, Officer Eugene Matthews, a white heterosexual man in his late 30s and a lieutenant in the Nemez Police Department, said:

They don't like them because, like I say, they honestly deteriorate neighborhoods. They really . . . You have to see the whole picture of what they do in neighborhoods. There's all these elements that you can bring into a neighborhood, and they all kinda like fuse together and then you've got a problem. And most of the time when it exists in the neighborhoods, your property values go down, the crime rates go up, the whole appearance of the neighborhood deteriorates rapidly, and then it's just a matter of time before it gets to the point where you have a complete skeleton of a neighborhood, where they've . . . It's just been . . . It's like a cancer: It takes over a neighborhood. It brings in other people because the good people move out. The criminals—the less, you know, responsible people move in, and then you've got a neighborhood that is seriously deteriorated.

In response to this same question, Officer Tom Hixson, a white 52-year-old heterosexual male and a former supervisor of the vice unit, stated:

Secondly [in terms of significant problems], the crimes that are involved. Car jackings, robberies, aggravated assault, shootings, stabbings, robberies, thefts, anything that is associated because obviously most of them are addicted to some sort of drug and the people that they hang out with kind of leech off of their profession are involved in all these drugs.

Russell, a white heterosexual man in his mid-30s and a neighborhood association leader, was most concerned about the people and activities associated with prostitution:

I would say the element it attracts. It attracts drug use. It attracts violence, domestic violence, that type of thing. I think those are the biggest problems our neighborhood faces or has faced with it. It seems like every time we've had problems with prostitution there's also been a house with drugs involved. [. . .] Because you not only had the johns and the prostitutes, you had the drugs that went along with it, and to buy the drugs there were burglaries, there were car thefts, there were shootings, there were beatings, there was just about everything that goes along with that type of crime, the prostitution and so forth. [. . .] We don't want prostitutes in our neighborhood because it brings in a worse element. I don't know, it seems if you were to have problems, prostitution is probably less bad of a problem than drug activity. Prostitution brings drug activity and drug activity brings prostitution. I don't know, it's a chicken and egg thing, I don't know.

The officer makes the connection between street-based sex work and drug use. He claims most of the women are addicted to drugs, and because the women both live and work on the street, this activity and its refuse are prevalent throughout the neighborhood. Inherent to those activities is violence and crime. Prostitutes are represented as using drugs, and there are other people around who sell drugs or want to "leech off of their profession" in order to use drugs. The cost of drugs leads to crimes being committed, and although the cause and effect relationship isn't entirely clear, the source of these problems is attributed to prostitution, not drugs, poverty, or the johns.

Joan, a white, 43-year-old bisexual woman and an activist with a sex worker rights organization, provides a minority opinion stating she is "happy to have them in my neighborhood":

Joan: No, I don't mind them in my neighborhood at all. Not at all. In fact I try to be really nice to them and make them feel welcome. I think everyone must walk down the street giving them dirty looks [. . .] because they're afraid of them or they think they're dirty and to me I think I'd like to get it decriminalized because I think they could work in better circumstances, but I'm happy to have them in my neighborhood. They could be in front of my house for all I care. I don't think they're bad for my children. They are women fully clothed walking down the street and getting in cars and getting out of cars. Lots of people walk down the street and get in and out of cars and nobody's the wiser for what they do in the car and where they go. They could be going to Target or they could be going to a parking lot and having sex. We don't see it, so who the hell cares what they're doing. I'm fine with them in my neighborhood, totally fine. I wish there was more of them in my neighborhood because I'd be really nice to them, and I've gotten my neighbors to be nicer to them.
Jill: How do you do that?
Joan: I've just talked to them a lot about them. I talk about them at the neighborhood meetings, in the neighborhood emails, the neighborhood association emails when people say things about them, I jump right on their cases and I'm like you know "Why don't you see if she needs a meal, why don't you see if she needs a ride somewhere? Why don't you see if her husband is beating her up?" I'm always trying to advocate for them to be compassionate and kind and treat them like neighbors.

In addition to their presence in the neighborhoods, the women who exchange sex are viewed by many public figures as vectors of sexually transmitted infections. In response to my question about the most significant problems related to prostitution, Officer Tom Hixson said: "First and foremost is probably the sexually transmitted diseases and the health-related various issues that get passed on, passed back and forth." Officer

Tom Hixson does not relate this issue to street workers' health, but rather the public's health in general.

"BROKEN WINDOW THEORY" VERSUS "PUSHING THEM DEEPER INTO THE SHADOWS"

> A lot of times what you'll get is . . . you know the broken window theory, if you let it alone, then people just think they can come in and do even more damage to that area. And that's why a lot of the neighborhood associations are not, are stepping up asking for assistance in ridding the area of that type of behavior. [. . .] We're not obviously driving around looking for the prostitutes, its because we've been summoned to a particular area because of complaints and these complaints can come from neighborhood associations, from businesses, and from the field officers who work the particular sectors. They can contact us and advise us that "Hey, we've got a prostitution problem here."
> —Officer Eric Johnson, a white heterosexual man in his mid-40s and the supervisor of the Nemez Police Department vice unit

Resident awareness is one solution to the prostitution and crime problems as explained by Russell, a white heterosexual man in his mid-30s and a neighborhood association leader:

> Awareness of the residents and that type of thing, making a concerted effort to try to solve some of our problems as a group. Calling the police more and reporting it more, and just people being more active. [. . .] We would just call the police four and five times a day and anytime we'd see a drug deal happen we'd call the police. Any time we'd see prostitutes walking up and down the street, we'd call the police. Just constantly calling, we finally got the city's attention and the city council office got behind it and they would authorize surveillance or whatever they did. Finally, they just found easier places to go.

As Sue stated: "Report everything. Don't think that they're not going to do anything because eventually, if you call enough, they will do something." This response was dictated by the police, Sue explained: "We would call and say 'I'd like to report.' Because they were saying report, report, so we'd call to report."

Because the problem is one of proximity and exposure, the residents are motivated to find a solution to these problems. The solution, then, becomes the removal of the people and activities from the location. Through the resident activities, the police are empowered to move into a neighborhood and solve the problem by arresting those who participate in these activities. Officer Jennifer Castillo, an Hispanic 34-year-old heterosexual female who had lived in Nemez for 29 years, worked as a Nemez Police Department undercover officer:

> Down in the Freemont Corridor, we have, um, the neighborhood; there's a certain lady that is very, very—she has a great relationship with us. She always calls and complains, which is good for us because then we're able to go down there and work a lot more than—I mean, we like to get complaints because then we know we can go down there, you know, we have a complaint. And she has actually seen a decrease in prostitution, which makes us feel good. And I've actually seen a decrease when I'm, you know, driving down First; Fifth and Coral is another area, and we can't find any over there now, which is good because we used to be able to pick, you know, three up in one night. But I would say the public perception is . . . People in Nemez know where to go to find prostitutes.

The problem is clearly defined as illegal behavior: if someone is doing something illegal, call the police, they will increase their presence, and arrests will be made, which removes those people participating in illegal activities from the area. The residents' actions are the beginning of the constructed solution, which are to recognize the illegal behaviors and call the police to make these problems a priority for the city that will lead to subsequent arrests. This construction of the problem places the blame squarely on the shoulders of the women, pimps, johns, drug users and dealers and protects the residents and neighborhoods from these people and illegal activities.

Chelley, an Hispanic heterosexual female in her late 40s who worked in community outreach for a mental health organization, critiqued these neighborhood responses: "Nemez thinks it's their problem. The ones that they're in their neighborhoods because they're infesting their neighborhoods. [. . .] The ones that want them shooed out should help take care of it and not just shoo them away." Rather than solving the problem or trying to "help take care of it," the neighborhood associations and police officers are depicted as simply scaring the women away from that particular area. Joan, a white, 43-year-old, bisexual woman and an activist with a sex worker rights organization, questioned the role prostitution is harnessed with in bringing other crime to an area:

> It's just too easy to say let's get the prostitutes off the street and the neighborhood would be fine. These are really poor demographics. [. . .] It's a lot easier to say if we get this defenseless weak woman off the street all the drugs are going to go away, all the crime is going to go away because she's bringing it all here. [. . .] Maybe it's not that simple, but [. . .] I think that they think that prostitution brings drugs to the neighborhood. [. . .] It's really easy to target sex workers because what are they going to do? Try to fix poverty in the neighborhood?

It's just real easy to gang up on the sex worker and politicians love it because it's really easy to swoop in and arrest a bunch of sex workers. [. . .] I think you can visibly look like you've done something, when really you've just pushed them to another neighborhood or put them somewhere for two weeks [. . .] They do go away for awhile. They definitely go away. You can definitely push them away, or push them deeper into the shadows.

Joan brings the argument back to the subject of poverty and how difficult it is to address. She also addresses the visibility of the women, admitting the women do go away, but rather than solving the dual problems of their presence in the neighborhood and the poverty compelling them to be there, they are simply being pushed "deeper into the shadows." By constructing the problem as poverty, she critiques the argument that prostitutes are responsible for bringing crime into a neighborhood. Rather, Joan views the women as scapegoats blamed for the problems related to poverty in general and drug use and crime in particular.

IMPLICATIONS: US VERSUS THEM

This depiction of the problem and the solution creates a resident versus criminal, or an "us versus them" situation, as revealed by Sue, a white heterosexual woman in her late 50s and a neighborhood association leader:

The people were very intimidated because the normal people weren't out on the street. My main objective was to get the prostitutes off the streets and get our residents back on the streets. That was a long hard road and it was a battle that was fought 24/7 to the point where there were days when I would get so disgraced and disgusted that I would just sit down and cry my eyes out. People were afraid to walk the streets, and rightly so [. . .] we had to take back our streets, literally take back our streets, and the only way we could do that was to hammer, hammer, hammer, get them arrested and work on ways so it wasn't just a revolving door [people arrested, fined, and released from jail].

Sue depicts the residents as "normal people" who were afraid to walk the streets. This language creates the prostitutes and others as "abnormal" because they were not afraid to walk the streets. The neighborhood associations align themselves with the police, who then work to arrest these women and other people participating in illegal activities. It is through resident surveillance and activity that the police are called and arrests made. Prostitution and drugs are the problem; the residents the solution.

Within this "Us versus Them" analysis, it is important to note the women participating in these activities are often assumed to live outside the

Who is the Victim?

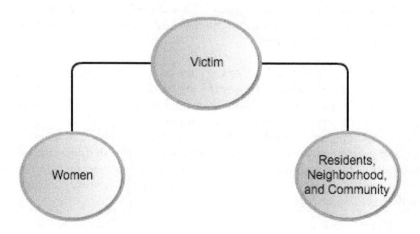

Figure 2.1 Who is the victim?

neighborhoods in which they work. Therefore, resident awareness and activity is ascribed as "us" and those participating in these activities "them." And yet making distinctions about residents and non-residents is often inaccurate, as the women in many cases are residents in the neighborhoods in which they work. Identifying prostitution as the problem and criminalization as the solution as the foundation for a law-enforcement approach often disproportionately targets and harms people of color as well as transgender individuals.[6]

I leave the discussion of the neighborhood as victim to present the context of woman as "victim" and its influence on how the problems and solutions surrounding street-based sex work are defined.

"Casualties of the Street"
(Nemez newspaper article headline about street-based sex work)

CONSIDER A BIRDCAGE

The experience of oppressed people is that the living of one's life is confined and shaped by forces and barriers which are not accidental or occasional and hence avoidable, but are systematically related to each other in such a way as to catch one between and among them and restrict or penalize motion in any direction. It is the experience of being caged in: all avenues, in every direction, are blocked or booby trapped.

Cages. Consider a birdcage. If you look very closely at just one wire in the cage, you cannot see the other wires. If your conception of what is before you is determined by this myopic focus, you could look at that one wire, up and down the length of it, and be unable to see why a bird would not just fly around the wire any time it wanted to go somewhere. Furthermore, even if, one at a time, you myopically inspected each wire, you still could not see why a bird would have trouble going past the wires to get anywhere. There is no physical property of any one wire, nothing that the closest scrutiny could discover, that will reveal how a bird could be inhibited or harmed by it except in the most accidental way. It is only when you step back, stop looking at the wires one by one, microscopically, and take a macroscopic view of the whole cage, that you can see why the bird does not go anywhere; and then you will see it in a moment. It will require no great subtlety of mental powers. It is perfectly obvious that the bird is surrounded by a network of systematically related barriers, no one of which would be the least hindrance to its flight, but which, by their relations to each other, are as confining as the solid walls of a dungeon.

It is now possible to grasp one of the reasons why oppression can be hard to see and recognize: one can study the elements of an oppressive structure with great care and some good will without seeing the structure as a whole, and hence without seeing or being able to understand that one is looking at a cage and that there are people there who are caged, whose motion and mobility are restricted, whose lives are shaped and reduced.

—Marilyn Frye, *The Politics of Reality: Essays in Feminist Theory*, 1983

When the woman is considered a victim, various events or influential material cause and more firmly entrench this "victim" status, including poverty; trauma, abuse or neglect; substance use and abuse; violence; poor health; and stigma, which can further exacerbate all of the above conditions. The cyclical nature of this status is often difficult to tease apart because of the complex interrelationships of influential and fixed material. For example, one's exposure to trauma, abuse, and/or neglect, either in the past or present, can place its object in the victim role. These experiences can then lead to other behaviors, for instance drug use, that can place the individual at further risk of becoming a victim of health problems, violence, or drug use.

Figure 2.2 outlines the problems and solutions that emerged from my data when the woman is the primary focus. Rather than provide an overly simplistic explanation of how I came to this understanding, the following presents several of my participants' stories. After presenting this context, their stories reveal how poverty and coping with trauma, abuse, and neglect

26 *Street Sex Workers' Discourse*

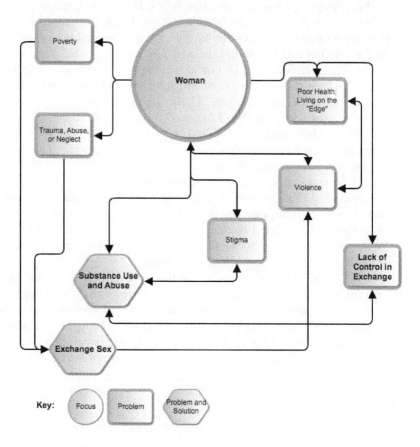

Figure 2.2 Problems and solutions related to woman as victim.

provides a foundation for the cyclical and inextricably connected material conditions that encage my participants.

Tiffany started exchanging sex at 29, when her daughter was 3 or 4. When I asked her what made her decide to start, she explained:

Tiffany: Involved with the men.
Jill: Okay. Tell me about that.
Tiffany: The brothers—or the black guys.
Jill: Okay. So you started, what, dating them?
Tiffany: I dated one and then I met another one. I never got rid of him because he came and parked it in the house. And then I got rid of the first one [laughs]. And then he had brought some girl up in the house and said, 'This was my daughter.' And it was raining the night she came, so I figured she could stay there. She started

living there. Then he brought some other woman up in there, and those two went out and made him money. [. . .] Making him money, and then he turned around and told me see how much I can make within an hour. I got mad at him. Well, I got mad at him first and told him, 'I ain't doing it because I've got two kids.' I just walked out front and some dude stopped and asked if I was working. And I said, 'Sure.' And it didn't take me more than 15 minutes to make 80 bucks. That dude gave me—I made more than 80 bucks, but that dude gave me 40, and then somebody else picked me up and gave me what was in his wallet, plus 70 more dollars after we went to the bank. [. . .] But I didn't bring him the whole money back. [. . .] I would never . . . I've always hid my money and brought back like $20, maybe $30 to the people I was with. Because I knew better.

Jill: So what made you decide to do that when he told you?
Tiffany: He didn't tell me. He told me, but then I was pissed off because he was feeding them the crack and he wasn't giving me any more until I made some money. So I figured, "Forget you."

Tiffany mentioned a number of men who protected her and also asked for money and/or crack after she did her "business."

Anna is a 43-year-old, white heterosexual woman who had lived in Nemez for approximately half her life. As a young wife, Anna had been training to be a medical secretary with only three months until graduation when her third child was born. When her husband died unexpectedly, his mother, who owned the house they were living in, told her she had to move out. Anna moved in with a friend and didn't have the education to get a job or home of her own. She ended up giving her mother custody of her children, and they lived with her mother until they were 18. Anna struggled with depression and got involved in a series of abusive relationships. She was also using drugs, exchanging sex for money, and later ended up homeless.

Denise is a 43year-old, white, heterosexual woman. Her father was an alcoholic who was physically abusive, and as a child she was "in and out of foster homes" due to her mother's medical issues and her father's alcoholism. She explained what it was like growing up:

Denise: My child life was bad, I mean bad. My dad was an alcoholic. He beat his kids all the time. I mean it was a very, very crucial [difficult] childhood.
Jill: Is that why you wanted to leave?
Denise: Yeah. Because I got tired of getting beat. And my sister, she'd beat me up. I was pregnant. I was 6 months pregnant and all I wanted to do was fry an egg sandwich. Big deal, what's an egg, you know? And she beats me up. I ran away. My dad had them throw me in jail. They sent me to an unwed mothers' home. They were going to take my child away, because I was too young.

Jill: How old were you?
Denise: I was 16. But my sister ended up going to court and getting guardianship of me, and I was able to have my child and I kept her.
Jill: Did you live at home when you had your child or did you live with your sister?
Denise: I lived with my sister, yeah. I was often in and out of foster homes because of my dad, and my mom's medical history. [. . .] My oldest sister, she was 13 when she got married. She got married so she could take care of us kids so the state wouldn't have us no longer. She got married to her husband and fought for us kids, and three of us got to go live with her. The other two didn't.
Jill: When she was 13?
Denise: Mmm hmmm [yes].
Jill: Wow. And how old were you?
Denise: Let's see. I was eight. I was a youngster.

Denise had finished eighth grade and had children at a young age, which led her to quit school. She said: "I have a learning disability that really is a struggle for me, that I get really humiliated and I won't even say anything; I'll just sit there and look at the people, you know, because it humiliates me. But other than that, I haven't had a desire to go back."

Lisa is a 47-year-old, Hispanic heterosexual woman who had just started a substance abuse program and was between places at the time of our interview. She was born in Nemez and had lived there her whole life. Her mother was Native American and her father was born in Mexico but grew up in the United States. Her father committed suicide, and Lisa was given up for adoption when she was two years old. She lived with her adoptive parents, who were from Mexico, until she was thirteen, started getting into trouble, and was taken away by the state. She left school during seventh grade when she ran away from home and ended up in juvenile detention. Lisa said:

> I ran away from home. I was in a foster home, and I was just real rebellious, you know what I mean? My parents, they didn't have a right to tell me what to do you, you know, I just had that attitude, and so I ran away and then I went to juvenile. Then I got out of juvenile, and that's when I met my husband, which was, I lied to him and told him I was 18. He was 21 and I ended up getting pregnant. I got married and that didn't work either.

Lisa had her first son at 14.

Lisa started drinking when she was eight years old and smoking pot at 12 or 13. She started doing heroin at 27 or 28, when a boyfriend was using it. She was a heroin addict for 17 years. Lisa had been arrested "probably 30 times" for prostitution.

Lisa first exchanged sex for money when she was "about 24." She said:

	I was in a bar and I met this gentleman in there and . . . we went out to . . . we went out, you know, and at the end he asked if I needed any money, if I needed anything, and I said "No," and he gave me some money. And he told me to call him, and I started calling him and that was my first john. [. . .] See, I wasn't on drugs. I mean, I would drink and I smoked pot, okay? But I wasn't like shooting heroin, doing crystal, or smoking that shitty-ass crack shit that just blows, you know, the mind.
Jill:	So when you started, you were just doing it for fun?
Lisa:	Yeah. Like I said, I met him at a club, we'd go out dancing. My sister was watching the baby, watching my son, and I was out having fun. I'd call this guy up and he'd come and see me, pick me up, and we'd go out, you know? It was like that. [. . .] I still don't see nothing wrong with it if it's a consenting adult.

For the three months prior to our interview, Lisa had been doing part-time work with a friend who owns his own roofing business. She earned her GED when she was nineteen. She was interested in getting more education, but was primarily concerned about looking for a home and trying to get situated financially.

Donna, a 47-year-old, heterosexual woman, identified as half Italian and half Cherokee, but because that was complicated, she told people she was white. Donna got married when she was sixteen and had a baby. She said:

> I was living with my parents until I was 16. I got married when I was 16. I had my first daughter exactly one month after I turned 17. My high school sweetheart is who I married. I did not love him. I wanted to get away from my father. That's why I got pregnant and got away.

Donna's father had been in the Navy and they moved around a lot when she was growing up. Her mother stayed at home and later worked at a factory. Donna's father had been adopted and they didn't know much about his family, and she believed that was where her addiction came from: "Because no one in my family is an addict. I'm the only one."

Donna called her parents [from the southwest state where she was residing] and told them she was "prostituting" and they came and got her and took her home. She had been raped several times while working on the street. When she returned to her home, she was drinking alcohol and smoking pot. Donna explained:

> And, um, my mother and father didn't know how to handle it. I didn't know how to handle it. I thought I had "prostitute," "dirty whore" written across my forehead, you know? It really messed me up, and I really got . . . I got raped a couple times really, really bad while I was out there

on the street. [. . .]And my parents didn't know how to handle it, and they ended up taking my kids to CPS [Child Protective Services].

When she spoke of her drug use, she said:

> I was using pot . . . I was doing a lot of alcohol for quite a few years. When I started doing cocaine, I started right off with the needles. Yeah, and I quit everything else. That was it, you know? And I shot dope for thirteen years. I started doing heroin and coke, and, um, I OD'd on coke really bad. I was dead for three and a half minutes; they brought me back.

Donna said she came from "a very dysfunctional" family, but she was raised with a lot of values and morals:

> I did come from a pretty good family, you know? So being out here in this world, it's been real hard for me because I do have a conscience, I do have a heart, I do believe in certain things. I know I'm better than a prostitute. I'm not just putting prostitution down, but I know that I'm, you know, I'm a good person. And it's been real hard to be a drug addict and a prostitute because I still have a lot of values and I do have a conscience. [. . .] And this last month that I started prostituting again, it's been really hard for me. Especially because of my age, my medical conditions and issues. You know, I don't walk with my head down. I'm not ashamed. I'm not proud, but I'm not ashamed. Because I take care of me. And if that's what I have to do at the time, that's what I do.

At the time of the interview, she had lived in Nemez for 20 years, where she had moved because her parents had retired there. As she said: "I'm stuck here. For the last ten years, I've been going to prison, probation, parole, so I haven't been able to leave."

Julie is a white, 42-year-old heterosexual woman who had lived in Nemez since she was 13 years old when her mother got remarried to her stepdad. Her father was in the Navy and her mother worked as a dental assistant. Her parents are both white, and she wasn't sure what levels of education they had completed. Julie dropped out of school during eighth grade and mentioned she had a learning disability, making it hard for her to spell and count. Julie was first introduced to drugs at thirteen by her brother and his girlfriend and had used them, as she said, "all my life." Julie first exchanged sex for money when she was 15 years old.

Ava is a white, 23-year-old heterosexual woman who had lived in Nemez for one year. Her parents had met in a bar and got pregnant with her. When I asked her what her parents did, she said: "My dad is actually now a police officer. He just became one within the past couple years [laughs]. It took him a long time to grow up. And my mom, she likes to . . . be a professional alcoholic."

Ava lived with her mom until she was 11, when she was removed due to her mother's alcoholism. The state called her father and told him if he didn't take her, she would be in foster care, so she went to live with her dad. She was resistant to her father, who had trouble handling her, and so her aunt stepped in and offered to adopt her, which they did when she was 14. But they "couldn't handle" her either, and so another aunt and uncle took her in. When she was 15 and living in the northwest she had "been involved in some crap [. . .] and was in a juvenile facility for awhile." The first time Ava exchanged sex for money was to buy Christmas presents. She was 14. Ava had never been arrested for prostitution.

These stories present the context and reasons for many of my participants' involvement in street-based sex work. From "having fun" to needing to support oneself and one's children, the women's stories stem from both individual choices and systemic influences that often resulted in drug use and abuse as well as criminal penalties for prostitution. Their need to leave difficult environments often led them to locate paths for survival that they had not initially intended. The lack of safety nets and support combined with trauma and increased substance use led many to a cyclical path of increased violation and victimization perpetrated by families, clients, and even the criminal justice system. These material conditions further jeopardized their health and control over the choices they made for survival and meeting their needs. Furthermore, substance use and exchanging sex are stigmatized, which can further isolate the woman, leading to an even greater risk of violence and less recourse if and when this violence does occur. These stories not only provide a context for the cyclical nature of the problems and material conditions surrounding street-based sex work, but they also provide a framework through which the problems and solutions can be understood.

SURVIVING POVERTY

The women I interviewed did not use the word *victim*, and yet they do address the issues of poverty, trauma, abuse, and neglect in their lives. Several stated they first exchanged sex for money to provide for their basic needs. Brenda is a white, 48-year-old lesbian woman who had lived in Nemez for 44 years. She was removed from her parents when she was 11 because her father was abusive. She started using drugs at this same time to "escape from getting beat." Her mother then "gave them up to the state." She was moved to a foster home and later a group home. At 14 she was sleeping with the housemother of the group home. The home was shut down by the state and at 15 she was on her own. She had completed eleventh grade. She started exchanging sex when she was 15 to "survive:"

> See when I started prostituting, I did it because I was only 15 and I was doing it to survive . . . to make money so I could have a place to

live. Because I was working at Wendy's two hours a day. That wasn't enough to pay rent and stuff. And I wasn't into drugs then. And then, once you start doing it, it just kind of falls into place, like, you have to do the drugs to be able to do the prostitution.

Brenda's older sister taught her how to do prostitution. As Brenda described: "Yeah, [she taught me] how to survive. Because she was the only one there for me—my family wasn't." Brenda struggled to find a way to support herself when her parents and the foster-care system failed her, and she turned to exchanging sex. This decision then led her into a lifestyle of drugs and exchanging sex in order to support her drug habit. This issue speaks to the conditions of abuse and poverty in which many children live.

Like Brenda, Anna first exchanged sex to support herself and her children. Anna had exchanged sex for money for almost half her life and had never been arrested for prostitution. At the time of the interview she was exchanging sex with only one "regular" client she had known for 11 years in order to supplement her income and support herself. She lived in an apartment with her boyfriend and often took care of her grandchildren.

Denise, a 43-year-old, white, heterosexual woman, exchanged sex in another state when her children were very young. She tells the story of her first time:

> I was at a motel, I was in a strange town, I didn't know where the hell I was at, and I had three little kids telling me that they were hungry. I didn't know who to go to or anything, so I did. Yeah, I went out and I sold myself five times just to take care of them three babies. And I feel guilty about it now, to this day. But at least I knew that my babies ate. [. . .] And back then, I didn't even think about it, you know? I wasn't thinking about it. But now, the more I sit, and yeah, I do, I dwell on sleeping with a man just to get food for my babies. You know, I do, I dwell on it. My children know. I mean, they were old enough that they knew mom was doing something, but they didn't know exactly what. [. . .] My oldest daughter, when she found out [her mom had exchanged sex for money], she goes, "Mama, next time, let the state take us. Don't do that." And I said, "I can't let the state have you babies. There's just no way. I mean, I had a way of feeding you guys, so I did it, you know?" Yeah, I know it was wrong and I feel guilty about it, but there's nothing . . . you can't change it, you know?

Like the three stories told above, many public figures understood poverty as one of the underlying causes of street-based sex work. Sylvia, an Hispanic lesbian woman in her late 30s, and a director at a mental health organization, said:

> I think that poverty is definitely a factor. I think that's probably the underlying factor . . . this behavior is born of a certain sense of

desperation that is frequently born of poverty. And poverty can happen to anyone. Poverty of spirit, poverty of wallet, poverty of language, of concern or care, of bankruptcy. The way I'm seeing poverty manifest is through the frustration, the violence, and the drug use.

Joan, a white, 43-year-old, bisexual woman and an activist with a sex worker rights organization, echoed these sentiments: "These are really poor demographics. These are demographics that are involved [with] social service agencies at a higher rate than any other neighborhoods in Nemez." Rosalie, an Hispanic, 43-year-old, heterosexual case manager at a women's homeless facility, said:

> And I hear a lot, too, that "Oh, she must be a drug addict." Right away they assume that these women are drug addicts. And sometimes okay, they are, but a lot of them, they're not, you know? There are some women that this is all she knows how to do, and she needs to feed her baby, you know? And it's not about getting her next high. You know, she needs to pay her rent, she needs to pay her light bill, she needs to feed her children, she needs to clothe 'em, and this is all she knows how to do.

Chelley, an Hispanic heterosexual female in her late 40s who worked in community outreach for a mental health organization, added often it was easier for the women to exchange sex rather than work a full-time job because of their commitments to home and family.

Chelley: Because they either have a family they need to take care of and they maybe can't get them into daycare whatever it may be, its just an easy way to make the money to take care of their families
Jill: Easy meaning ... ?
Chelley: Not nine to five, eight to five—an hour, they've already got what they need. Two hours, they got what they need.
Jill: Less long-term responsibility? Or it's just quick?
Chelley: No, its quick. Its quick for them, and then they can stay there and do what they need to do with their family. They're just gone for an hour.

Like Rosalie explained above, the first time Donna exchanged sex for money wasn't for drugs, but for her kids. She was 21 and living in her car with her kids. Her husband had left her, leaving a note saying "he didn't want the responsibility of me and my kids anymore." She was living in a southwest state away from her parents. She ended up living with a man who required she make a certain amount of money before she could come home:

> I was 21. I had to make a $1,000 a night or I couldn't come in. And anyway, I brought my kids out there [to a southwest state] and he ended

up molesting my kids. I was police-escorted away from him. From that day on, everybody in Nemez, when I started prostituting for drugs, everybody in Nemez knows that that's something that I will . . . I'd flip, 'cause, you know, this man, I made a $1,000 a night and he was hurting my children.

The public figures define poverty on many levels. Poverty can be the foundation of someone's existence, based on spiritual, physical, and perhaps drug-dependent behaviors. It occurs when one does not have the resources needed to provide the basic necessities for oneself and one's children. Poverty also exists when one does not have the resources, the education, or the support to find employment for which she is qualified while simultaneously shouldering the responsibilities of a family. These definitions of poverty are material conditions of many people's lives, and for some, exchanging sex for money is a solution to that problem.

The Nemez newspapers also reveal poverty as a central reason for exchanging sex. A subset of twelve articles within the newspaper corpus includes those whose stated purpose is to provide an in-depth exploration of street prostitution, including its causes, consequences, and possible solutions, within the ten-year period examined. Within this subset the women are described as becoming involved in prostitution due to their desperation or as a way of taking care of themselves. For example: "Prostitution was her method of survival"; and "I didn't consider it prostitution. I was taking care of myself—I didn't have to beg or steal or depend on someone else." Within this corpus, women become involved in prostitution because they are leaving abusive home lives, either as children or adults, and/or due to their involvement with drugs. Notably, words such as *poverty* (118 occurrences), *victim* (247 occurrences), or *safety* (265 occurrences) occur much less in the newspaper corpus compared to the terms *prostitute* (1,135 occurrences), *crime/criminal* (1,212 occurrences), and *drug* (1,061 occurrences).[7] The lack of these words and their ideas also influences how people understand the central problems and solutions surrounding street-based sex work.

COPING WITH TRAUMA, ABUSE, AND NEGLECT

> The most significant problems, I think generally trauma related to . . . just trauma in their lives. Their place in society and access to resources, their sense of self. I don't see that these women have access to things that others might take for common. They live in the margins.
>
> Dr. Veronica Alvarez, a 48 year-old heterosexual Latina woman and the Project Director of an HIV-prevention program

Dr. Annie Shepherd, a 51-year-old white heterosexual woman and a psychology professor who had directed several research projects with substance users and women who trade sex for money or drugs, provides an overview of the most significant problems associated with women who exchange sex for money or drugs, focusing primarily on the women:

> I think that a lot of women—not all women, but there's a lot of women—who have addiction problems, and to support their habit, so to speak, they trade sex for money or drugs. I think, beyond that though, I believe there are a host of related problems, including past and current sexual and physical abuse, trauma in a number of different ways, not necessarily sexual trauma, but just traumatic life experiences. That could be being homeless as a kid. I think that a third is grief and loss. I think that a lot of the women that we come across—again, we work more with women who have addiction problems—is a lot of grief and loss in their life, both current and past. And then I'd say mental health issues are probably next. And then more concretely, employment, housing, immigration. And child custody.

Dr. Annie Shepherd describes trauma as a significant underlying reality, in its various forms, for most of her clients.

Julie is a white, 42-year-old heterosexual woman who had lived in Nemez since she was 13 years old when her mother got remarried to her step-dad. Her father was in the Navy and her mother worked as a dental assistant. Her parents are both white, and she wasn't sure what levels of education they had completed. Julie dropped out of school during eighth grade and mentioned she had a learning disability, making it hard for her to spell and count. Julie was first introduced to drugs at 13 by her brother and his girlfriend and had used them, as she said, "all my life." Julie first exchanged sex for money when she was fifteen years old, and she spoke directly to the relationship between sexual abuse and her reasons for exchanging sex for money:

> Some people don't understand that that's what some people have to do. That's the type of lifestyle that they're used to. They've been doing it, or they've been sexually molested when they were kids, so they figure if they turn around and they go out there and give their bodies away, they still feel like its ok, that they're not doing anything wrong.

Jill: And is that how you feel about people that do it?
Julie: Well, I was sexually molested too. When I was a kid. And that's why . . . [long pause]
Jill: You think that's why you do it?
Julie: That's why I did it.
Jill: Oh really?
Julie: Yeah. That's why I did it. I haven't done it in quite awhile. [. . .]
Jill: When did you first do it?
Julie: 15.

Jill:	Yeah, and you did it because you were molested?
Julie:	Yeah.
Jill:	Really? Why, what makes you think that?
Julie:	Because if I was, because I thought it was the thing to do.
Jill:	Oh really?
Julie:	I thought it was the thing to do. It wasn't the money outlook on it. I thought it was the thing to do. If I go and have sex with this man then he's going to have more affection toward me, and he's going to think more of me. That's the way it is. I mean, it's not a good thing and it's not a bad thing.

Historical sexual and physical abuse of both my participants and their children was prevalent in the interviews.[8] Julie attributes her participation in these activities to early child sexual abuse, saying exchanging sex is not good or bad, it just is. Rather than emphasize the problems associated with this initial sexual abuse, she presents it as a lifestyle choice based on her own and others' experiences. In response to this reasoning, one might argue sexual abuse is wrong, and therefore hope life decisions surrounding sexuality and exchanging sex in response to this abuse would also be considered wrong. And yet by separating the two, Julie bases her choice to exchange sex on her lifestyle and experiences, stating there is nothing wrong with these activities. In Family Studies Professor Rochelle Dalla's (2001) in-depth interviews with 31 streetwalking prostitutes (her term) to examine their interpersonal support systems, she explores the literature surrounding the correlates between early sexual abuse and participation in prostitution and states: "Inconsistency and contradictory evidence reveal the complexity of identifying causal, developmental paths leading from childhood experiences to adult prostitution" (p. 1069). As Ronald Weitzer (2009) states:

> Childhood abuse (neglect, violence, incest) is part of the biography of some prostitutes, though it is more common among street workers (Jeal and Salisbury 2007; Perkins and Lovejoy 2007) and also occurs within at least one-fifth of families in the wider population (National Research Council 1993). Studies that compare demographically matched samples of street prostitutes and nonprostitutes reach mixed results; some find a statistically significant difference in experience of family abuse, while others find no difference (Nadon et al. 1998). (p. 219)

Rather than attributing participation in street-based sex work as being primarily related to sexual abuse, understanding that in many cases the conditions may become unlivable, and because the resources are not available for support, the individuals end up "on the street" which then leads to participation in street-economies for survival—economically, psychologically, and otherwise. As 'Juliet' (2006) stated: "the problem is coercion . . . lack of choices, not prostitution itself" (p. 245).

The sexual and physical violence is then often exacerbated once involved in street-based sex work. Lily, a white lesbian woman in her mid 40s and an activist and former HIV outreach worker, discussed the role of sexual trauma in many of the women's lives:

> The other interesting thing that they do, and one of the reasons why I started working at the center against sexual assault is that among some street sex workers there's a huge amount of sexual trauma—both predating their entry into sex work and then also after they've been in sex work. Probably the majority of street sex workers were sexually abused within their families while they were growing up, and are, or have been in abusive relationships as adults. And then that just gets extended, that sort of becomes their expectations of it, if they're sexually abused within a commercial transaction, then its, that's sort of part of it, its more sexual trauma but its still the same degree of sexual trauma.

Officer Tom Hixson, a white 52-year-old heterosexual male and a former supervisor of the vice unit, responded:

> They're everybody, they're young girls, they're old girls, they've been around forever, there's prostitutes that just started, there's prostitutes that have been doing it years, twenty years or so, its seems like the majority of them. Something happened to make them start this, and it was usually a boyfriend, husband left them and they had absolutely nothing, they were stuck in the middle, usually the boyfriend or the husband, he was a doper, a junkie, he's the one that got them started. I would guess almost all of them were abused some way as kids or had a dysfunctional upbringing because they talk about that, "Yeah my dad beat me, my husband beat me, my father beat me, my father's molested me" and they're actually down, absolutely addicted to mostly crack cocaine, so they have to have their money to buy their dope and this is the quickest and easiest way to do it. Most of them have kids, most of them have had their kids taken away at some point, most of them have been married, some of them were professionals. I've talked to prostitutes, you know, they were engineers, they were professors, and they just got into this dope and it took them down, nurses, doctors . . .

Officer Hixson outlines the personal and systemic abuse that occurs in multiple cases and the connection made to drug use and abuse while also emphasizing these conditions affect individuals from all walks of life. Rather than focusing on systemic poverty and neglect, the women focused more on their own individual situations and choices. This perspective is consistent with the public figures I interviewed as well as much of what is revealed in newspaper media.

The following is a presentation and analysis of substance use and abuse as understood and connected with street-based sex work that further creates a framework of the woman as a victim.

> "She's a prostitute, addict, and abuser, but she's a mom and he misses her"
> (Nemez newspaper article headline about street-based sex work)

The words *crime*, *drugs*, *neighborhood*, and *police/cops* all appear well over 1,000 times in the newspaper article corpus.[9] These numbers are significant relative to the word *prostitute*, which occurs 1,135 times. Therefore, the reader associates these other words with the information contained in these articles roughly equivalent to the word *prostitute* itself. The word *drug* appears slightly less than *prostitute*, at 1061, and the other terms *crime*, *neighborhood*, and *police*, occur more than the word *prostitute*.

The most popular cluster, meaning words commonly grouped together, was variations of the phrase "drugs and prostitution." In other words, the most popular noun clustered with the word *prostitution* is the word *drugs*. After searching for all of the possible permutations of prostitution and drugs (e.g., "drugs and prostitution," "dealing and prostitution," "drug use and prostitution"), the drugs/prostitution cluster occurs 157 times in the corpus.[10] Therefore, within this corpus, when someone reads an article that mentions street-based sex work or prostitution, they are very likely to see prostitution clustered with drugs and sex work discussed within the context of law enforcement and community safety. This context has implications for the public's understanding of street-based sex work as a whole.[11]

A subset of twelve articles within the Nemez newspaper corpus includes those whose stated purpose is to provide an in-depth exploration of street prostitution, including its causes, consequences, and possible solutions, within the ten-year period examined. In general, the women get hooked on drugs and then end up selling themselves in order to support their habits. For example: "Desperate for cash and with little forethought other than getting well [sickness due to drug withdrawal], she turned her first trick—selling her body for quick money." The reverse is also prevalent: the women turn to drugs or their drug use escalates in order to provide a mental escape from prostitution. Within these articles, prostitution was their means of supporting themselves and is portrayed as a means of survival. For example, Rebecca is "tired of working the streets"—as her "harsh history" includes "six years as a prostitute and twice as long as a heroin addict." She says she was "looking for a legitimate job, but didn't have any luck." She doesn't know if it's her past, but "it's hard to get a job." She goes on to say, "I'm trying as hard as I can." Similarly, Angie was "dragged under by drugs and knows of no way out." She thinks of trying to create a new life for herself, but she "doesn't know where to begin." And again, "life on the streets and on drugs is all she has known for several years." Both of these women are described as long-time drug users who are trying to get out of street work but aren't able to due to their circumstances. This representation of being "dragged under by drugs" is somewhat consistent with my research participants because most of them had been deeply involved in drugs when they were exchanging sex and their drug use often escalated in order to provide a mental escape from exchanging sex.

Drugs were considered to be the primary motivation and problem for most of my participants. Sandy, a 46-year-old, white heterosexual woman, began by talking about her addiction to crack:

Sandy: After I took my first hit of crack cocaine, rock cocaine . . . That's another funny thing. I always tell people, "I have class. I don't smoke crack; I smoke rock cocaine." Crack is just street lingo. I never wanted to snort again. Yeah. I stopped playing softball. I used to play at the Sports Park a lot. I was very competitive. We were a very competitive team. As soon as I took that first hit of crack, softball was no more important. I stopped showing up for games, I would miss games, I would use that excuse.
Jill: Use what excuse?
Sandy: To get out of the house: "I'm gonna go play softball." I'd go straight to some user's house, somebody that used. [. . .] And once I took that first hit, I didn't want to do anything. [. . .]
Sandy: October 31st of '97, I dressed my kids up . . . I was just gonna go to the bar and have some drinks. Dressed myself up as Sheena, the Ultimate Warrior . . . Xena. Won the contest—well, 2nd place, got some money, got picked up by a trucker, wanted to go to the casino. Sure, I'll go. He gives me money to gamble with, you know, because I've decided I don't have enough yet. I wasn't doing the drugs.
Jill: You were just drinking?
Sandy: Yeah. So, the casino, sure. I go and I win money, so I have him take me to Planter's Park and drop me off.
Jill: What's Planter's Park?
Sandy: Planter's Park is an area where I can go and cop now. Because now I have some money. I never returned.
Jill: You never went home?
Sandy: Never. Never. I mean, I'm talking never.

Ava, a white, 23-year-old heterosexual woman, talked specifically about her involvement with drugs and how she lost everything:

Ava: Because before I got involved with all of it, I had two cars and I had a house and I had my son. And it all . . . That's why I would never do meth again, because one by one—I owned both my vehicles, and I was buying the trailer and the land, and one by one, I lost them all. [laughs]
Jill: Yeah. How old were you when that happened?
Ava: I was 20. And then . . . I was 21 when I lost my son and 21 when I went to prison.

Later in our interview, Ava refers to being caught by the police and her subsequent arrest:

> But I was happy because, like the cop said, "We're gonna read you your rights. You're under arrest for this and this and this," and I was just like, "Thank God." Because I was tired. I had been just running amuck because I didn't, you know, I felt like I didn't have my son anymore, I felt like I didn't have anything, so . . . It was just kinda I was riding that car until the rims fell off, and I didn't care. But when they finally got me, I knew I was gonna go eat, I knew I was gonna sleep. I didn't know where I was gonna go from there, but I knew I wouldn't be all strung out and busting my ass to get nowhere in this world.

Officer Jennifer Castillo, an Hispanic-34-year old heterosexual woman who worked for the Nemez Police Department talked about the power drugs held over many of the women's lives:

> The girl that has her Master's degree has three kids, and they've all graduated from college. She lost contact with them, though, because they want nothing to do with her. And it's sad because when she's telling me this, she's crying, you know, so you can see the pain, but drugs are so overpowering. And it's just like they know that they're not doing the right thing, but you know, the drug just takes over. It's really sad . . . It's really sad . . . It's really sad.

Drug use or addiction is often considered the motivating factor for involvement in street prostitution where a worker must exchange sex for drugs or money to support her habit. It can undermine a worker's control while also making her less discriminating when it comes to clients and services. Women who work primarily to support their habit are often seen as "undercutting the market by working below the going rate and offering unsafe sexual services (sex without condoms, for example)" (Chapkis 2000, 189). Sociologists Judith Porter and Louis Bonilla (2000) found the use of crack had a tendency to drive down the price of sex, as there was competition among the women and increased competition with women who exchange sex for drugs (p. 172).[12] Substance abuse has also been correlated

Who is the Victim 41

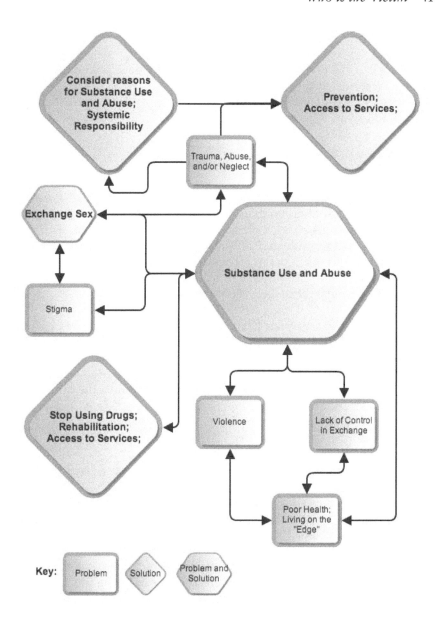

Figure 2.3 Problems and solutions surrounding substance use and abuse.

with increased risk of HIV and other drug-related harms.[13] Although all three examples emphasize the importance of drugs in the women's lives, the reasons for this use are largely unaddressed. Figure 2.3 demonstrates the complexity of the problems and solutions surrounding substance use and abuse as represented by my research participants.

The following subheadings and examples provide more detailed explanations and analysis of these problems and their corresponding solutions as my participants understood them.

"I Wanted to Hide My Feelings"

Although considered by many to be the central problem related to street-based sex work, drug use and abuse is often used to ease the underlying problems of previous abuse, trauma, and neglect; violence and victimization; exchanging sex; and stigma. Using drugs as a way to mask pain and problems was a prevalent theme throughout most of the interviews. I asked Brenda, a white, 48-year-old lesbian woman: "What is the problem? You said there's a problem out there. What is it?" Brenda replied:

> The problem is the drugs. For the women. The women have to be high to be able to have sex, because then they, how can I put this? I got high because I wanted to hide my feelings. I didn't want to have to deal with the pain that I was going through. And that's what they do. They're out on the street [. . .] where they have an old man doing the same thing that they're doing. But what support is he to them? So they get high to forget about who they are or where they're going or what they don't have. And that's the same thing I did.

Brenda discussed a recent relapse and why she chose to use drugs:

> I think it was a relapse because of me and my girlfriend breaking up and her moving and us trying to work it out and her being up there and me being down here [. . .] When I got high those two weeks, I was trying to hide my feelings from losing my girlfriend, to getting on probation, and then I realized, what am I doing? Because when I came down that night, everything was still there. So I knew I had to deal with it.

Jill: Everything was still there? The problems?
Brenda: All of my problems were still there. All of my feelings were still there. I still sit here and cry. [. . .] That's what they're doing, they're hiding the way they feel. And I think that if we have someone out there telling them that you don't have to do this, you don't have to hide your feelings. Go to detox, go to rehab, y'know, there's housing all over the place for these women, if they're willing to get clean and stay clean.

Brenda defines the central problem as drug use, which, for her, is rooted in pain. The women feel pain, whether it is due to abuse, relationships, or life conditions.

As she discussed working out of motel rooms as well as on the street, Sandy emphasized how her use of drugs allowed her to "cover up what she felt":

Sandy: But then the next day, you can go back out, you know, and then you get your money and then you come back in. But once you have your hotel room, you could run back and forth; it was okay. But when you got up in the morning and realized that you had smoked all your money or used all your money on drugs, then you were like, "Oh whoa, now I got a certain amount of time. Am I gonna carry all this stuff?" So the first thing that was on your mind when you woke up in the morning was to go get your money for your room. And if you were mind-set enough, you wouldn't go and get high first, because then you're carrying all your possessions, if you had any. You know, I didn't have any. So then once you got your hotel room cleared, you know, you could take a shower and then go back out. But that's all you did. That's all I did: Once I got settled, or if I lost the room and was camping out in someone else's room, once I turned my first trick and got high, it was . . . And I cried going to the streets. There wasn't times that I wanted to go out there. But I knew once I took that first hit, it was on.
Jill: And you didn't care.
Sandy: I didn't care. There was no worries, no thoughts, no hurting, 'cause that . . . and then I wouldn't cry anymore. Because all the pain was gone. I could cover up what I felt. And then it was on, all day and all night, until, you know . . . Even times there'd be three- or four-day stretches that I would continue as long as I could make the money. And then, you know, who needed a hotel room? Because you didn't take most of your dates to your hotel room anyways. You did 'em in cars or . . . Because unless you were real sly—and a lot of these hotel rooms you can't go in and out with a lot of people, especially late at night. 'Cause unless you had a . . . And I never did that, but I think the hotel manager knew what some of the girls did, but he didn't allow them to do it in the rooms, but, you know, he knew what we did, he knew how we lived. He knew how we made our money. Just as long as we didn't bring the heat to the room.

This extended description not only reveals Sandy's lifestyle, but her desire to numb herself at the expense of everything else.

"We Had to Get High"

Although potentially closely intertwined with using drugs to escape one's feelings, most of the women discussed their choices to exchange sex as a way to support their drug use. Sandy talked about what led her to start working on the streets:

Sandy: The way I was introduced to working on the street was I got strung out for like 6 days, by a dealer, and I got cut off. So he's like telling me, "Well, you need money. You know, you're gonna have to go out and get some money," and I'm like, "Money?" I never thought... You know? I don't have a job. I had just lost my job, asked to resign.
Jill: From where?
Sandy: From a school.
Jill: As a campus monitor?
Sandy: Yeah, because I got caught in a lie. 'Cause I had already been warned by my principal: "Sandy, we can't let you come back if you're going to continue your attendance record. So you've got to, you know, promise me that next year when school starts, you're gonna be okay." "Oh no, I'll be okay." And so that's when I left my family. I just like went out one day and never went home. So then I was introduced by a guy, one of the guys that stayed in the hotel, which is, you know, a very small hotel: "Well, I'll take her out and I'll, you know, kinda show her the ropes or explain to her and stay out there with her." So once I went out [laughs] and stood there for two-and-a-half hours and... Because, you know, he told me this and told me that, like "Don't go in the car if you feel... weird. Don't go underneath a certain amount of money, you know, stick to your goal. I mean, stick to your limit; don't go because it will come." So two-and-a-half hours. Then once I did it, it was, um, it was like wow. I mean, it was 15 minutes, $40, then I got to go cop.
Jill: Cop?
Sandy: Cop, get the drugs. So I got to go and score and get high.

At the time of our interview, Sandy was no longer exchanging sex for money or drugs, but the following excerpt reveals her and others' desperation:

> But I was there, I was them [women who are still "out there" exchanging sex]. It didn't matter how many times I had to do it or who I had do it with or how gross it was or how... ugh, sickening it was. It didn't stop me. We had to get high. That was the easiest way for women to get the money, without trying to hold a job.

Brenda started using methamphetamine again and relates her return to exchanging sex with her addiction:

Jill: What made you get back into prostitution?
Brenda: I lost my job. Lost my house.
Jill: Were you doing drugs?
Brenda: Yeah.
Jill: Oh.
Brenda: I started doing meth again.

Lisa, a 47-year-old, Hispanic heterosexual woman, is an example of someone whose relationship with exchanging sex was directly influenced with her use, abuse, and addiction to drugs. When Lisa first started exchanging sex, she liked it and told stories about how she felt good about herself. And yet, in response to my question about what she disliked about exchanging sex, she said "Um, the abuse, the drugs. The drugs, what I became. What I became. What I became at the end."

As Brenda, Sandy, and Lisa testified, Sylvia, an Hispanic lesbian woman in her late 30s and a director at a mental health organization, stated:

> The most significant problem is that they have an addiction. I've not met, of the population I work with, and it's a very specific segment of the population, they have a substance abuse problem. [They] self-identify. So the biggest problem is that they're not coming to this decision to exchange from a place of empowerment because frequently it's to feed a need and not necessarily one that they want. And I find that unfortunate. As I said, if these women decided to do this for a living and weren't doing it as a means to get the next fix, they'd probably be relatively successful and it would be a step in a better direction for them. They would probably be at less risk of violence, which is the other issue. So I think the factors for me that influence the population as I see it, the two that come up over and over and over are violence and substance abuse.

Substance abuse is of primary importance in this example. Sylvia not only clearly delineates these women as largely involved with drugs, but states they self-identify as drug users. Based on this drug use, the problem then is not one of exchanging sex, but of the motivation for the exchange for sex. The motivation issue is even further removed from empowered or agential choice because the woman is motivated by a need she does not necessarily even *want*. If the women were "choosing to exchange from a place of empowerment," they would not be identified as victims at two levels: due to their choice to exchange sex for money or drugs, nor based on their addiction to drugs. Sylvia identifies the primary problem as addiction, which implies the solution is treatment for addiction. And yet by examining the discourse and the related material conditions more closely, the central problem appears as one's motivation or choice and one's ability to act from a position of power in order to make a choice that feeds something she may truly "want."

Most of the public figures and the women I interviewed defined substance use as a central problem. Some women discussed their own drug use as a reason for exchanging sex and drug addiction as a central barrier to changing their lifestyle. Similar to the newspaper articles, the women I interviewed became involved in exchanging sex in order to escape abusive lives as a way of survival or became involved in using drugs to mentally escape feelings related to physical and/or sexual abuse, which then led to exchanging sex. Their experiences also reflected those explored in the newspaper articles where the women's drug use escalates in order to provide a mental escape from exchanging sex.

Dr. Annie Shepherd, a 51-year-old white heterosexual woman and a psychology professor who had directed several research projects with substance users and women who trade sex for money or drugs, discussed the different feelings the women had about using drugs while both using them and after becoming sober:

Jill: So would you say it's an issue [drug use] if it's an issue for them? If they don't want to be doing it.

Dr. Annie Shepherd: Right. Although I have to say that, with addiction, that women will say that they're very happy being addicted, but once they've cleaned up for awhile and looked retrospectively, they are not happy with where they came from. But in the moment in your addiction or one's addiction, you think you're having fun. And if you think about where, you know, the different centers that the brain is affected by drugs, it's usually those pleasure centers. And you'll often find women laughing—you know, not often, but, you know, you'll be talking about, you know, some kinda drug-using episode and . . . You know, like one of our young girls, they're laughing, "Yeah, I can't believe I got so drunk and I was so screwed up. Like, you know, I don't know what happened, and then I came back and I had like this big black eye and ha ha." They're laughing, but that's where those drugs hit those centers. Different regions of the brain.

Valarie, an Hispanic heterosexual female in her mid 30s and a program manager at a behavioral health agency, echoed these sentiments, stating their behavior is a coping mechanism the community does not understand.

Valarie: Well, they don't really understand that their behavior is a coping mechanism. I really don't think they understand, because

	even the officers that come to our advisory group—because they are part of our advisory group—see it more as their hobby or just something that they like to do. Our women don't like to do this stuff; they don't. Yes, they do it. Yes, they get on our nerves sometimes because they keep doing it 10,000 times. It doesn't mean they like it.
Jill:	They don't like to exchange, they don't like doing drugs, or they don't like—what is it that they don't like?
Valarie:	They don't like either one. I mean, it may seem good at the time, but it doesn't make them feel good. You know, our women don't want to continue using. They didn't grow up saying, "Yeah, I wanna be addicted and I wanna be exchanging." I mean, no one wants that. They do wanna be helped. And a lot of the officers will have that mentality of "Yeah, that's just the way they wanna be and that's what they're always gonna do." And that's not true. It really isn't true. And that's why we have been trying to keep having one of women at least tell their story or tell who they were and who they are now, you know, just to remind them, yeah, they are human and really, you know, one of us could be there, you know, at any point in time. It's difficult. And I think, like I said, a lot of these officers really don't know. They really don't understand.

Like Valarie explains, many of the women I interviewed did not identify as choosing to exchange sex, but rather were driven to it because they needed to support a drug habit. Valarie's framing of the behavior as a "coping mechanism" reveals there is an underlying need or pain that is not being addressed. When the problem is understood to be solely one of drug use, the solution is "access to substance abuse treatment," which may not address the underlying trauma.

"You have to do the drugs to be able to do the prostitution"

Brenda explains using drugs was almost a prerequisite for exchanging sex because she had to be high in order to exchange.

> When I started prostituting, I did it because I was only 15, and I was doing it to survive. To make money so I could have a place to live. Because I was working at Wendy's two hours a day. That wasn't enough to pay the rent and stuff. And I wasn't into drugs then. And then, once you start doing it, it just kind of falls into place. You have to do drugs to be able to do the prostitution. And I used to have a 500 a day habit. Never did heroin, but I did every other drug that they made.

This process was often cyclical. The women would be using drugs, would then exchange sex in order to get more money to buy the drugs and would also want to use drugs to feel comfortable exchanging sex, which then led to the purchase of more drugs, which led to more exchanges of sex.[14] For example, in response to my question about how often the woman would exchange sex for money or drugs, Julie, a white, 42-year-old heterosexual woman, said: I don't know. Every day if I could.

Jill: Yeah?
Julie: For dope. Yeah, when I was a crackhead. I'd do stupid stuff just to get that next hit.
Jill: What affects it, how often you did it then?
Julie: Well, it depends. If I was straight, if I wasn't floating crack, I wouldn't do it.

And in response to my question about others she knows who exchange sex for money or drugs, Brenda said: Their [lives] are totally different from mine.

Jill: How's that?
Brenda: Because they don't want a house. They're too interested in getting high all the time. And they're just out there to get the money to go get high or drunk. And that's like the friend that was over here, that tried to get me to get high the other night with her. She's not interested in cleaning up or getting a house. She's just interested in getting that money and worrying about the next rock [crack cocaine] she's going to get or the next bottle of beer she's going to get. And her old man is the same way.
Jill: Is it mostly connected to drugs, would you say? The friends that you have?
Brenda: Yeah.
Jill: Did you have friends that did it that weren't involved with drugs?
Brenda: No, because everyone I met was . . .
Jill: [Interruption] Doing drugs?
Brenda: Yeah.
Jill: So you were pretty rare.
Brenda: Yeah.
Jill: At 15 . . .
Brenda: [Interruption] Yeah.
Jill: To be doing it and not being involved in drugs.
Brenda: But it only took me about a year. And I was into doing coke and meth and downers.
Jill: What do you think led you to the drugs?
Brenda: Prostitution.
Jill: Really?
Brenda: Because you get so sick of always having to go out to make money, and having guys on top of you. And it's like it turns you into doing drugs. Because it's easier to do it when you're high.

And I see a lot of women, that's why they get high, and then they go out and pick up the guys.
Jill: And it's easier?
Brenda: Yeah.

Olivia, a 43-year-old Hispanic heterosexual woman, reflects on how she felt about exchanging sex before and after these exchanges, specifically in relationship to using drugs in order to be able to exchange sex:

Olivia: I felt dirty afterwards. I felt . . . I felt no self-esteem. I hated myself. Afterwards, I hated myself. But before, I was like, "Yeah, girl, you can do it. It's okay. It's okay. Don't even think about it. Just get ready." I mean, I had to be high to do it. I could not be sober, like wake up and have no crack, no nothing, and I go up and "You wanna a ride?" No, no. I just could not do it sober. I had to be high to do that.

Drugs and street prostitution are often intimately connected because the drugs drive one to exchange sex to support the drug habit, and drugs are often needed in order to exchange. Within the above statements, using drugs is seen as both a cause for and an effect of exchanging sex for money or drugs. Exchanging sex leads to using drugs because it is part of the lifestyle in their milieu and it makes it easier for the women to exchange sex. Drug use leads to exchanging sex because the women need the money or the drugs to support their habits and can easily turn to exchanging sex in order to locate these resources.

The solution, as Brenda explained it, was to tell those who are exchanging sex and using drugs they do not have to hide their feelings. If this situation is in fact the case, then the underlying cause is the need to repress feelings—which led to drug use and addiction. The solution Brenda offers involves no longer using drugs by going through detoxification, rehabilitation, and then finding housing—all of which are dependent on continued abstinence from drugs. How does one feel her feelings or get to a place where she can feel her feelings if she doesn't have the resources required to achieve a security that allows her to be vulnerable enough to feel? How does one achieve that state without housing, support, basic necessities, and in the throes of an addition to drugs?

Choosing Not To

Several of the women stated they had stopped using drugs due to their fear of losing what they had and the daily consequences of drug use. Brenda, a white, 48-year-old lesbian woman, explains:

Brenda: It was like everybody was coming to my door wanting me to get high. And then I had a friend of mine come over the other night and she was like, "You can just do a rock [crack cocaine] with me. You can just do a rock with me." And it's like "No, Linda. No, I can't." And I said, "You've got to go." And I sent her on her way. And I think I hurt her feelings. But its like, I'm too strong. I just can't do it. And I think of my house. I think of my animals. Who's going to take care of them? Who's going to pay my rent? And I'm looking at sixty days in jail if I mess up.

Jill: Because you're on probation?
Brenda: Yeah, and I'm not willing to do that. I'm too old. I've had my days of partying and doing what I needed to do. I'm just not willing to do it. [. . .] Jail doesn't scare me. I've been there, done that. But what scares me is that I don't want to die, and I don't want to lose what I have. Those two little things are my favorite little things [referring to her animals]. [. . .] I'm doing it for myself, not because of probation and all that. Because I've tried to do it for everybody else and all I've done is relapse.

Donna, a 47-year-old, white, heterosexual woman, expresses the difference between "choosing" to do it for herself as opposed to being "forced". When we spoke, she wasn't using as much crack as she had in the past:

Donna: But I'm kind of glad because I don't want to be . . . It's like I'm smoking again, but I don't want to be out in that world again, and I see myself slowly slipping there because of the prostitution thing. And I know what that'll eventually do to me, you know, with my emotions. That's why I think I started going to the Women Restored Program, and I'm still going to my one-on-one counseling. I don't have to do none of this stuff; nobody's making me anymore. But I feel I have to have some kind of . . . something to keep my stability or my mind, you know, focused, so I don't go all the way back out there, you know? (sigh) Well, it's something that I'm not really wanting to do.
Jill: Prostitution?
Donna: Yeah. And I don't want to be back to where I'm on the street and in a hotel (crying). I don't want to go back. No. [. . .] But I'm too old, I'm too tired, you know, I'm really tired. And my personality is so angry, you know. I'm going to end up getting killed out there [laughs] because I just don't . . . you know, like fuck you. I'm just, you know . . . and if somebody tried to come up and rob me, I'm going to kill them, because you're not taking from me. You know, I'd rather die first. And, um, so that kind of mentality is not healthy, you know. [. . .]It's just . . . I'm tired. I'm tired of my addiction, you know, and I'm so tired of people saying, "Well, you know, you can stop, you can stop, go to meetings, da da da." I've done everything with my addiction. I've

been to seven rehabs, prison four times. I've been SMI [Severely Mentally Ill], you know, I've been on . . . I've been through it all, and I'm still using. You know, what part haven't I gotten? I don't know, you know. I don't even know why I use anymore. I don't enjoy it. I do not—I've got to where I want to be alone when I get high, you know, I isolate really bad. I mean, it's hard for me—like all these people out here make me nervous [laughs], you know what I mean? I just . . . When I'm walking down the street, it's hard because people are staring. I've isolated to really extreme, and it's not good. And . . . so right now, I'm kind of like lost, you know? I really don't know where I'm at right now. And it's hard. It's hard, you know. But there's that one little piece of me that was raised right and believes right and has hope, you know, and that's the part, I guess, that keeps fighting. But even that part's getting tired, you know? [. . .] When I went to *Casa Segura* yesterday, they offered to put me in a rehab for ninety days, and I was like, "I'm not doing no more rehab." I don't want to be confined no more. I'm really, really . . . If I can't . . . Structured, I know I can do, but I need to know that . . . because somebody's not telling me or I'm not forced, I need to learn to do it for me. And that's what I'm trying to do by going to these meetings. I'm doing them on my own. I don't want to be told that I have to, because it doesn't work. It just doesn't work with me. I rebel. You know, I need to know that somehow . . . if I'm gonna do this, I got to do it for me, you know? And that's what I'm trying. [. . .] Reality is, I've been an addict for thirty-five years. I've been prostituting twenty-five. And it's like . . . I really don't believe I'm going to go to school and have a career at this late state of age, okay? I really—I mean, you can say, "Oh, you can do it." Well, me, knowing me . . . I'm still battling my addiction, and I have been. And I really don't see it happening [. . .] I wanted to be a part of society, you know? [Referring to her veterinarian technician job] And it was good for a while, but I know now that I can't—you know, I've got a bone degenerative disease in my spine, and I got a lot of things going on. I'm just not . . . I'm not going to be able to function, and I know it, and I finally admitted it and said, 'Okay, look, you know. Let's get back on medication, let's get your head together. You know, you're still battling this addiction. Let's just go from here.' And I can't just sit around. I don't want to prostitute the rest of my life, you know? So I'm going to try to do what I can."

Donna clearly demonstrates the struggle she faces with drugs. The difficulties are compounded because of the issues at play—mental health, poverty, history of drug abuse, and experiences with exchanging sex. Making choices is convoluted and complicated, and yet ultimately her goal is to "choose not to" for herself, on her own.

Julie, a white, 42-year-old heterosexual woman, talked about how her addiction related to their daily life and how she struggled to break it:

Jill: Is it hard for you to not do it?
Julie: No.
Jill: No?
Julie: No. After three days it's not.
Jill: Really? Is it hard the first day?
Julie: It's all up here [points to head]. It's all up here in your head. It's just like if you turn around and you do something and you really, really want something in life. You want something for I don't know how long. You turn around and you use your head. You know it? I can't think of the word I'm trying to say.
Jill: Determination?
Julie: Determination. You gotta put your foot down and say "You know what? Is this what you're going to do? Are these the consequences you want to deal with? Do you want to become broke with no food, money, or nothing?" It gets old.

Sandy, a 46-year-old, white heterosexual woman, talked about how she made her decision to stop using drugs and exchanging sex:

So he's [Sandy's boyfriend] like, "You gotta get up. You're not staying here anymore." 'Cause I'd been down here [Nemez] for two months, not looking into the interviews, doing what I used to do: just lay around, go out all night, sleep all day, get up and make him dinner, you do whatever. Some nights we'd get high; some nights we wouldn't. So before I laid down, I said, "God, please, if you open . . ." I know about God. I know about the AA program, Cocaine Anonymous, Narcotics Anonymous. I know about all these programs because I been in them, you know, all this time. "If you open a door, I promise I will shut one." And I meant my relationship with my ex-boyfriend. So the next morning, I get up, he's already on a rampage, you know, because he says, "Okay, I'm gonna allow you to sleep here tonight and that's all, you know? Then you've gotta go." So I get up. He hears the phone call. And this is typical behavior: "I changed my mind. You don't have to." Because they say, "Come on." I'm packing my stuff now. I'm going.

Jill: So you're going to Carlie's Place [a residential treatment center for women who are experiencing homelessness and may or may not have experience with substance abuse].

Sandy: "There's a bed available. You can come." I'm packing my stuff. He had somebody that offered him a side job: "Come over and do it." [He says:] "I changed my mind. You can stay. When I get home, it's okay for you to be here." When he left, that voice in my head, which I know now, today, is my Holy Spirit: "Honey, you asked for a door to be opened." And I knew then I had to go. I was so tired, Jill. I'm so tired of having to do what I have to do to get high. There's never enough money and there's enough dope. That's where I got in my addiction. [. . .] I couldn't turn enough tricks, I couldn't have enough money, and there was never gonna be enough dope—whether the drug dealer had it or the guy that wanted to get his dick sucked while I—we got high, and my high was very little compared to theirs. Because it's a sensation. They're gonna smoke a whole lot and get that rush while they're getting their dick sucked, while I'm getting very little to smoke. It was very frustrating, you know. I don't want to be this person anymore. My kids aren't taking my phone calls because they know; they know what I'm doing. I'm losing my family, my dad. [. . .] and I just said, "I'm broken." They let me in, and for the last 4 months, I've battled. I haven't used. I've had sex with him [ex-boyfriend] one time.

Sandy reveals the battles she faces on a daily basis. Drug use is embedded in her history and patterns of behavior, which compounds the struggle. And yet in spite of the challenge, she reveals that she doesn't "want to be this person anymore," and wants to do things differently. Her struggle, even with the resources available to her, is paramount.

The women talk about their many different reasons for not using drugs, which range from fear of arrest to losing what they have gained since not using drugs. This loss is directly related to the daily consequences many of them face while using drugs—being broke and not able to provide for their basic needs. They also discuss what they have lost as a result of using drugs, such as jobs and housing. For most of the women who exchange sex in my study, drugs and prostitution are intimately connected. A primary reason for no longer using drugs was to be able to see their kids, which meant they stopped exchanging sex. And yet because the two are so intimately tied, it is hard to separate out the emotions—the material reality that creates the conditions upon which this choice to no longer use drugs is one that can be made.

All three sites clearly define the central problem as substance abuse. The sources of this drug use are mentioned in the newspaper articles and in the interviews with public figures, and yet these roots are made more palpable through the interviews with the women. Many women clearly explain they encountered systemic abuse and violence that led them to use drugs to escape from the pain and make it easier to exchange sex. This cycle then led to increased exchanges of sex and drug use.

When I began this study, I thought I would find, primarily through my interviews with the women who exchange sex for money or drugs, that the central problem was *not* rooted in drug use. I thought perhaps that belief was just a stereotype not grounded in reality. My focus was on exchanging sex for money, and yet I soon found these exchanges were more of an afterthought for most of these women, while the drugs were the primary concern. Once the women stopped using drugs and gained some distance from these activities, they presented exchanging sex and drug use as separate entities. While engaged in exchanging sex and using drugs, however, the two were irrevocably intertwined, with the drugs as the focal point and the exchanges of sex as a means to an end. Those who were addicted to substances did not "choose" to exchange sex as a lifestyle or an occupation. This statement does not imply the women were being forced to participate in these acts; they did choose, but the underlying motivation was often to maintain their drug use.

The preceding analysis led me to believe I had been mistaken in my initial premise and, in fact, the central problem *was* drug use. And yet just because drug use is rampant and is a dominant factor in the women's stated primary motivation does not mean drugs are in fact the root cause. This conclusion may reveal how ubiquitous ideology can be: people in the United States are encouraged to believe their successes and failures are the result of personal choices rather than based on multiple complex factors influenced by a global transnational capitalist system. Again, this statement does not imply the women are deluded victims of the insidious system unaware of what they are saying and feeling, but rather that ideology is powerful, and an ideology of personal responsibility is emphasized in the language surrounding street-based sex work. Most specifically in relationship to drug use and abuse, the emphasis on the individual woman, or victim, to make a change is prevalent and often masks systemic influence and responsibility. I now turn to an examination of the woman as criminal or victim within the context of criminalization.

3 Is She a Criminal, a Victim, or a Victim of the Criminal Justice System?[1]

> Unlike middle-class escorts, they [women on the street] might feel really crappy about doing sex work, they might feel like really, maybe its against their morals, or something like this . . . I don't know, but I think that that population, and also it just doesn't get them the services that they need, it makes, it makes, yeah, I guess what it does with them is it makes it like it's a moral failure to be where they are and have the problems they have when in fact they've got a disease of addiction, or the social disease of poverty.
> —Joan, a white, 43-year-old bisexual woman and an activist in a sex worker rights organization

The intrinsic intertwining of sex work and (im)morality seriously complicates understandings of the nuanced power relations surrounding sex workers' victimization, legal status, and relationships with clients and those who exploit people on the street who exchange sex for money or drugs. Teela Sanders (2005) notes, for some, sex work "signals a failure in individual morality, a breakdown of cohesive institutions such as marriage and the family" (p. 158). This reality is inseparable from broader gender norms regarding female sexual expression and propriety, as was exemplified in the second-wave feminist debates of the 1980s. Sociologist Wendy Chapkis traces the antecedents of this debate to the early 1900s by drawing upon feminist historian Sheila Jeffreys' characterization of the beliefs of many prominent suffragists. Such activists were of the opinion the sexualization of women led to her being considered fit for no other career than that of sexual object and affected the opportunities of all women from the "degradation of her temple to solely animal uses," so she might take a full part in all the areas of life previously arrogated to man (Jeffreys, qtd. in Chapkis 2000, p. 11).

Women were either recognized as sexual objects or civil subjects and being recognized as the former obviated the latter. Nonetheless, women's rights activists who opposed these beliefs argued "sex could and should be an area of expanded freedom for women" (Chapkis 2000, p. 11). It was through these debates, Chapkis observes, the "prostitute thus comes to function as both the most literal of sexual slaves and as the most subversive of sexual agents within a sexist social order" (2000, p. 12). Against the fabric of such historical neglect, my participants provide varied understandings about morality, sexuality, and the "wrongness" or "not wrongness" of exchanging sex for money.

CRIMINAL STATUS AND ARRESTS

Prior to 1910, prostitution per se was not a crime in any state until the federal government enacted the White Slave Traffic Act, also known as the Mann Act. This act criminalized interstate travel of women and girls for "immoral purposes," focusing specifically on "prostitution or debauchery, or for any other immoral purpose" (US Congress 1910). Sociologist and Research Consultant Melissa Ditmore (2011) points out:

> the codification of these social mores reflected changing attitudes that arose in the context of migration, including both urbanization and immigration. The history of prostitution in the United States features recurring themes of sexual morality, racism, and the protection of women and children, and legislation typically reflected a desire to control women's sexuality and autonomy. (p. 795)

Within ten years of the Mann Act, most states passed laws criminalizing prostitution, and although passed as a way to protect women from what was then known as "white slavery," these laws "reflected stereotypes of the day and were used to exclude particular ethnicities and were selectively enforced along racist and political lines" (Ditmore 2011, p. 795). Sociologist Brian Donovan (2006) points out in his historical analysis of the "white slave crusades":

> White slavery narratives offered different images of the white slave that pivot on the question of women's sexual agency: the extent of control women have over their sexual practices. The white slave's lack of sexual agency distinguished her from willful prostitutes, yet white slavery narratives revealed a range of opinions on how much responsibility a woman should assume for entering the vice trade. [. . .]White slavery narratives had not single political valence but were an elastic cultural resource for a range of political agendas. (p. 20)

The creation of this concept and subsequent criminalization has encouraged and solidified the marginalized status of people who participate in these activities. Criminalization of prostitution is currently the dominant legislative approach in the United States.

Is She a Criminal, a Victim, or a Victim of the Criminal Justice System? 57

The increased emphasis in the media on international sex trafficking—a commercial sex act induced by force, fraud, or coercion, or in which the person induced to perform such acts has not reached eighteen years of age—is also increasingly conflated with prostitution and the material conditions of exploitation (*Victims of Trafficking and Violence Protection Act of 2000*). Although these acts have existed for thousands of years (Kempadoo and Doezema 1998), during the past 20 years within global, transnational, and capitalist contexts, governments, the media, non-governmental organizations (NGOs), and individuals have increasingly brought the issue to the world's attention.[2] To help combat trafficking both domestically and worldwide, the US government has responded with the *Victims of Trafficking and Violence Protection Act of 2000* and subsequent reauthorizations.[3]

The definition of sex trafficking is different from that of prostitution by choice, although various political and academic groups based on their own moral and political agendas often conflate the two.[4] And at times, the two are not easily separated.[5] Women and men who are trafficked and forced to perform sexual acts are not free to choose their work, and therefore, they are not identified as sex workers or women and men who trade sex for drugs or money but rather as "slaves" or "victims." Women and men who choose to perform sexual acts for any kind of economic gain or security are defined as sex workers. Melissa Ditmore provides an overview of the distinction between sex trafficking, labor trafficking, and sex work, and explains the danger in conflating sex trafficking with sex work:

> [. . .] treating sex work as if it is the same as sex trafficking both ignores the realities of sex work and endangers those engaged in it. Sex workers include men and women and transgendered persons who offer sexual services in exchange for money. [. . .] Sex workers engage in this for many reasons, but the key distinction here is they do it voluntarily. They are not coerced or tricked into staying in the business but have chosen this from among the options available to them. ("Sex Work, Trafficking: Understanding the Difference" *Reality Check* 2008)

Ditmore (2008) continues: "A key goal of sex worker activists is to improve sex-working conditions, but self-organization is impossible when sex work is regarded as merely another form of slavery. Then authorities and laws trying to stop true slavery—trafficking—get misapplied to sex workers, clients and others involved in the sex industry." In their analysis of the US legislative response to trafficking, Lerum et al. state: "the decade following the passing of the TVPA [Trafficking Victims Protection Act] in 2000 has been marked by intense political advocacy from well-funded conservative groups who have incrementally defined trafficking as prostitution."[6] These policies have also had a detrimental impact on marginalised communities of youth (INCITE! 2011).[7]

Because prostitution is illegal in the United States (except for a few counties in Nevada), women and men who exchange sex for drugs or money are concerned about being arrested in addition to trying to earn a living. This concern leads some workers to have what are commonly referred to as "pimps," or men (most often) who either look out for the women who are exchanging sex for drugs or money or require the women they "look out for" to exchange sex for drugs or money and bring a certain amount of this money home in exchange for security, housing, food, and/or drugs. Many women have a husband or boyfriend who works as a lookout against police and/or violence. The illegality of the profession requires that a worker surrender some control over her working conditions. In addition to legal harassment by the police and the fear of arrest, the illegal status undermines a worker's ability to protect herself from dangerous clients and then dissuades her from filing charges if such violence does occur. The illegality also requires negotiations and transactions are speedy and occur in vulnerable locations like cars, parks, or alleys.

The discussion of "pimps," or those who are understood as exploiting and further victimizing women who exchange sex, must also be addressed and is far from simple. There are boyfriends or partners who may be defined as pimps who may not necessarily exploit the women who share their money with them, whereas there are those who are violent and further isolate women who exchange sex for money. And these relationships are not static, but may shift based on individual, even daily, circumstances. My participants, except in one or two instances, did not rely on or include partners or pimps in their negotiations of or proceeds from exchanges of sex.[8]

The Federal Bureau of Investigation (FBI) reports there were 79,700 prostitution/commercialized vice arrests made each year ranging from 98,800 (1994) to 71,400 (2009) in the United States.[9] According to the *Sourcebook of Criminal Justice Statistics*, approximately 90,000 arrests are made in the United States each year for violations of prostitution laws. This number does not include the arrests also made for disorderly conduct and loitering, two of the crimes for which workers on the street are often arrested (Weitzer 2000a, p. 159). Most scholars believe the number of arrests vastly underrepresent the number of people who are currently working, as many workers are never arrested. And trying to compare the number of arrests to the overall number of people participating in these exchanges is in many cases futile, as many are arrested multiple times. Statistics regarding the number of arrests primarily serve to reveal how much money is spent on arresting and prosecuting these types of crimes.

Some researchers have estimated approximately 20 percent of the prostitution that occurs in the United States includes street prostitutes (Porter and Bonilla 2010, p. 163). Activist, filmmaker, and spokesperson for COYOTE (Call Off Your Tired Old Ethics) Carol Leigh (1994) in "Prostitution in the United States: The Statistics" claims street prostitution comprises between 10 and 20 percent of all sex-for-hire arrangements in larger cities such as Los Angeles and New York. In small cities, Leigh estimates the percentage to be much larger, somewhere in the neighborhood of 50 to 70 percent in areas where there are limited indoor venues (p. 17). Despite these percentages, women on the street make up the vast majority of arrests. Leigh cites that 85 percent of those arrested work on the street. This number is disproportionate to the number of street sex workers, as 80 percent of sex workers work off the street in saunas, massage parlors, or as call/outcall escort services (p. 17). These statistics are difficult to determine and are contested.[10]

Specific problems and solutions emerge from prostitution's illegal status. First and foremost, if something is defined as morally wrong, it is usually defined as a problem. The solution, in the US context, therefore, is criminalization, which then leads to arrests. In other words, based on the material condition that exchanging sex for money is illegal, the problem could be defined as immoral behavior, whereby the solution resides in making this behavior criminal as a deterrent or punishment. The problem then shifts to locating and arresting those people who are violating the law, and the solution to this violation is either fines, jail time, or increased penalties. This solution also solves other specific problems, such as removing people from areas in which these interactions occur.

This chapter explores my participants' perspectives of criminalization as both a solution and a *problem*. I begin by presenting my participants' beliefs about prostitution, which are defined as immoral, wrong, or not wrong, as well as a combination of these ideas. Because arrests are often the result of this criminal status, arrests are defined as both a solution and a problem. Alternatives to arrests often cycle back to the victim or criminal status of those participating in these activities. The contradictions in this duality locate criminalization as cause for increased problems and harms related to street-based sex work while simultaneously an ineffective solution to the "problem" of prostitution.

WRONG, "NOT WRONG," OR SOMEWHERE IN BETWEEN

Prostitution exists on a gradation between "wrong" and "not wrong" for the women I interviewed. Very few of them argued prostitution was wrong. At times, the women contradicted themselves and their beliefs within the same conversation. The explanation was often as follows: prostitution is morally wrong, yet, under certain circumstances (which vary based on the viewpoint of the speaker), its immorality does not deter the woman from participating in these activities. As a way to begin to sort out the different ways my participants discussed the morality, wrong-ness, and non-rightness of prostitution, I present their stories and their words.

Prostitution is Morally Wrong

In our conversation about exchanging sex, Olivia, a 43-year-old Hispanic heterosexual woman, said:

> I was raised—not religious, but my mother read us the Bible and I read my kids the Bible, and . . . I just knew morally that [prostitution] was wrong, you know? But I didn't care. I didn't care. And now I feel bad . . . I find it hard to believe—no, I don't find it hard to believe, because I know I was doing that; I just find it hard to believe that I was doing that.

Later in the interview, in response to my question about police arresting women who exchange sex for money, Olivia said: "Oh, I think they're doing a good job, and I think they're in their right. Because [. . .] It's wrong. It's wrong to do that. I think it's . . . It's against the law, you know? Prostitution."

Denise, a 43-year-old, white, heterosexual woman, offers a more contradictory perspective on the morality of prostitution because she views the situation as complicated based upon the circumstances of the individual.

Denise: I mean, at least use protection; if you're going to do it, use protection.
Jill: And if they use protection and they want to do it, that's okay?
Denise: Yes. Yeah, I'm not going to downgrade on it, no, because it's . . . I don't think it should be wrong.

Here, Denise clearly states she does not think prostitution should be considered "wrong." As she said in response to my question, "Do you think—not that [the police] do it, but do you think that they're . . ."

Denise: Doing wrong by arresting them and locking them up?
Jill: Mmm hmm [yes].
Denise: On some of them, they do right; some of them, they do wrong to them. You know, some of them are out there because that's the only thing that they do to make a living, you know? And other people, they do it just because they want to do it to have the extra money or extra drugs or whatever extra that they want.

Denise went on to explain more fully:

> Well, it all depends to a certain point on it. Now if it's for drugs, I sometimes, it all depends. You know, its ridiculous, you know, but its just an addiction and they've got to have that drug, so they're going to do it in any way they can get to it. Okay. That's on the drugs, but . . . the other, man, it's just hard, you know, I mean, money-wise. Like I

Is She a Criminal, a Victim, or a Victim of the Criminal Justice System? 61

said, I mean, I did, and that's because I had three little kids and my old man went to jail and I had no way of supporting these kids.

Denise states exchanging sex was clearly wrong for her and she still feels guilty about it, although she did not regret the decisions she made to support her children. Although women would state it was wrong, there were often qualifiers based on the reasons for exchanging, or the woman's own personal circumstances, that showed exchanging sex for money was far more complicated and could not fit into a simple category of "right" or "wrong."

Denise makes a clear distinction between needing money for drugs and money to survive. One choice is wrong, whereas the other is, while not right, at least somewhat understandable. And Denise ties these moral beliefs to the criminal justice system, stating if a woman has no other means to make a living, then she should not be arrested for these activities, but if she has other means and is working for "extra" money or drugs beyond what she needs to survive, then she *should* be arrested. Denise's argument is grounded in her own experience and her reasons for exchanging sex for money. Her statements and their underlying ideologies are complicated at best. And yet they speak to the needs of the individual, with which all of my participants were intimately familiar. Here, the "victim" status becomes more apparent, rather than an offender who commits crimes.

Not Wrong, but not "Right"

When Laura, a 36-year-old, white, heterosexual woman, and I talked about exchanging sex, she said: "I know it's not right, and I know it's not right when I do it." In response to Laura's statement, I asked, "So do you think it should be illegal?"

Laura: Illegal, yes.
Jill: You do?
Laura: Yeah.
Jill: Okay. So you're okay with cops arresting people. You think that's okay.
Laura: Well, I don't think that's okay either.
Jill: No?
Laura: I don't want to be arrested.

At my prompting, and in order to clarify her statement, Laura said she believes prostitution is "not right" and it should be illegal, but when the subject of arrests is addressed, especially in terms of her own arrest, she doesn't want that "wrongness" of prostitution to be realized. This conversation is the only instance wherein one of my interviewees used the word *right* in the context of morality and prostitution, and in this case, it was to specify these activities were in opposition to "right" beliefs and actions.

No one used the word *right* to refer to prostitution as a correct or morally acceptable action, but rather, they referred to it as "not wrong," which underscores the powerful connection that exists between morality and prostitution even in the minds of those who participate in these activities.

Prostitution is "Not Wrong"

Lisa is a 47-year-old, Hispanic woman who had just started a substance abuse program and was between places at the time of our interview. She was born in Nemez and had lived there her whole life. Her mother was Native American and her father was born in Mexico but grew up in the United States. When she was two, Lisa's father committed suicide, and Lisa was given up for adoption. She lived with her adoptive parents, who were also from Mexico, until she was 13 when she "started getting into trouble." She left school during the seventh grade. As Lisa said:

> I ran away from home. I was in a foster home, and I was just real rebellious, you know what I mean? My parents, they didn't have a right to tell me what to do, you know, I just had that attitude, and so I ran away and then I went to juvenile. Then I got out of juvenile, and that's when I met my husband, which was, I lied to him and told him I was 18. He was 21 and I ended up getting pregnant. I got married and that didn't work either.

Lisa started drinking at age eight and smoking pot at 12 or 13. She had her first son when she was 14. Lisa first exchanged sex for money when she was "about 24." She describes her experience:

> I was in a bar and I met this gentleman in there and . . . we went out to . . . we went out, you know, and at the end he asked if I needed any money, if I needed anything, and I said "No," and he gave me some money. And he told me to call him, and I started calling him and that was my first john. [. . .] See, I wasn't on drugs. I mean, I would drink and I smoked pot, okay? But I wasn't like shooting heroin, doing crystal, or smoking that shitty-ass crack shit that just blows, you know, the mind.

Jill: So when you started, you were just doing it for fun?
Lisa: Yeah. Like I said, I met him at a club, we'd go out dancing. My sister was watching the baby, watching my son, and I was out having fun. I'd call this guy up and he'd come and see me, pick me up, and we'd go out, you know? It was like that. [. . .] I still don't see nothing wrong with it if it's a consenting adult. [. . .]
Lisa: But me, I was going to work, dude, you know what I mean? I had fun. You know what I mean? [. . .]

Is She a Criminal, a Victim, or a Victim of the Criminal Justice System? 63

Jill: So you liked doing it?
Lisa: I did. I did.
Jill: What did you like about it?
Lisa: Meeting these different people. Just the way they treated me. They didn't look at me the way my so-called friends were looking at me.
Jill: So your perception is different from the public's perception because why?
Lisa: Because I've lived the life, I guess, and if there's someone that speaks so bad about them it's because they don't understand it and they don't know it, you know, to me. And I lived it. You know what I mean? So it wasn't all bad.

Other women present the issue as a personal choice—it is up to the individual and her chosen lifestyle. In response to my question: What do you think of women who participate in sex for money or drugs? Anna, a 43-year-old, white heterosexual woman, said: "I don't see anything wrong with it. It's their body, y'know." Anna offers the argument the woman owns her own body, rather than the state or society that creates laws against these activities. Julie, a white, 42-year-old heterosexual woman, agreed with these sentiments when I asked her about her friends who exchanged sex for money: "Oh yeah, that's fine. It's each individual for themselves."

Tess is a 41-year-old, white, heterosexual woman who had lived in Nemez for 35 years. Her mother had moved her to Nemez when she was six, and she didn't know who her father was because her mother wouldn't tell her. Tess had completed eleventh grade when her mother kicked her out of the house for "partying" too much. She moved in with her boyfriend and didn't return to school. Tess said her addiction had "pretty much killed [the relationship with her mother]." Tess started using drugs at 15, primarily marijuana, and at 19 started using cocaine. She used cocaine until ten years prior, when she started using crystal meth (crystal methamphetamine). Tess would exchange sex for money or drugs when she needed to get high, and she had never been arrested for prostitution.

Tess had met her husband in high school, started dating him after high school, and got married around 25. They had used drugs together, and had gone through times where they were both trying to quit. He was from a wealthy family and so they didn't have to work, but ultimately his family told him he had to choose his wife or the money, and "he chose the money." Tess said: "I wasn't done using yet, you know?" They were married for three years and didn't have any kids.

She eventually ended up living outside and was using drugs and exchanging sex to support herself. During this time, she took a job as a receptionist at a car dealership. She was able to maintain that job until she was hospitalized, shortly before Christmas, with MRSA (methicillin-resistant Staphylococcus aureus). During her stay, her company replaced her, and she was fired. After being fired, she returned to living outside and using drugs. She had been in and out of multiple programs, relapsing in between, and after working several programs, she qualified for an apartment through a social service agency. At the time of our interview, Tess hadn't used drugs in six months, and she wanted to attend Vocational Rehabilitation School to become a secretary.

When I asked Tess what the public thinks about women who exchange sex for money, she said: "I don't care, you know? I know that, the things I've done aren't who I am. And you know, I'm proud of who I am, no matter what I've done. We all make mistakes. And if women need the money, that's their decision. But it's not for me."

On the whole, the women expressed little moral indignation against street-based sex work. And when they did discuss their reasons for exchanging sex in relationship to its morality, they often talked about them in terms of survival—of themselves and/or perhaps their children. Denise, a 43-year-old, white, heterosexual woman who had argued some should be arrested and some should not based on their reasons for exchanging sex, spoke about her own experience:

Denise: To me, it was, you know, a way of feeding my kids because I didn't know nobody and I was too afraid to ask. And I know if I would've went out and asked I wouldn't have had to do it, you know? But I was too afraid.
Jill: Mmm hmm. How'd you feel about it?
Denise: I felt good because my babies were getting fed. You know, I knew my kids were getting fed.
Jill: Mmm hmm.
Denise: But then afterwards, you know, it didn't bother me; it just kept on going through my head, "At least you did it so the babies could eat. At least you did it. You guys got to stay in another motel." You know, the motel for two more nights, you know? Because I didn't know what was going on. I didn't.

In contrast to the women who stated prostitution is wrong, many of the women who participated in this study stated prostitution is *not* wrong. These responses varied from simply saying it was not wrong to adding certain conditions, such as it occur between consenting adults or is based on a participant's past or present circumstances.

Prostitution Should Not Be Illegal

Some of my participants explicitly argued prostitution should not be illegal. For example, Vicki, a 43-year-old Hispanic heterosexual woman, states:

> If the men wanna do it, let 'em do it, okay? That's all I say. If they wanna spend money on the girl to go do something, let him be, let him

Is She a Criminal, a Victim, or a Victim of the Criminal Justice System? 65

>do it, you know? The police should just go catch crime, you know? Not get us, you know? We're not doing nothing. I don't have AIDS and I use rubbers, condoms, you know? I'm not . . . If they don't want to wear a condom—I get 'em for free, okay? If they don't want to wear a condom, I say, "Let me out the door and you've gotta pay me $5 for my time."

And in response to my question about how she feels about the police arresting women who exchange sex, Vicki went on to say:

>I don't like it because they have to wreck our lives, just throw us in jail, when they got other crimes out here that they should be taking care of, you know? Instead of prostitution, you know? There's some people that wanna have sex because they don't like doing it with their women or the women don't like to do it with them, you know? Well, you know, I think they [police] should just stay out of it, really.

Julie, a white, 42-year-old heterosexual woman, looked at exchanging sex in terms of cause and effect, or what would cause someone to exchange sex for money, as well as one's individual preferences:

>I thought it was the thing to do. It wasn't the money outlook on it. I thought it was the thing to do. Ok, if I go and have sex with this man, you know what I'm saying, then he's gonna have more affection towards me and he's gonna think more of me. That's the way it is. You know, I mean, its not a good thing and its not a bad thing. I know a lot of people look at it in a bad way, and they're wrong. They're wrong because each individual in life has their own lifestyle. And they're gonna live their own lifestyle the way they want to.

Joan, the activist quoted at the beginning of this chapter, expressed some of the difficulties related to participating in prostitution as a moral issue versus meeting one's immediate needs. Ultimately she views the problem as one of addiction and poverty. The women I interviewed viewed exchanging sex through the lens of morality, but it often took a back seat when other needs were more pressing. The problems lay in access to particular resources, which led to the following three perspectives: Prostitution is the problem because it is illegal, and therefore it should be criminalized; Criminalization is the problem, and therefore prostitution should be either regulated or decriminalized; or Drugs are the problem, and the solution is access to services.

IS CRIMINALIZATION THE SOLUTION OR THE PROBLEM?

One cannot discuss the criminalization of prostitution without considering arrests and their impact on the women's lives. This subject of arrests, in addition to the circumstances of these exchanges, also led to contradictions about the "wrongness" or "not rightness" of prostitution. Of the seventeen women I interviewed, seven had been arrested for prostitution. One of the women did not mention arrests at all, and nine were never arrested for prostitution. Thirteen of the seventeen women had been arrested for something other than prostitution, including the possession or sale of drugs, trespassing, fraud, or driving under the influence. Less than half of those interviewed had been arrested for prostitution, and yet the possibility of arrest for exchanging sex for money was a great concern for all of the women. Anthropologists Roche, Neaigus, and Miller (2005), in their study of sex work and the risk experiences of 28 women in low-income New York neighborhoods, found women to be more concerned about prostitution arrests than drug-related charges because a "drug-related charge could, in time, be glossed over as a careless act associated with a misspent youth—whereas a charge of prostitution carries more extreme connotations, implying a significant level of drug addiction" (p. 157). This distinction was not made among my participants, nor was the morality of arrests for drug-charges addressed. Some of the women were more indignant and angry about prostitution arrests than drug-related charges, and yet the morality of the latter was not addressed.

Donna, a 47-year-old, white, heterosexual woman, links the criminalization of prostitution directly to drugs and officials' hopes that they will be able to eradicate both:

> I think the cops are making such a big deal about it because they think if they stop prostitution, they'll stop drugs, which is never gonna happen. You know? I mean, prostitution has been going back since Mary Magdalene, you know, with Jesus. I mean, I don't think it's ever gonna change. You know, I think they make a bigger deal out of it than they should at times; but because of the way the crimes have gotten behind the drugs—not so much prostitution, but the drugs—has made it . . . Or this is a concern to some people: um, the STD thing, because prostitutes don't give a shit. I knew a girl that had AIDS, and because she was dying, she didn't give a shit: "I'm gonna die. They can have it, too." You know? She didn't care. And that's murder, you know? So yeah, there are concerns somewhat, you know, with anything you do in life, you know? But people out here just trying to do their thing and not hurt anybody and be protective about it, I don't think people should interfere with it.

Here, Donna's primary emphasis is on the drugs rather than prostitution, and yet the link between prostitution and drugs is clear both for those who exchange sex as well as for those who enforce criminalization of both drugs and prostitution.

When my participants discussed the violence they experienced at the hands of clients, prosecuting these acts through legal channels was never

Is She a Criminal, a Victim, or a Victim of the Criminal Justice System? 67

mentioned. Rather, several women stopped exchanging sex for a long time as a result. The police were also aware of these situations. When I asked Officer Jennifer Castillo, an Hispanic 34-year-old heterosexual female who worked for the Nemez Police Department as an undercover officer, about the most significant problems associated with women who exchange sex, she answered:

Officer Jennifer Castillo: The drugs, I would say. Um, the drugs; the violence that they can come across.
Jill: What do you mean by violence?
Officer Jennifer Castillo: Well, a lot of them will get beat up, um, whether after they've completed the sex act, um ... And depending on—I know there's a lot of johns that pick up these prostitutes that are married men, um, but a lot of them are the drug ... you know, the drug users also, um, and I know ... I've spoken to a couple of them that have been beat up pretty severely because they wouldn't do a certain sex act.

Here, the officer discusses the violence as a significant problem, explaining these women are victims of violence because they wouldn't participate in a particular sex act. In another interview, Officer Eugene Matthews, a white heterosexual man in his late 30s and a lieutenant in the Nemez Police Department, simply states if the women were to try to report this violence, they would be caught participating in prostitution:

Officer Eugene Matthews: I think there's some gender issues with it, too. Some males just like to just dominate a woman or have some power over a woman. It's like a rape thing, you know? Some of them will go, you know, have sex. And by the way, sexual assaults are commonly done in these transactions, and many times they're not reported.
Jill: By the clients or the johns?
Officer Eugene Matthews: Yeah, the johns would be sexually assaulting the, you know ... I know of one particular instance where we were doing a john sting and there was a girl brought into a hotel room that we were with, and of course, we don't let it go that—I mean, we're prepared to arrest, but ... The guy contacts the girl, the girl goes into the hotel room, the guy comes in with her, they make a deal on the street for this sex for this much money, he goes in the room, and, you know, I won't get into all the tactical thing, but it turns out when the arrest is made, he has no money on him whatsoever and that he has got a history of sexual assault and had been in prison for sexual assault and is a registered sex offender. So it doesn't take any rocket scientist to figure out what was gonna go on in that room. He was gonna sexually assault her

and then out the door he would go, and it would've never been reported.

Jill: Why?

Officer Eugene Matthews: Well, because you have to, um . . . You know, I'll say, in many cases, sexual assaults are reported, and then it'll come out that, you know, the officer goes out there: "Okay, you met this guy. You don't know his name. He told you his name was Larry. You know, you went to the hotel at such-and-such a place." And then, you know, things just start adding up, and then you finally confront the girl: "You're a hooker and this was a john?" "Well, yeah, that's what it was."

Jill: And they're afraid of that?

Officer Eugene Matthews: Well, what they're doing is basically admitting that they're engaging in prostitution.

Jill: But they wouldn't necessarily be arrested for that.

Officer Eugene Matthews: No. But like I say, they don't come forward for a lot of reasons. And some of them will come forward, but they lie about what occurred.

Both officers discuss the problem of violence as central, and yet the women's fear of reporting these crimes is viewed as commonplace—not a problem to be addressed systemically, but rather a problem the individual woman must confront and perhaps accept given her participation in illegal activities.

Joan, a white, 43-year-old, bisexual woman and an activist with a sex worker rights organization, argues for decriminalization as a way of contributing to the safety of these women:

> I think it would make them safer. I do, I think it would be a good thing for them. I think that right now they make so little, on the street, I mean these women can make, I've heard of women getting $3 for a blow job. I mean, honest to God that's ridiculous. So they don't make a lot of money, they operate in the shadows because they don't want the police to see them, which puts them in a good position to be raped or robbed or hurt. I think that if it was legal than they could operate in the light of day, so to speak. I don't mean necessarily in the light of day, but they could ply their trade in a zoned area out in the open and if someone beat them up then they would have legal recourse, they wouldn't be afraid to go to the police, they could have a system where the guy coming in has to give a driver's license, or whatever. They could just be a lot safer, and so I think it would make their work a lot safer for them.

I asked Lisa, a 47-year-old, Hispanic heterosexual woman, if she thought making sex work legal would increase their safety. She said:

Is She a Criminal, a Victim, or a Victim of the Criminal Justice System? 69

Yeah. I wouldn't be like so ashamed or embarrassed or . . . Once something happens, when rapes or someone takes advantage of us, that we couldn't call up . . . Like the time that the dude beat me over the head with that wrench: I thought he was putting his arm around me and he kinda started beating me in the head with a wrench. [. . .] Maybe he got ripped off by another prostitute, I don't know, but I was the one to get it that day. And I didn't want to call the cops because I was scared that I would go to jail for prostituting, number one, you know? Yeah, he beat me, you know what I mean? There was, you know, times that it went a little too far outta hand, you know what I mean? With the slapping and kind of abusive type of thing, you know? Where if it was in a place that, you know, maybe you wouldn't get hurt or you wouldn't find so many dead bodies.

Figure 3.1 outlines how criminalization can actually create conditions that decrease the women's safety as well as recourse if violence does occur.

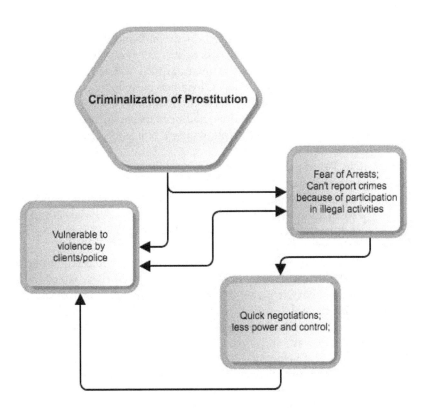

Figure 3.1 Criminalization of prostitution impacts safety.

Criminalization leads to lack of control, not only in terms of not being able to prosecute violence and crimes against them, but because perpetrators know it is extremely unlikely the women will prosecute because of their participation in an illegal act combined with their extremely marginalized status in society. And because their negotiations must be furtive and fast, the women are often not able to take time to evaluate a situation for safety. Therefore, the criminalization of prostitution may create fixed and influential material conditions that not only allow for this violence to occur, but simultaneously prevent a person from feeling protected and "safe." The criminalization of the activity, in some ways, can even lead to "blaming" the person for becoming a victim of this violence.

"A DOOR TO THE OUTSIDE"—CRIMINALIZATION AND ACCESS TO SERVICES

The social service agents and activists discussed access to treatment for drug addiction as a way of "helping" the women, and the women also viewed this access as a way of "getting help." And yet how one attains "access" to drug treatment services differed based on the individual's perspective. The relationship between arrests and access to services is complicated. Olivia, a 43-year-old Hispanic heterosexual woman, argued arrests provide access to services. At the time of our interview Olivia had been homeless for "a couple of years" and was currently living at a shelter. She had been arrested for prostitution "three or four times," and we had been discussing police activity in response to prostitution when the following exchange took place:

Olivia: Oh, I think they're doing a good job and I think they're in the right. Because, like now, like I said, in the community . . . It's wrong. It's wrong to do that . . . It's against the law, you know? Prostitution. And now that I have a clear mind, if they could banish it completely, these girls could get help.
Jill: If they could what?
Olivia: They could get help, you know? Because they're doing it because of the drugs. If they don't have a job, then they can't buy . . . kinda theory. I mean, it's not a good theory, but I mean . . . I think the police are . . . I pray for them. I mean, I'm glad they're doing that. I'm glad they did that to me, because it helped me, too, in a way.
Jill: How did it help you?
Olivia: It opened my eyes more. It made me more observant, made me [feel] more guilty, more like, "That's wrong," you know? "I can't do that. It's wrong," you know?
Jill: Oh, I see.
Olivia: "I'm going to jail." It made me think more, scared me more.

Is She a Criminal, a Victim, or a Victim of the Criminal Justice System?

The underlying belief operating here is Olivia's fear of going to jail as well as the guilt she felt about participating in these activities. Because they were judged "wrong" by society and the criminal system, she felt increased pressure not to participate in these activities, which in turn helped her to stop. Olivia tells her story as achieving what is morally right, or no longer participating in these activities and using drugs, based on her fear of jail or prison. And yet my experiences with Olivia, which occurred over my two-year period of fieldwork, revealed something different. At the time of our interview, Olivia had experienced an extended period of sobriety and movement toward achieving her goals of reconnecting with her family. In our interview Olivia told me she attributed her sobriety and current status to Mark, a friend and social service agent who had found her on the street and helped her gain entry to the shelter in which she was currently living. As she states:

> [Mark said] "We've ... been out there for eight months looking for you. We've been worried about you." I said, "No, no, no." Then I was like, "I'm going back out there" [to use drugs]. He said, "No, that's going to kill you," because they already talked to the doctors that day [about Olivia's pneumonia], you know? "Because you'll die, Olivia," and he says, "I'm not going to let that happen." He says, "Give me two weeks. Stay clean for two weeks," he says, "and I'll get you a bed." And the week before, I had already talked to my counselor and she said, "It's two to four months, you know, the waiting list. I cannot get you in until then." I said, "I'm going to relapse and then I'm going to die." She says, "I can't [help you]. There's a long wait." So I said, "I'll go see Mark," and I was like, "If you guys don't help me, I'm going to go get high and die ... So Mark said, "Please just give me two weeks. If I can't do it in two weeks, then go ahead. But just [do it] for me, please just this one time." I said, "All right, Mark." But twelve days [later], I'm already unpacking in here [the shelter]. [Mark] can move mountains.

The contradictions in Olivia's statements reveal the complications inherent in the narratives told about criminalization and accessing help—even when the women stated exchanging sex was wrong and people *should* be arrested for it, when it became personal, arrest was not necessarily the best course of action. Olivia's story also reveals the role services and access to them plays in one's ability to stop using drugs and exchanging sex. She was told there was a two to four month waiting list when she asked for help and access to services. Mark was able to decrease this wait considerably.

Avery Gordon's (2008) "complex personhood" may offer insights into the contradictions that become apparent:

> Complex personhood means that all people (albeit in specific forms whose specificity is sometimes everything) remember and forget, are beset by contradiction, and recognize and misrecognize themselves

and others. Complex personhood means that people suffer graciously and selfishly too, get stuck in the symptoms of their troubles, and also transform themselves. Complex personhood means that even those called "Other" are never never that. [. . .] At the very least, complex personhood is about conferring the respect on others that comes from presuming that life and people's lives are simultaneously straightforward and full of enormously subtle meaning. (pp. 4–5)

In light of the stories we all tell ourselves and each other to better understand our lives, not all stories are valued equally, especially when it comes to what are commonly defined as immoral and illegal behaviors. Therefore, the statements my participants made that may have appeared to be "contradictions" in beliefs may, in fact, be based on the need many people have to tell a story that is validated or even rewarded in society, for example, "I did something wrong, I reached my lowest point, and then I was redeemed by something or someone". Although I do not believe my participants were consciously telling me lies, I acknowledge their stories may have been told in certain ways for my "benefit." In order to counteract this concern and its effect on my ethnography, I spent extensive time with many of my participants and knew them over several years, thereby encouraging their trust and openness in our conversations as well as fortifying my own ability to understand their lived experiences.[11]

The neighborhood responses to prostitution are well known to social service agents and activists and are explained by Sylvia, an Hispanic lesbian woman in her late 30s and a director at a mental health organization:

The community itself is very, very interested in resolving this issue. There's community members, the neighborhood associations are extremely active in trying to address alternatives to continuing pursuing this issue in the neighborhood plans. [. . .] Prostitution is identified as something they would find a solution for by creating access to substance abuse treatment. So the neighborhoods in the community in that area are very, very savvy about what the real deal is.

Here again, the problem is defined as drug use and addiction, the "real deal" is the connection between prostitution and drug use, and the solution lies in "access to substance abuse treatment." What is not mentioned are the avenues that provide access to treatment. Public figures often expressed hope that through their arrests the women would "get some help" from social service agencies and substance abuse treatment programs, and this "help" is directly related to drug addiction.

Is She a Criminal or a Victim?

Unlike other crimes viewed more clearly as having perpetrators and victims, street-based sex work is complicated because those who exchange

Is She a Criminal, a Victim, or a Victim of the Criminal Justice System? 73

sex, especially on the street, are often viewed not as perpetrators of a crime, but as victims themselves in need of services ranging from housing and employment that provides a living wage to counseling and rehabilitation from systemic and personal violence and abuse. Following from this perception, sex workers' bodies and identities have been presented as both sites of oppression and objectification (Jeffreys 2008; Raymond 2003) as well as the basis for social justice and human rights (Kempadoo and Doezema 1998; Weitzer 2010). When viewed through the eyes of people on the street who exchange sex for money, each of these perspectives can be validated. As Teela Sanders argues: "Few other jobs attract stigma and marginalization to the same extent as sex work. Also, the fact that selling sex, particularly on the street, is criminalized and continually policed by law-enforcement agencies and community protesters increases the stress and stigma experienced when trying to earn money" (2005, p. 40).

The following excerpts reveal the perspectives on criminal and victim status, as well as how the criminal system, itself, victimizes the women. Officer Eugene Matthews, the former supervisor of the vice unit, stated:

> I've dealt with some individuals in dealing with all these other entities that will believe that it's poverty, it's . . . And it could have aspects of that, but sometimes I think that you've got people that are politically motivated and forcing agendas on these type of issues. Same thing with drugs. I always get, um, you know, when it comes to the narcotic-type thing: Oh, it's a victimless crime [. . .] legalize everything. And they just don't see the whole picture, you know. And sometimes with prostitution, I've seen it so many times where I've talked to people at social agencies: "Well, prostitutes, are nothing but victims and . . . and . . ." There's probably some that are victims that are probably following when they're doing it, you know, because they're being forced into it or whatever, but I think that's very insignificant. I personally believe, just from my personal experience, that there's some women that would be doing it anyways, regardless, because they like it.

Dr. Veronica Alvarez, a 48-year-old heterosexual Latina woman and the Project Director of an HIV-prevention program argues the women are victimized by the police and the legal system, and this victimization is grounded in gender bias:

> *Dr. Veronica Alvarez:* I don't know what drives the—well, certainly the focus . . . I don't understand the police focus. Making women the criminal. Yeah, I don't understand that. [. . .] It's really biased.
> *Jill:* Because they're going after the women more than the men? Or more than . . ?
> *Dr. Veronica Alvarez:* Right. Well, that it's criminalized the way it is and that it's certainly gender-biased. [. . .] I mean, it's so very blatant.

Jill: How would you have it be, or what would you say would be a better . . . I'm not saying it's good.

Dr. Veronica Alvarez: Yeah. No, I'm saying that I think the women deserve protection. And they're not getting protection; they're victimized. That's what I'm saying.

The victim status of the women was readily accepted by those who were in favor of criminalization, largely because they viewed criminalization as the avenue through which women make changes in their lives. Officer Tom Hixson, a white 52-year-old heterosexual male and a former supervisor of the vice unit, discussed his involvement in creating a diversion program and how it contributed to the women's future:

> Because I kind of developed a prostitution elimination program, I called it, for the city of Nemez. Now obviously we're not going to eliminate prostitution, but instead of just arresting them and throwing them in jail, arresting them and throwing them in jail, that's not working, and it's the same with the johns too, you have to keep in mind the guys, what we really want to do is to get it to reduce and eliminate it. Part of the problem is, the girls need to have . . . the people arrested for prostitution need to have some way to get out of this, some assistance to get out of that life. And the vast majority problem is, number one, they're addicted to drugs, crack cocaine, so they're in need of those services and then following that there's the other basic needs like food to eat, a place to live, and then I found out that one of the biggest leverages we had with a lot of these female prostitutes was a good majority of them had kids that they lost, and that was usually the trigger that got these ladies to finally accept some of the services. If you really sit down and interview them after you arrest them, which I did hundreds, just conversations with them, how'd you get into it, what are you doing, you'd almost always find that a boyfriend, a husband left them, they had no other choice, and do they want to get out of this, oh absolutely—they hate the life. Now, many of them would say that, and then you'd see them next week, but eventually, they would accept the services if they were there—so that's why I did it.

After enough opportunities to access services through their arrests, Officer Tom Hixson implies these women would eventually "accept them." Officer Eugene Matthews, a white heterosexual man in his late 30s and a lieutenant in the Nemez Police Department, also explains this approach:

> You have to have a very comprehensive approach that works not only in areas of enforcement, but also something that I think even goes beyond the scope of the police department, and that is diversion-type programs

Is She a Criminal, a Victim, or a Victim of the Criminal Justice System? 75

to break the cycle of prostitution. I believe that the enforcement is critical. I don't believe that any diversion program or any social program works in and of itself, because they will not . . . They simply won't choose that solution.

Without the arrest, the women won't "choose that solution," which implies the woman is not making a choice, but rather being forced into circumstances that may encourage her to "choose to change." Based on the solution arrests offer in this framework, Officer Eugene Matthews refers to them as a "door to the outside":

There are programs that the courts offer. I'm not sure what the standard benchmark is now, though, but you know, there's diversion programs other than they do the jail time. *Casa Segura* is always a resource for them; in fact, I understand that *Casa Segura* makes contact with many of them at the jail and then offers that type of activity. Now, the police department, although we work directly with *Casa Segura* and we have meetings with [them]. But the police work is basically . . . The enforcement side is kept separate. I mean, we have our, you know, our responsibilities and we have to . . . The integrity of our enforcement initiatives have to remain separate, but also, it's kind of like the door to the outside for them. You know, the arrest sometimes starts the process of them getting out of it. And there's been a lot of women that have been very successful, where they have got out of it.

Officer Eric Johnson, a white heterosexual man in his mid-40s and the supervisor of the Nemez Police Department vice unit, talks about how arrests help to facilitate the process of no longer exchanging sex for money:

I mean obviously they don't like being arrested, and they kind of figure that there's other things that we could probably be doing that are better suitable for society, but, that's our function and unfortunately we cross paths and we try to get along with them. Not only do we, I mean, we're not out there to cause them harm, obviously, we don't want to keep taking them to jail and throwing them in there in the jail. What we do now is we have, we refer them to *Casa Segura*, and *Casa Segura*, helps them with, they contact them at the jail and try to schedule appointments with them, and I'm not sure if you're familiar with *Casa Segura*, but a lot of our prostitutes are, suffer from poor self-esteem, um, they're drug addicts, they have no marketable skills, so what they [*Casa Segura*] try to do is they try to help them, number one, get off the drugs, number two, is give them self-esteem, show them some self-worth and number three, to try to give them some skills that they can go out and do something where they can make money legitimately.

76 Street Sex Workers' Discourse

These examples reveal the underlying hope that through their arrests the women will be offered services and ultimately "get some help." As Russell, a white heterosexual man in his mid 30s and a neighborhood association leader, stated: "We've talked about it, we're always saying, if they get arrested and that type of thing, hopefully they'll get some help from some other agency so they don't have to, they'll be able to go to a drug treatment facility or something like that." When stated this way, arrest is a vehicle through which the woman will hopefully receive services. The "help" is primarily depicted as access to substance abuse services. The process the officers lay out (arrests lead to services that will help the women "get off the drugs [. . .] give them self-esteem [. . .] show them some self-worth [. . .] and give them some skills [to] make money legitimately") is not as simple as it might appear. The women are arrested, by force, provided services, again by force, they can "choose" to accept or not. In the scenarios above, they are then "given" self-esteem and "shown" self-worth—which implies passive recipients of attributes central to making an empowered, or agential, choice.

Valarie, an Hispanic heterosexual female in her mid 30s and a program manager at a behavioral health agency, did not see arrests as providing this access to services:

Valarie: And when you say they want help, what does that mean? I mean, they want to be offered some type of treatment program. They do want—but not something that is just gonna tell them, "Yeah, go here." A lot of our women here come and tell us, "You know what? I need more structure. That's not gonna work with me." They really do want that. And it may have not worked in the past. Maybe they were given the opportunity. Who knows? We know not everyone's the same, but they don't want to be arrested and let go in 3 hours. That's really not what they want. [. . .] In the very beginning, we dealt a lot with people that didn't agree with what we had. And we still get it sometimes where they say, "You know, this center just enables them, and this center doesn't really force them to change." We still get it. But I think, now more than ever, they're understanding our perspective as to we can only do so much, and you can lock them up as many times as you want; obviously, it's not helping. NPD [Nemez Police Department] makes sure to repeat that every meeting that we have.

Jill: What?

Valarie: The fact that arresting them isn't always the answer. And they get pretty tired. They get pretty tired of arresting the same women over and over. They tell them every time. And they've asked us, you know, "If we're arresting someone, can we just bring them over here instead of locking them up for the seventh, eighth time?" And of course, you know, that's always welcome.

Is She a Criminal, a Victim, or a Victim of the Criminal Justice System?

Lisa, a 47-year-old, Hispanic heterosexual woman, offered an example of how her arrest and time in prison helped keep her sober, even when she was offered increased access to drugs:

> For the times I've gotten away, 5 years and 10 months, I guess is good, you know what I mean? It saved my life, you know? Prison is not always bad, you know what I mean? It helped keep me clean for 5 years and 10 months. I was working visitation for 5 years, and that's where the dope usually comes in is through our visits, you know what I mean? So I had access to it. They put money on my book so I could have dope, regardless of whatever. But I managed to stay off of it. I got put on medications for my anger and kind of being shy and not feeling sociable. And the medications seemed to help, so . . .

Jill: Even though you had access to it while you were in prison, you didn't do it?
Lisa: No, I had no desire to, even though it was there in my hands.

In prison, even though given access, Lisa chose not to use drugs.

Although arrests and time spent in jail or prison were viewed by some of the women as helpful, overall, the implications of criminalization were problematic for most. As Kristina, a 34-year-old Hispanic heterosexual woman and outreach coordinator for a mental health organization, said:

> A lot of barriers that I run into is when you're trying to help an individual with housing or job placement, a lot of agencies and apartment complexes don't like to rent to anybody that has felonies; they don't like to provide anybody with an opportunity for job placement, you know, because of their history. So that's a huge problem and I think something I would love to see [our mental health organization] work on, as far as the housing portion, just because we have so many women that may be willing and ready to change, and you get there and they're ready to get an apartment and they can't because of their felony; and the places where they can get housing . . . Back to the old lifestyle, and I think that's difficult.

The women wanted access to social service agencies and substance abuse treatment programs, and in most cases they did not identify their arrests as the vehicle through which they achieved this "help." Some women found relief and support in the mandated non-drug use of prison/jail, and yet most women placed their movement away from drugs and exchanging sex to their own personal choice to do it for "themselves." Arrest is often not a gateway to services, in part because the services do not exist. The person arrested then has the additional burdens that have surmounted due to criminal charges, fines, court dates, and criminal records.

Once an individual is moved away from or off of the grid of "mainstream" life, she must either survive off of this grid, or get back on it through the processes developed and made available to her through the system. These are physical, material conditions that must be managed if one is to live as a documented citizen with a job, place to live, bank account, etc. The systems that helped to create the conditions through which these women chose to exchange sex, as well as the systems to which they are subjected when they use drugs, exchange sex, and make other non-"mainstream" choices, become barriers to movement back onto the grid. In other words, these systems can actually prevent an individual from becoming an "upstanding" citizen that contributes to society.

In most cases, the women do not want to be participating in these illegal activities, and in some cases, criminal charges more firmly entrench the women in a marginalized lifestyle because it inhibits access to more legitimate jobs, housing, and other mainstream pursuits. Although in some cases fear of arrest was a deterrent to exchanging sex, in most cases the women participated in these activities because their immediate needs outweighed the potential consequences.

The arrests serve to move people away from the given location, as well as to inculcate fear in the person participating in these activities, perhaps so they are less visible to those on the street. Therefore, this threat of arrest is somewhat successful because it requires individuals not be seen by those who may arrest them or call someone to arrest them. If the woman is already a "victim" of poverty, neglect, abuse, and drug use, why penalize her further in order to try to move her into the treatment system? Accessing treatment programs and social service agencies through arrests serves to "blame the victim." In all cases, the women disliked the police, felt they were not fairly represented, and had very few resources when dealing with the judicial system. Although many of the women stated it was a deterrent, Julie, as noted earlier, had been arrested an estimated "forty or fifty times" and continued to exchange sex in spite of her fear of going to prison. In no case did the women state the reason they accessed help and decided to change their lifestyle was due to arrests; rather they all stated they stopped using drugs and exchanging sex due to personal choices related to their desires and the responsibility they took for their lives.

A Solution that Isn't One?

In this description of the problem, the options are to arrest or ignore. Two of the officers stated explicitly the arrests for prostitution wouldn't solve the problem, but the activity could not be ignored, and therefore, they seem to operate in a middle ground. As Officer Eugene Matthews, a white heterosexual man in his late 30s and a lieutenant in the Nemez Police Department, stated:

> Because it is a task that I don't believe it'll ever be eradicated. It can't be ignored. It simply can't be ignored. It can't be viewed as—as much as

Is She a Criminal, a Victim, or a Victim of the Criminal Justice System? 79

sometimes I thought, you know, "Oh, gee, just let it go," sometimes we did let it go until the complaints became so prevalent. In fact, what we do in many cases is we do our other activities and the prostitution complaints would stack up, then we'd zap it. [. . .] It's a pain in the butt.

When I asked him to clarify his statement he said:

We know that it's necessary. We know it's a necessary thing. I say "a pain." We know that it's a vital enforcement area. We know that it is important that we do it, but it's like, we know that the girls, we arrest them, we'll see them again. We know that we continually see them. They absorb a lot of resources.

Ironically, the zone restrictions usually included with an arrest for prostitution (mandating a person not be allowed within a given distance of the point of arrest) were attributed to increasing the women's presence in the neighborhoods. Officer Eric Johnson, a white heterosexual man in his mid-40s and the supervisor of the Nemez Police Department vice unit, explained the restrictions to me:

There are zone restrictions and those are that they've been arrested in a particular area before and the courts say that you cannot come within 1,000 feet or whatever they deem of that particular area again. [. . .] And that's what's kind of pushed the prostitution problem throughout the whole city is because they keep getting these zone restrictions that they can't go back to this area so they just move a little bit further away, so then you get a zone restriction for there, and then you end up going a little bit further out.

Sue, a white heterosexual woman in her late 50s and a neighborhood association leader, attributed the women's presence in her neighborhood to the zone restrictions put in place to protect the local businesses:

The business owners got fed up with losing customers because the prostitutes and johns were lingering in front of the businesses so they raised cane, went to the mayor and council and so forth and [. . .] there were some restrictions imposed on the prostitutes and the johns, which was [. . .] to be back a thousand feet of a business, which pushed them off into the neighborhoods. They went off the strip and over into the neighborhoods.

Although Russell, a white heterosexual man in his mid-30s and a neighborhood association leader, was very much in support of criminalization, he mentioned the police presence in other areas of the city could actually increase the women's presence in his neighborhood: "I think there's kind of consensus in the neighborhood that the prostitution isn't as big a problem for us as it is for the neighborhoods directly north of us. But if the police chase them out of those neighborhoods they might come down here, so that's something we're always trying to keep an eye out for." The solution, then, is to have the police "chase" the women to another neighborhood, as long as it is not the neighborhood in which the speaker resides.

Valarie, an Hispanic heterosexual female in her mid 30s and a program manager at a behavioral health agency, argued that most people do not understand arrests will not solve the underlying problems:

Valarie: A lot of them are still not very sensitive to the population that we target. A lot of them still don't even understand the nature of the problem. They really do believe that we should be calling NPD [Nemez Police Department] and arresting more of these women as they come in. I think to this point we haven't seen eye to eye on a lot of these issues.
Jill: And what does that do in their minds, by arresting them?
Valarie: Get 'em off the streets, which is really their primary goal.
Jill: To get them off the streets?
Valarie: Just get them off the streets, get them out of my neighborhood.

Officer Eugene Matthews agrees with this perception when he discusses the visibility of the "prostitution problem" and how criminalization is more likely to move the women around rather than stop their participation in exchanging sex:

You know, we see them out there, we need to give them attention. The more attention they get, they're less inclined to be so visible. After a lot of police activity, they may kind of retreat, but they don't go away; they just change their tactics a little bit. You know, there was a period where we hit an area real hard, and so instead of being on the streets and on the sidewalks, they retreated to convenience stores and they would get the crowd coming in to get the Big Gulp and stuff.

Figure 3.2 presents the problem and solution framework as outlined above, which create cycles, as stated by the police themselves in this study, that do not solve the problem.

Criminalization may solve the problem immediately for the neighborhood in question based on proximity alone. The attention then is largely paid to the women's visibility and making them less so, which implies the ultimate goal is to hide the problem, or, as Joan, a white, 43-year-old, bisexual woman and an activist with a sex worker rights organization, argued, the penalties can make the problem worse by "push[ing] them deeper into the shadows." Not only are they pushed "out of sight," but as Lerum et al. (2012) argue:

Is She a Criminal, a Victim, or a Victim of the Criminal Justice System? 81

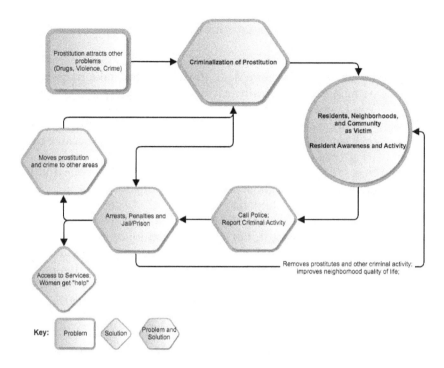

Figure 3.2 Problems and solutions related to criminalization of prostitution.

economic marginalization due to the deep impact of racism in the United States means that people of colour make up the majority of sex workers in public spaces, and are relentlessly targeted by the police in their efforts to clear the streets. Arrest and subsequent conviction for prostitution-related offenses intensifies the homelessness or housing precariousness experienced by people from low-income communities because people with criminal records are barred from accessing, or may lose, their public housing. (p. 89)[12]

As Duff et al. (2011) argue: "an array of health problems have been associated with being homeless, including mental illness, physical violence, and substance abuse. The convergence of these factors may elevate an individual's risk for homelessness, leading to the concept of 'hard to house' individuals" (p. 2). These examples exemplify the cycles in which individuals who exchange sex are continually caught.

Alternatives to Arrests

When the women mentioned help, it took a variety of forms and was not accessed primarily through arrests, as I explore more fully in the conclusion.

82 Street Sex Workers' Discourse

Ava, a white, 23-year-old heterosexual woman, discusses alternatives to arrests she believes would be more helpful for women:

Ava: I don't know why they go arresting girls for it. I think they should try to help them more than arrest them and take them to jail, because that's not really teaching them anything; that's just . . . You know, if they're doing it, they're probably needing money for bills or something that day. If you arrest them that day, while they're doing it, and you throw more fines on them because that's what they do: they throw fines. Then they're just gonna go do that [exchange sex] to pay the fine. I think the police and law enforcement goes about it the whole wrong way.
Jill: How would you think they should do it?
Ava: Based on the girls individually, you know? Not necessarily as to why they're doing it, but like . . . what kind of mental history they have, what kind of drug history they have, you know? And then they should put them in a program and make that mandatory instead of giving them, "Hey, here's another fine. Good luck paying it because you don't have a job. Good luck getting a job because you don't have a home." You know?

Ava argues arrests, fines, and criminal charges only add to the women's difficulties and become additional obstacles to living free of the criminal justice system. The root causes, mental disabilities, or drug histories must be addressed or the behaviors will not change. And adding additional fines and criminal charges only makes it that much more difficult to break free from the criminal justice system. In the final two chapters, I present two collages: one with a foundation in responsibility to and for change and the other based in agency, or agential choice.

4 "An Opportunity to Change"
Responsibility and Choice

These girls are given an opportunity to change and some will and some won't. The ones that have are the success stories for those that may [change], but the opportunity is there for them if they want to and are willing.
—Sue, a white heterosexual woman in her late 50s and a neighborhood association leader

You know, if you give them the right chance and you give them the right tools, you can change it. If they are willing to change. And some of them are, you know? Some of them say, "You know what? I've had enough." And they wanna get out. But nobody ever took the time to maybe show something different or open the door for them and say, "You know what? Come on in. There are programs here. You can do something." You know? What I tell the women sometimes, "You know what? Do your GED. What's your dream? What do you want to be one day? So what is keeping you away from becoming, you know, a counselor, for instance?" You know?
Adele, 53-year-old heterosexual white woman and Assistant Program Director at a federal residential re-entry center

All three of my research sites focus primarily on the women and their need for change, or more precisely, the responsibility they have to "change"—meaning they no longer use drugs and/or exchange sex for money or other gain. This change is addressed explicitly in the newspaper articles, and this theme reverberates throughout almost all of my interviews with public figures and the women. Everyone's focus, including the women themselves, is on the individual woman and the changes she needs to make in order to achieve a better life. The way these changes are accessed is a point of discrepancy, as the neighborhood association leaders and police officers often argue these changes occur through arrests and thereby subsequent access to treatment and social service agencies, whereas the women see this change as occurring based on their own personal choices. What is clear is the women are the focus. The following presents several excerpts that emphasize this change based on my participants' perspectives.

"YOU'RE THE ONLY ONE WHO CAN CHANGE IT."

Numerous examples emerged within my conversations with the women and public figures that placed the need for change squarely on the women exchanging sex. Julie, a white, 42-year-old heterosexual woman, for instance, discussed others who participated in these acts:

Jill: Do you have friends who participate in sex acts for money?
Julie: Yes, quite a few of my friends.
Jill: Are their lives similar to yours?
Julie: Similar to some of them. It just depends.
Jill: How are they different?
Julie: Because they're not willing to change. They do the same thing. They like doing the same thing, and they don't have, they're afraid to accept that if you want to change your life you're the only one who can change it. Nobody else can.

"But its all what they want."

In my interview with Brenda, a white, 48-year-old lesbian woman, she said: "I talk to them [women on the street who exchange sex for money or drugs] all the time like that. And they know that I had a relapse and that I got back up on my feet. And they're all proud and stuff and they're looking at me and saying, 'If she can do it, I can do it.' But it's all what they want." During our reflection on the interview process, Brenda suggested I ask:

Brenda: What the women would do who were prostitutes. How would they change their life if they had a chance? Would they be willing to stop doing drugs if they could change their life?
Jill: Would you answer those questions? I know you've already stopped doing drugs.
Brenda: How would I answer those questions? How would I change my life? I would get help from the programs. I mean, how would I stop doing drugs? I'd start going to meetings.

Rather than emphasizing how an individual must decide to change, the public figures often focused on the reasons why the women did not "choose" to take responsibility and change their lives.

MOVING FROM A VICTIM TO TAKING RESPONSIBILITY

One's ability to move from victim status to taking responsibility for one's self was apparent in many interviews with public figures, who not only placed the responsibility on the individual, but emphasized the women's *choice* in taking this responsibility and changing their lives. Evelyn, a 60-year-old heterosexual white woman and the director of a mental health counseling agency, outlined the relationship between claiming victim status versus taking responsibility for one's "place in society [. . .] and where that's gone wrong."

"Sometimes that's just too hard to do."

Jill: And what about the differences between the way you see them [women who exchange sex] and the way they see themselves?
Evelyn: I don't . . . (long pause) for the most part, there are reasons why women are victims, and they're valid and they are victims. At some point in their lives, you want to hope that they get past that. There are other areas where women perceive themselves as victims that aren't valid, and so I'm not as apt to see them as victims, especially in the beginning, as they are, because . . . Did you get set up? Maybe. Were you doing anything right or wrong? Who knows? I don't know. But you put yourself in a place where somebody could make the assumption that you were doing something wrong and you got arrested. That's a reality. That doesn't make you a victim. That means that that was, for whatever reason, a choice you made at that moment. So from the arrest standpoint, you're not a victim. So I'll listen to your story about how the arrest happened, but I'm not going to reinforce the fact that you were victimized by the police, unless you can come in here and show me that they beat the crap out of you. And that's a whole different ball game [laughs]. Beyond that, you may be a victim, and then let's look at how we help you get past that or learn to live with it. But I think that's the difference. I'm not . . . When it comes to . . . There's two things: in domestic violence and in these kinds of criminal charges. Were you a victim? Yes. But did you have a part to play in the whole thing? Most likely. Even in domestic violence, the first or second time somebody really hurts you, you might not have seen it coming. But after awhile, you're in the place with them, so there's two people. You may not be the primary mover or the primary guilty party, but you were there and so you had a role to play, and that's the same thing: You have a role to play in your arrest, and you played it, so . . . And believe me, I get in a lot of trouble for saying that [laughs].
Jill: Oh, yeah? Why?
Evelyn: Well, because most women's programs don't want you to . . . a lot of women's programs reinforce the idea that women are victims and powerless and that if you're involved in domestic violence, if you're involved in prostitution, if you're involved in drug use, it's because some male—primarily—person has control over you

	and is doing things to you. And it's almost like you're a doll and you just stand there, which is never the truth; you react somehow. And so as soon as you react, you become part of, to some degree, whatever is going on. But there are a lot of people that don't want to look at it that way.
Jill:	I see.
Evelyn:	So I get in trouble [laughs].

Later in the interview, we talked about a specific program her agency offered:

Jill:	Do they learn [. . .] in the course of the 12-week [program], that it was a good program [and] that they're not just here to beat a charge?
Evelyn:	I think so. I think they do, mostly. You know what? If they're not learning that, they don't come back, they don't complete the program; they just stop coming, you know, it's not worth it to them. Or if they decide that it's gonna be too painful, that they're going to have to look at too many things they don't wanna look at, then they don't come back. Everybody who starts doesn't finish.
Jill:	What percentage would you say?
Evelyn:	Mmm . . . That finish?
Jill:	Yeah. Or that don't finish. Either way.
Evelyn:	Oh, maybe . . . Maybe 30 percent finish. [. . .] They're looking at their place in society as a woman and where that's gone wrong and what that means to them and how they can make it different. And sometimes that's just too hard to do.

Evelyn places the emphasis on the women and how difficult it may be for them to "look at their place in society" and "where that's gone wrong." These phrases place the responsibility on the shoulders of the women. And if they choose not to return to the program, Evelyn attributes that choice to the difficulty she has in taking responsibility for herself. Even in her acknowledgement that the women can at times be victims, she encourages them to "get past that" while she simultaneously tries to help them decide if their behavior actually warrants victim status.

"Can't see the big picture."

Officer Jennifer Castillo, an Hispanic 34-year-old heterosexual female who worked for the Nemez Police Department as an undercover officer, saw her role as helping these women take responsibility for their lives and change. I asked Officer Jennifer Castillo what her role was in working with women on the street.

I personally try to make an effort to help tell them that there's other things out there to do. The majority of them come from abusive relationships. They're all meth heads, crack; they're on crack. Those are the two drugs that they do. They all have kids. The majority of them don't have custody of their children. I would say more than half of them are homeless just trying to support their habit. So me, personally, my role, I feel, at least I want to try to help them, to make them look at the big picture, that they have choices. That they don't have to be doing what they're doing. And I'm very honest with them, you know. I tell them, "I can't relate to you because I've never been in your shoes, but I know that, you know . . ." I try to encourage them the best that I can, I really do.

Officer Eugene Matthews referred to the cycle of exchanging sex for money or drugs as an inability to "see the big picture":

It's really sad that they can't see the big picture in life. [. . .] That there's another side to life that's more productive. They don't see that they—I don't think they really fully understand, or even care, about the activities . . . how, you know, it is basically impacting their lives, their health, their children, and their whole ability. I believe that there are some out there that may not have had a high education level but are pretty smart, and that, you know, you look at a person like that and you say, "Well, it sure would be nice if she applied herself in another, you know, task and probably could be very successful."

The big picture is "productivity" as well as the women's health, abilities, and children. The assumption is the women do not look beyond their microcosm of drug use and/or exchanges of sex, which implies if they could only see beyond their immediate needs, they would choose something different. The power lies in their ability to see. The responsibility placed on the individuals often manifests as a personal character flaw within the women because if they are not able to "choose" to change and take responsibility for their lives, their circumstances, and their emotional and physical health, then there must be something wrong with them. As Sylvia, an Hispanic lesbian woman in her late 30s and a director at a mental health organization, says: "There's a segment of them, certainly, that's impacted them to believe 'I have a personal character flaw and that's why I do this.'" This statement is consistent with my interviews with the women when they talk about wanting to change and create a better life. This social service agent went on to say: "It's important for them not to relax themselves into that and believe that's their truth. It's nice to be somebody that hopefully can remind them that you can change your truth anytime you like." This statement is also consistent with those made by many of my participants. The women

88 *Street Sex Workers' Discourse*

echo these statements by talking about making changes, being determined, becoming role models for others, and creating a better life. Like Sylvia, who likes being someone who can remind these women they can change their truth, many of the women interviewed also like being someone who is a role model for others and can encourage them to change and create a better life.

SOLUTION: PERSONAL RESPONSIBILITY TO AND FOR "CHANGE"

"A Way Out for Prostitutes"
[Headline from newspaper article about prostitution/street-based sex work]

According to the newspaper media in Nemez, the pathways the women who exchange sex for money or drugs have traveled as well as those paths available to them in the future are limited.[1, 2] Specifically, 10 women who are or were actively working as prostitutes are quoted directly, paraphrased, or discussed in some detail. All ten of the women were cited by either their real or street names. Five of the 12 articles are in-depth explorations of street prostitution and organizations working with women on the street. All of these articles focus on women who are currently using or have a history of using drugs, have been sexually and physically abused as children or as adults by johns, have been in jail/prison on charges ranging from drug paraphernalia to manslaughter, and are vulnerable to diseases and general violence. These women include those who currently work as street prostitutes and want to leave, those who had previously worked and were victims of violent crimes resulting in their deaths, and those who left prostitution and offer a message of hope to others.

Four of the articles focus on street prostitutes who have since left this environment and now work with and inspire others to leave street prostitution. Through personal strength and programmatic support, these four women found their way out of prostitution and are now active role models, working to help others who are involved with drugs and prostitution. One article includes the story and perspective of a director of a diversion program for street prostitutes who, prior to her work as the director, was a street prostitute for more than twenty years. Another former prostitute became the director of a diversion program in another city for women arrested for prostitution.

One article focuses on *Casa Segura*, a program working with street prostitutes, and two women are interviewed and describe their current status in detail. The first woman is unsure of her options, wants to leave prostitution and drugs, but is not sure if she'll be able to. The second woman talks about her history of prostitution and now works with *Casa Segura* in order

"An Opportunity to Change" 89

to help others get out of prostitution. Only one of the five articles includes the voices of women who are currently working as prostitutes, and these women are unhappy and want to leave this work. This same article also includes the stories of three prostitutes who were found beaten and killed—violence attributed to their work as prostitutes.

In all of the stories, the women who are working on the street want to leave prostitution. In four out of the five articles (80%), the reader is offered a message of hope. Individuals remove themselves from street prostitution and subsequently work to help others do the same. Only in two cases does the reader see women working as prostitutes who do not necessarily plan on leaving prostitution, but who say they would like to leave and are worried about their futures. And because these messages saturate the newspaper media, the public is likely to associate these stories with all women who work in street prostitution, and most likely all people in sex work.

One of the stated purposes of the in-depth articles is to explore potential solutions to the "problem" of prostitution. Although the women may have entered prostitution due to desperation and the need for survival, the articles focus on women who have made choices to get "help," change their "lifestyle," and are no longer involved in prostitution. They are represented as heroes and role models for others who are still involved in prostitution. By emphasizing the personal choices made by the women involved in prostitution, the newspaper articles construct the *individuals* as the source of the problem, which constrain the potential solutions.[3]

AGENCY AND REPRESENTATION

In addition to examining the stories told about prostitution in these articles, I explore how the women who exchange sex are represented in the newspaper media, who is given a voice within that media, and the implications for street-based sex work and street economies as a whole. The questions asked of those interviewed in the Nemez newspaper articles both construct and constrain the answers given as well as how these individuals are represented. The types of information solicited from those interviewed include whether the interview participant is anonymous or named in the article; their current relationship status with significant others and children; their reasons for and length of time participating in prostitution; their histories with illegal substance abuse; the length of time and/or cause of incarceration; their status as a victim of physical or sexual assault; and a physical description specifically related to drug use.

Only one of the five articles includes interviews with and specific information about the johns or clients who employ street prostitutes—one who is famous and not local and two who are local and anonymous. Mike is a "lonely" man because his marriage ended over ten years ago, but he never thought his "search for comfort" would land him in jail.[4] He is described as "just wanting to talk" and "to be with somebody for a little bit." Mike states he's "not just a pervert." The second man quoted in the article is Tommy, a mechanic who "lives with his girlfriend and their one-year-old daughter" who says he's "satisfied with his love life." Nonetheless, he stopped to proposition a woman standing on the side of the road, although he says he doesn't know why. Later, Tommy suggests his choice has "probably something to do with men." These two examples of men who purchase sex are the only ones the reader sees within this corpus. Although the men are portrayed as responsible for their actions and are obviously choosing to participate in acts of prostitution, they are also portrayed as somewhat confused and pathetic.

The johns commented on their relationship statuses and why they participated in prostitution, whereas the prostitutes were not asked about or did not discuss their relationships. The articles included information about how long the women had worked as prostitutes, but did not include how long the men had been soliciting them. The length of time using, as well as treatment for, drug use was attributed to the women, but there was no mention of the men's current or previous drug use or treatment. The articles also included physical descriptions of the women's skin due to drug use ("arms showing scars of track marks left by needles"; "her face is pocked because, while under the influence of drugs, she picked at imaginary bugs"; and "pock marks scar her shoulders where she punched needles into her skin"). The descriptions don't denote the quality of the men's skin in the same way the women's skin is identified: they are regular, everyday guys who don't wear the physical signs of drug use and its correlation to the exchanges of sex for money or drugs for everyone to see. Unlike the sex workers who are physically marked and clearly identified, their clients are anonymous in both name and appearance. Professor of Women's Studies Vivyan C. Adair (2002) examines both ideology and economy in her analysis of the welfare mother and poor working women and argues "systems of power produce and patrol poverty through the reproduction of both social and bodily markers" (p. 452). She goes on to say "In addition to coming into being as disciplined and docile bodies, poor single welfare mothers and their children are physically inscribed, punished, and displayed as the dangerous and pathological other" (p. 452). The newspaper descriptions are consistent with Adair's analysis of poor women, warning others of prostitutes as the "dangerous and pathological other."

Details about the women's length of time in jail/prison were also included in this corpus. The men in the articles were both experiencing their first arrest for prostitution, and previous arrests or incarceration for other crimes were not mentioned. The articles offered information about the women as victims of physical or sexual abuse or assaults, whereas the men's victimization or perpetration of abuse or assaults was not mentioned. In fact, there is no overriding narrative about the men's lives related specifically to prostitution, drugs, or jail/prison.

"An Opportunity to Change" 91

Overall, there is a much greater focus on the negative aspects of the women's lives than the men's. While the women are depicted as having lives ravaged by addiction, abuse, and social ostracism, the men are depicted as lonely or unfulfilled, but essentially harmless to both themselves and their community. The women and their paths are revealed and made public, while the men remain unknown. The women are also much more in the spotlight in terms of their actions, both past and present, that led them to participate in prostitution, whereas the men's motives and history are vague. Based on the information provided, the reader is encouraged to envision the women as a "dangerous and pathological other," while the men remain undescribed and unseen.

WHO GETS TO SPEAK?

Seven of the twelve articles focus on penalties for prostitution, plans to decrease prostitution, and a planned diversion program for men and women arrested for prostitution.[5] Within the Nemez newspaper articles about penalties, plans to decrease prostitution, and diversion programs, the women's voices are not heard, nor are those of their clients.[6] Instead, the reader hears from police, attorneys, program directors, legislatures, researchers, and others who talk about street-based sex work, its penalties, and its implications on the health of the women actively involved in the trade, their clients, and the neighborhoods in which street-based sex work is transacted. These articles included an editorial about increased penalties for prostitution, two letters to the editor responding to proposed and actual changes to the law, and four articles that focus on city and neighborhood association plans to decrease prostitution in specific areas, state-wide changes in prostitution policy that resulted in increased penalties, and diversion programs for people who are arrested for prostitution and want an alternative to spending time in jail and are therefore offered counseling. They include the voices of city councilmen and women, police officers, attorneys, residents, neighborhood association leaders, business owners, activists in the sex-worker movement, senators involved in the proposed and contested bills regarding penalties for prostitution, the governor, program directors (of programs designed to help women in street economies and provide diversion services), statistics regarding the number of women in street-based sex work and arrests both locally and in other areas, proposed laws, and research from nationally known researchers involving street prostitution. They do not include the voices of women who exchange sex for money or drugs.

Therefore, when the public hears the voices of these women, it is only in response to in-depth articles about prostitution rather than about neighborhood plans to rid the area of prostitution or the penalties for prostitution. When the articles focus on policy and programs for women involved in prostitution, the women are silent, as are their clients. They aren't interviewed, aren't asked what they think of the programs and penalties, and aren't asked how this might affect their lives. Readers do hear from those working to implement the programs and policies, such as city council leaders, police officers, attorneys, and neighborhood association leaders. The readers hear from researchers about the problems associated with prostitution, residents and workers who live and work in the areas where prostitution is more visible, and local business owners and neighborhood association leaders who believe prostitution is decreasing the value of their properties and businesses. In two articles, sex worker activists and sex worker activist organizations are also mentioned—in one article briefly as an aside, and in another a more in-depth description of the organization and the issues surrounding sex work activism.

Based on these articles, when prostitution is examined, street-based sex work is the primary focus. And when an in-depth look at prostitution is offered, the participants exchanging sex are included, but when penalties, laws, and plans to decrease prostitution are discussed, neither the prostitutes' nor the johns' perspectives are included; instead, the reader hears from police, social service agency leaders, lawyers, and legislators. Therefore, when the public does hear from these women, it is only in response to in-depth articles about prostitution rather than about neighborhood plans to rid the area of or penalties for prostitution. When the articles focus on policy and programs for women involved in prostitution, the women are silent, as are their clients. They aren't interviewed or asked what they think of the programs and penalties and how these programs or penalties might affect their lives. Those working to implement the programs and policies, such as city council leaders, police officers, attorneys, and neighborhood association leaders have a voice.

Readers also hear from researchers about the problems associated with prostitution, residents and workers who live and work in the areas where prostitution is more visible, and local business owners and neighborhood association leaders. The voices of the men and women engaged in these acts are silenced further still when concerned citizens who are marginally involved in sex-work issues are nonetheless asked to offer their opinions for print. This trend is also consistent within the hundreds of articles contained in the larger corpus of articles. In very few cases were the women and men who were directly involved in exchanging sex asked to express their opinions about the laws and penalties surrounding street prostitution. In two articles, sex-worker activists and sex-worker activist organizations are also mentioned—in one article briefly as an aside, and in another a more in-depth description of the organization and the issues surrounding sex-work activism is given.[7] As a whole, the johns receive the least amount of attention in terms of biographical detail and the reasons for their participation in prostitution, while the prostitutes receive the greatest amount of exposure, especially about their drug use, criminal pasts, jail time, and statuses as victims of violence.

From this perspective, a reader might conclude it is only necessary to hear from those on the law-making and enforcement side of the policy—in terms of how it will affect a neighborhood and its residents, and in some cases the business owners—because these are the only people who are given a voice in terms of proposed plans and solutions. The men and women who participate in exchanges of sex for money are directly or indirectly silenced when matters of policy are discussed and are only given a voice when the subject matter of the article is an in-depth look at prostitution and the programs created to "help" prostitutes.

This presence, and lack thereof, further marginalizes these women and their clients while also depriving the public of their expertise and insights that could potentially address many of the concerns raised. Removing the reader from the lived experiences of those participating in these activities when their political, legislative, and criminal attributes are discussed, while simultaneously providing an up-close and personal understanding of the individuals' lived experiences when the issues of personal choice and experience are explored serves to place the responsibility in the hands of the individual making these choices, rather than in the community responding to these issues systemically and legislatively. Their invisibility, especially in discussions of policy, penalties, and solutions to prostitution further invalidates them and indirectly locates them as "the problem" because they are not part of finding and creating solutions. The "problem" of prostitution, therefore, becomes one of personal responsibility for "change."

Several of the women who participated in my study were no longer using drugs on a regular basis and had not used them regularly for years. My participants' "success" stories in many ways mimic the women who are portrayed as breaking the cycle and becoming role models for others in the newspaper articles.

Figure 4.1 offers a visual representation of the trajectory from victim status to taking responsibility and changing one's life. The personal choice and responsibility framework encourages the public to focus on the individual as the solution to the "problem." The expectation of change is aligned with the viewer's focus, and larger systems of poverty, abuse, and violence are not considered.

Ironically, the story is one of "escape" that hinges on personal choice. The term *escape* positions the women as prisoners or captives of the drug and prostitution lifestyle. The women become involved in prostitution because they are desperate—desperate to escape from an abusive home life, to support a drug habit, or to support themselves in general. And yet once involved in prostitution, it is up to the individual woman to *choose* to remove herself from this "lifestyle." As stated in the articles: it is up to them to "choose drugs on the street over a new lifestyle"; there are "options that exist to help prostitutes break their cycle of danger and despair, but the choice is up to them whether they will change their lifestyle"; and "it is up to them if they want to change their lifestyle." Within these statements

94 *Street Sex Workers' Discourse*

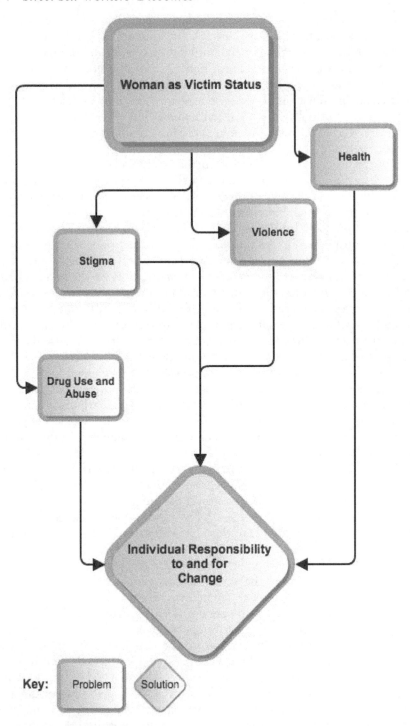

Figure 4.1 Trajectory from victim status to taking responsibility.

lie the assumptions these women *should choose* to change their lifestyle, programs exist to help them change their lifestyle, and ultimately it is their *personal* choice to change or not. The women who advocated for change expressed these same sentiments, accepting personal responsibility for their choices. They stated they made the change for themselves, not due to fear of jail or pressure from others, but because they wanted a different and better life. As Julie, a white, 42-year-old heterosexual woman expressed, a person has to have determination to stop using drugs and change one's lifestyle. Although social service agencies and family can offer support, ultimately the decision is up to the individual.

This construction simultaneously positions the women as prisoners or captives of the drug and prostitution lifestyle while also agents of their own change. The focus is on the individual—individuals make choices, they escape prostitution and drugs, and they become role models and provide hope, both for those who are still in prostitution and want to find their way out and for the general community who wants to find solutions to prostitution. These beliefs defer the responsibility from the public to the individual—which is akin to blaming the victim.

This framework makes sense in the United States where individualism, self-reliance, and the ideology of "pulling oneself up by one's bootstraps" pervade mass culture. And yet this focus becomes ironic and contradictory in an analysis of the newspaper rhetoric concerning street-based sex work: prostitutes shoulder the harshest blame for the evils of sex work, while johns are allowed to shirk their collusion in the same transactions; prostitutes are celebrated for their eventual choice to leave prostitution, but no celebratory voice is ever given to their initial (and in many cases, life-saving) choice to enter into prostitution; and prostitutes are commended for their strong will in leaving the sex trade while virtually ignoring the deep and damaging socio-economic roots that make prostitution a viable option for desperate people in the first place.

The problem is one that primarily involves drug use and focuses on the women who choose to participate in these activities. The reader's attention is not brought to focus on the cycle of abuse, both as children and as women, in which many of them have been subjected, their perceived need for drugs, nor the issues of poverty and difficulty supporting oneself and perhaps one's children. The newspaper articles focus little attention on the men who have chosen to purchase sex—they are assumed to be nowhere near as desperate as the women, perhaps because they are paying for rather than receiving money for sex. But readers never learn their histories as intimately as they do the women's, nor are they considered the primary problem. These relationships between the men and women, the selling of sex, its status as illegal, and the advantages of selling sex over other choices—none of these issues are questioned, critiqued, or even acknowledged.

A number of messages about street prostitution become clear. The construction of the woman and her role in the "problem" of prostitution maintains the system in which prostitution exists—or even thrives—by placing the public's attention on the individual and the choices it expects her to make. This framing of the intimate details of these women's lives accompanied by the message of personal choice and responsibility then encourages the public to view the prostitution "problem" as one that can be solved by the individual, and, more specifically, by the individual prostitute. This focus on the individual both diverts attention from and maintains mainstream systems of hierarchy and power. When the individual woman is presented in the spotlight, her role is to show how other individuals can take responsibility for themselves and change—on an individual basis. Not only applicable to women who exchange sex for money or drugs, this construction of the individual nature of street prostitution contributes to the public's understanding of other marginalized groups.

Likewise, the women do not look at larger institutions of equality, poverty, abuse, and so on, in considering where the change should occur. For example, the women I interviewed did not argue they should have been better provided and cared for as children and therefore not subjected to physical and sexual abuse. They did not argue there should be additional ways to support oneself other than exchanging sex. They most often viewed the problem as personal, rather than systemic, and fully accepted the responsibility placed on them to change and create a better life.

This narrative of one who can change, achieve success, become a role model, and help others is also prominent in the social service agents' language and definition of success. If a person believes in this narrative, then she is likely to place herself in it and define herself according to it—which necessarily follows women who exchange sex need to change, and if one does change, is a role model for others. If one does not define exchanging sex in this way, then she has less of a need to fit herself into this version of "success." Do the women embody this narrative because it is what they are taught through social service agencies and in the general media, as is apparent in the newspaper articles? This story is told again and again, and therefore it makes sense the women would also define themselves in this way.

An underlying narrative of the "reformed" or "recovered prostitute" is maintained throughout these interviews and in the newspaper articles. Why is this story so prevalent? Lily, a white lesbian woman in her mid 40s and an activist and former HIV outreach worker, discusses claiming this unrepentant "whore" identity:

> I think that the other thing that I can do is to say that, yes, women do get raped, and women do get abused, and it happens most often in their homes, and a lot of women who are doing sex work don't get raped and don't get abused and they are doing what they do and they deserve respect for the work that they do. Because I think its really hard for sex workers to come out. "You know what? I'm a whore and I'm fine with that." Because if you're a whore you're supposed to feel guilty about it,

and if you don't, then you're a really nasty whore, because you're not feeling guilty about it.

Sociologist Gail Pheterson (1989) echoes this idea while arguing for the legitimacy and agency of prostitutes in her introduction to *A Vindication of the Rights of Whores*: "Never have prostitutes been legitimized as spokespersons or self-determining agents, both by those who defend them against male abuse and not by those who depend upon them for sexual service. It is a radical political stance to assume prostitute legitimacy" (pp. 3–4). As English and Gender Studies Professor Anne McClintock argues, "Empowering sex workers empowers all women, for the whore stigma is used to discipline women in general; and encouraging society to respect sex workers encourages society to respect all women" (p. 3). I would revise this sentence to state empowering sex workers empowers all people, because the whore stigma can be used to discipline anyone; and encouraging society to respect sex workers encourages society to respect all marginalized identities and individuals who are choosing to participate in the commercial sex industry. Kaleidoscopically, when the viewer changes what is viewed, new possibilities and material realities can emerge. When we reframe the problem, we see different solutions.

5 Systemic Violence Perpetuates Victim Status

When somebody else calls me a 'ho,' I don't like it. I don't like it at all. You haven't walked in my shoes; don't condemn me. You know what I mean? I don't like when a man pulls up to me and says "Hey, ho, come here." No. Don't do that shit because I will go off, you know? Now I could say, "Well, I'm a ho." I could say it. But I know who I am. But when other people try to do that, I don't like it.
—Donna

But if we're really working with the women, we try to not use that [prostitute] as an identity, because we think the identity of the woman is so much above and more complex than what she does for a living or what she does on the side of her living. Like I'd hate for somebody to come and identify me as only "Oh, she's one of those researchers." I mean I would hope that they would identify me as more than the sum of one particular part of my being. So we really try to stay away from that, and in some of our trainings, we've really emphasized that. For instance, we were doing a group at the jail, and we asked everybody to identify themselves. Most people said, "I am Joe Schmoe" or whoever, "I am Sally Sue" or, you know, whatever their name was, or "Here's a little bit about me." When we got to one woman, she said, "Well, I'm a Homeless Woman," no name, no nothing. And you really try . . . you know, stories where people really connect their entire identity to a particular behavior, to me, is . . . I guess it could be good if it's a great behavior. But for me, most of the time, it's limiting.
—Dr. Annie Shepherd, a 51-year-old white heterosexual woman and a psychology professor who had directed several research projects with substance users and women who trade sex for money or drugs

Jill: What do you call it when women [exchange sex for money]?
Olivia: I call it . . . Let me think. I call it "surviving," "survival."
—Olivia

This analysis is grounded in the constructed nature of terminology as well as material reality—case and point, the language surrounding sex as a commodity. The terms *prostitute* and *sex worker* are constructions that serve particular interests.[1] Examining the "prostitute" and "sex worker" constructs reveals the ideological perspectives about the right one has to sell sex versus the exploitation one experiences in a patriarchal system where women's bodies are objectified, brutalized, and largely valued as "less than" men's bodies.

A VICTIM

According to *The New Oxford American Dictionary* (2001), the word *prostitute* came from the Latin word *prostituere* meaning "exposed publicly, offered for sale," from "*pro-* 'before' + *statuere* 'set up, place'" (Jewell and Abate, "Prostitute," p. 1369). The *Online Etymology Dictionary* dates the word *prostitute* as first recorded in written form in approximately 1530 and was used as a verb to mean "to offer [an individual] to indiscriminate sexual intercourse (usually in exchange for money)" (Harper, "Prostitute"). In 1613 this word was used as a noun based on the Latin word *prostituta* or prostitute, the feminine version of *prostitutes*. According to this dictionary, the concept of "sex for hire" was not "inherent in the etymology, which rather suggests one 'exposed to lust' or sex 'indiscriminately offered'" (*ibid.*). This same definition is the first one listed in *The Oxford Dictionary of English Etymology* (1967) without the same level of detail, simply stating, "offered or exposed to lust"; "woman given over to indiscriminate sexual intercourse for hire" (Onions, "Prostitute," p. 717). Within *The Perseus Digital Library*, the first definition for the term *prostituo* is "to place before or in front" and secondly "to expose publicly to prostitution, to prostitute" (Crane, "*Prostituo*"). Its root word is *statuo* which means "to cause to stand" or corporally, "To cause to stand, set up, set, station, fix in an upright position" ("*Statuo*"). The root definitions of "plac[ing] before or in front" and "to cause to stand" are foundations of the word *prostitution* today as used in the English language. These traditional definitions imply the prostitute does not have agency in making this choice, but is "exposed," "placed," and "caused to stand" by someone else. The person is thereby not making his or her own decisions. Likewise, *The New Shorter Oxford English Dictionary on Historical Principles* defines prostitute as "Exposed or subject to a destructive agency" or "Exhibit shamefully or degradingly to public view" (Brown, "Prostitute," p. 2386). The passive voice results in the construction of a prostitute as weak and helpless, and this powerless position is equated with dehumanization because the individual is not viewed as a person who is capable of making his or her own choices, but is instead controlled by other forces.

Today, the most common understanding of the word *prostitute* is used as both a noun and a verb: the noun indicating an identity (the "prostitute"), and the verb ("prostituting") as participation in the activity of "sex for hire." Although often considered the world's oldest profession, some scholars argue the concept of prostitution as a social construction is relatively modern, created as an identifiable concept within the last 200 years (Karras 1996; Lerner 1986; Otis 1985). Anthropologist Laura Agustín (2005c) argues the term and identification of the prostitute was invented to create a pathetic victim who required "saving." Prior to the late eighteenth and early nineteenth century, Agustín argues, "the buying and selling of sex was treated as one of an array of social offences" and there "was no word or concept which signified exclusively the sale of sexual services" (pp. 9–10). She argues middle-class women created the classifications of prostitution and prostitute in order to have someone to "help," providing not only employment for these rescuers but also an activity that helped them feel good about themselves. This construction also created a formalized avenue through which these women were able to pass "down" their own "middle-class" values of the family to those whom they identified as prostitutes.

Debates surrounding the word choice of *prostitute*, *sex worker*, or v*ictim of sexual exploitation* reflects the speaker's moral and political standpoint regarding the subject's agency and position in society. For example, people who are in favor of the abolition or prohibition of sex work often use the words *prostitutes*, *prostituted women*, and *victims of sexual exploitation* to refer to people who exchange sex for money or drugs.[2] Prohibition, related to the criminalization of sex work, "is the system in which prostitution and all activities that surround it are criminalized and prohibited by law" (Thukral 2006). The language choice often underscores one's belief and argument that these women are victims rather than agents making an occupational choice. Research Coordinator at Framework Housing Association, Rachel Harding and Criminologist Paul Hamilton pay particular attention to the language used in their study and explain their reasons for using the term *working girl(s)*: "Throughout the research process, women typically referred to themselves as 'working girl(s)', occasionally 'sex workers', but never 'prostitutes' and it seems appropriate to adopt the linguistic construction that respondents felt to be the least value-laden and stigmatized" (Harding and Hamilton 2009). The term, *prostitute*, narrowly identifies an individual based on one activity and reproduces the stigma associated with it.

AN AGENT

In order to challenge the derogatory representations of prostitution, activist and spokesperson for COYOTE Carol Leigh invented the term *sex worker* to "create an atmosphere of tolerance within and outside the women's movement for women working in the sex industry" (1997, p. 225). As Sociologist Kamala Kempadoo explains in her introduction to *Global Sex Workers*, the term *sex worker* "suggests we view prostitution not as an identity—a social or a psychological characteristic of women, often indicated by 'whore'— but as an income-generating activity or form of labor for women and men.

The definition stresses the social location of those engaged in sex industries as working people" (Kempadoo and Doezema 1998, p. 3). In addition to the emphasis on choice, this explanation shifts the focus to labor rather than identity alone. The term *sex worker* is intended to be more neutral in describing a type of work, similar to holding a position in other fields that contain both positive and negative aspects. Leigh states this construction was an explicit appeal to change people's perceptions of the work—both those inside and outside the feminist movement.

Sex worker rights advocates argue those who choose not to use this term are making a concerted effort to silence sex worker voices because of the agency implied in its use that an individual can *choose* to participate in these activities as a way to make a living.[3] Those who ideologically oppose exchanging sex for money, in choosing *not* to use the term *sex worker*, discursively render sex workers invisible, another type of violence that mutually reinforces oppressive systems. And yet, Secretary of State Hilary Clinton's statement that meeting with "'sex workers' in the cause of protecting LGBT [lesbian, gay, bisexual, transgendered] rights is an example of 'people to people diplomacy at its best'" signals its use may be becoming more commonplace (Starr 2011).

The term *sex worker* is also fraught with underlying assumptions implying equality and choice. Many who identify as sex workers do not exchange sex on or near the street, but rather enjoy the privilege of consistent housing as well as Internet and telephone interactions with clients. Although the term *sex worker* is well known in academic and activist communities, many who are identified as sex workers do not identify as such. As Lerum et al. (2012) site in their analysis of the sex worker rights movement:

> Another strand of organising against repression wrought by anti-trafficking approaches and heightened policing emerged from harm reduction organisations, local service providers and communities of colour. Many coming from these sectors did (and do) not embrace the term 'sex work' as a way of describing their engagement in sexual commerce. (p. 93)

This non-identification is particularly applicable to my research population, who did not identify as sex workers, and often did not identify as prostitutes either. The phrase *women who exchange sex for money or drugs* places the women, rather than the acts in which they participate, at the center of the discussion. They are women who participate in lots of activities, including exchanging sex for money or drugs. Although still defined in many ways by their behavior, the intent is not to define them *solely* by this behavior or action.

Sociologist Gail Pheterson (1990) questions the category "prostitute" and argues the deconstruction of this category "is necessary to counter prejudice and to conduct scientifically valid inquiry" (p. 397). She suggests that even "the category 'prostitute' is based more upon symbolic and legal representations of the bad woman or whore than upon a set of characteristics within a population of persons" (p. 398) and she argues it is "the basic paradigm of a prostitute profile that is faulty, either in its reinforcement of classical stereotypes or in its reversal of those stereotypes" (p. 403). Sociologist Wendy Chapkis (1997) dismantles the prostitute concept as well as the black and white categories often attributed to it:

> There is no such thing as The Prostitute; there are only competing versions of prostitution. The Prostitute is an invention of policy makers, researchers, moral crusaders, and political activists. Even sex workers themselves contribute to the creation of a normative prostitute by excluding those from their ranks who are not "real" enough or "good" enough. [. . .] [T]here is no one overriding narrative spoken by prostitutes on prostitution. There are instead competing and sometimes conflicting stories, each with its own integrity. Accounts of sex work presented in these pages, as elsewhere, are often contradictory, without one being "true" and the other "false." Discussions of sex—commercial and otherwise—necessarily reveal both victimization and agency, exploitation and engaged complicity; in short, both the violence and wild defiance of sex. (pp. 211–12)

STREET-BASED SEX WORK

The "victim" status is central not only to the debates surrounding prostitution, but in particular to the discourse about people involved in street economies. Sylvia, an Hispanic lesbian woman in her late 30s and a director at a mental health organization, explains this victim status:

> I think that the fact that the police are starting to say "We have a john problem" and progressively creating programming to enforce the anti-john environment has changed the public's perception of the women. They are able to see more [of them] as victims, which, quite frankly, I would never say seeing someone as a victim is a good thing except in this case. It's a great thing because it moves the process forward in a better way. If they're able to see [them] as victims, then they're able to see them potentially as survivors and that's what I mean by that. So I'd rather they see them that way, and then I can assist them, as can the staff or other community members, and the women themselves in saying "I was a victim of poverty and neglect and child abuse" and I mean almost every woman that we work with has been molested or raped and has a history of child abuse or neglect. And now I'm a survivor and tomorrow I will be empowered to help others, to thrive. So I'm hoping they will go from both, in the consciousness of the public as

well as within their own consciousness, from a victim to a survivor to someone who thrives.

Sylvia argues focusing on the "john" is beneficial because the public then views the women as victims. The forces victimizing the women are "poverty and neglect and child abuse." Therefore, if the public and the women define themselves as victims, they can then work toward becoming "survivors." Sociologist Stéphanie Wahab's (2006) evaluation of a prostitution diversion project emphasizes this victim status as a vehicle for obtaining services: "Those perceived as 'real' victims were given opportunities to enter into the diversion program (i.e., avoid jail time) that were not granted to those perceived as more empowered. Furthermore, service provider stakeholders reported exercising more compassion and empathy towards women who were perceived as victims" (p. 86).

Not all of the public figures I interviewed relied on the victim status to describe women who exchange sex. Lily, a white lesbian woman in her mid 40s and an activist and former HIV outreach worker, stated:

> I see them as women who are doing the best they can with what they've got, which I think is pretty much how I see everybody. I see them as women who are having to live really often dangerous lives where they're trying to find as much value as they can within the limits that they've got and that they're incredibly limited. But I see them also as women who despite everything else have found terrific ways to survive and even flourish. [. . .] I think they wanted to see themselves as a lot more mainstream than most people thought of them as. Do you know what I mean? What they do was completely normalized for them, it wasn't a big deal. I think that they saw themselves as resourceful because they had figured out ways to survive under conditions that you and I probably wouldn't, I mean, it would be really difficult, we'd figure it out but it takes, you know, they have a lot of special knowledge that isn't shared.

Here their victim status is not central, as they are already survivors, without the help of social service agencies or a required exit from street-based sex work.

Social service agencies are central, perhaps even required, for a victim to transform into a survivor. *And yet this relationship locates both the victim status, as well as the help she can receive, outside of the woman.* In other words, she is named a victim by others and then offered services in order to achieve survivor status. In "helping" these women, the social service agency, in part, becomes the savior. Although many women do want the services these agencies provide, constructing the women as victims echoes Agustín's (2005c) discussion of benevolent identities. These identifiers often perpetuate the power relations embodied in the terms. When the prostitute is always considered a victim and the john and/or pimp is always considered the exploiter, then the speaker ideologically removes power from the prostitute and condenses the exchange into narrow possibilities that may not reflect the reality of those persons participating in these exchanges.

In my research, there is a connection between the language the public figures use to discuss street-based sex work and its related problems, which potentially directs how the solutions are envisioned and implemented. Those public figures who use the word *prostitute* tend to focus on the neighborhood as the victim and look for solutions that will rid the neighborhood of these problems. These solutions include resident awareness and activity, law enforcement, and arrests, which then create access to social service agencies and substance abuse treatment programs for the women who are arrested. Those public figures who use the terms *women who exchange sex for money or drugs, women,* or *sex worker* tend to focus on the woman as the victim and look for solutions that address the woman's needs. These needs include not only access to social service agencies and substance abuse treatment programs, but also the systemic frameworks of poverty, abuse, and violence. These public figures tend to view the women as victims of poverty, abuse, substance abuse, and also neighborhood, city, and state politics. Because causes of poverty and violence are ephemeral, the solutions are not clearly delineated.

The language used reveals the ideology of the speaker as residing on one side or the other of this debate, while also positioning the object of the discourse as one who is acting or being acted upon. But each "choice," as Agustín (2005c) underscores, "essentially asks whether a woman who sells sex must by definition be considered a victim of others' actions or whether she can enjoy a degree of agency herself in her commercial practice" (p. 1). These concepts are inadequate and the dichotomy far too simplistic to define any one individual or group of people in general, especially when it comes to people who are working in an area so fraught with the moral and political ideologies surrounding sexuality, gender roles, commerce, and social/sexual relationships. Sociologist Ronald Weitzer's (2012) "polymorphous paradigm" is "sensitive to complexities and to the structural conditions shaping sex work along a continuum of agency and subordination" (p. 16). By taking the many varieties present in sex work, he creates a framework that moves beyond sex work as simply either "oppressive" or "empowering." Weitzer's polymorphous paradigm most accurately depicts the varied nature of selling sex as a commodity, although his overview of street-based sex work represents these workers in ways that reinscribe powerless and uneducated positions that lie within the oppression-based context (p. 19). Examining these ideologies, as well as the policies that govern its many facets, reveal how the identities surrounding street-based sex work as well as the related material conditions are mutually reinforced.

My findings reveal the women do not occupy a "victim" or "agent" status because choice, responsibility, and personal and systemic circumstances

Systemic Violence Perpetuates Victim Status 105

combined create material conditions in which individuals are continually co-creating themselves based on their existing circumstances and opportunities. Notably, many of the women who exchange sex also expressed this belief that women who exchange sex need "help," and not one of them used the word *victim* to describe themselves or others.[4]

Sarah, a white, bisexual, 25-year-old woman who works with non-profit groups that provide services to sex workers, explains how her feminist values inform her perspective on viewing sex workers as more than either victims or empowered individuals:

> I'm a very committed feminist and very committed to taking action on things, and I feel like the prohibition of prostitution is very deeply connected to the repression of women, and using sexuality to discriminate against women specifically. [. . .] I think that feminism, at its core, is about recognizing equality among the genders and not equality of privilege, but equality of responsibility. And I think that I take the responsibility of being a human woman very seriously, like I think that . . . To really say that you're a feminist means that you're going to work toward that equality, and so I think that every day I'm working toward that equality and being very mindful of the power differences and things like that. So I think, at its core, feminism is about recognizing equality of rights and responsibilities and making that about everybody, and not allowing gender and sex to define what choices people have. And so in terms of advocating for sex workers, I think the truest feminist value is to say, "We want you to be able to choose the conditions in which you engage in sex." And . . . the other really sincere sense of justice that if somebody is forced into a sexual situation that they don't want, regardless of gender, that is, you know, it's a sexist act and it has to be addressed by the community. And so I think that message is so often missed when I think about sex workers. It's like, well, feminists say you can never do it, and sex workers say you can do it anytime; and I think, you know, real feminism is in the middle somewhere, where, you know, we're saying, "No, we all get to choose and establish that." And laws that criminalize our ability to negotiate are not feminist values. I mean, we have to—if we say we're feminists—we have to step up and address that.

Using language that creates space for choice honors the individual agency of those who participate in these activities, which simultaneously honors their agency to make many choices in life.

None of the terms are clear or uncontested, but trying to inhabit my participants' perspectives allowed me to understand how language and perceptions can change based on one's stance. Using terms such as *sex worker* and *client* opens up the discussion to one of professional terminology, and although not clearly representing all situations where sex is exchanged for money, it allows for more agency of both the person exchanging sex and the client.

A cautionary note: I do not mean to imply there is a simple cause and effect relationship between language and the material conditions of street-based sex work or any constructed entity for that matter. I am not arguing if people change their language practices, then material conditions will necessarily change as well because the material conditions are layers upon layers of belief systems, language choices, and fixed and influential material difficult to unravel and break apart. Discourse is a departure point. This examination and disentangling uncovers information that can then impact the material conditions surrounding street-based sex work.

I strive to give the voices of my participants room to speak, argue, and ultimately create varied understandings about the representations of street-based sex work without trying to recreate a "truth" about the words *prostitute* or *sex worker*. This analysis can then inform policies, resources, and even one's own speech and thoughts about people who exchange sex for monetary gain, as well as the power words have to define and reproduce these thoroughly contested concepts.

"LIVING ON THE EDGE": VIOLENCE, SAFETY, AND HEALTH

In addition to the past trauma, abuses, and poverty the women experienced, their exposure to violence and other physical health issues were a primary concern. These areas included the control and protection they had over their bodies during an exchange and how this control or lack thereof impacted their safety as a whole, their vulnerability to violence in general, their ability to prosecute crimes if committed against them, and the impact criminalization of sex work had on their safety.

Sylvia, an Hispanic lesbian woman in her late 30s and a director at a mental health organization, offered a poignant example of sleep as a privilege:

> People go to see the program and you know a lot of times as you know, the ladies [clients at the drop-in center] will be sleeping on the couch. So I've had like two different people say "My god, you let them sleep here?" [laughs] This is the safest sleep they've ever had, in years, so sure, and possibly their whole life. You know, they don't have to worry about getting raped, they don't have to worry about getting their crap ripped off. You know what I mean? So its so interesting to me because people just interpret that, you know, it's the smallest thing. I mean people have no idea what a blessing you know, or a special moment, or something to celebrate, is just being able to fucking sleep. Without worrying. And some sense of safety. Some of them are exhausted probably,

I'm assuming emotionally because they're constantly vigilant. They're gonna get arrested, or they're gonna get beat up or somebody's old man is gonna find them and be mad at them because they looked at him the wrong way or there's all kinds of drama, you know, and very genuine circumstances that are negative. But, I do want to highlight the fact that people really amaze me in their interpretation of the most simple acts. You let these women sleep here? Hell, yeah. Hell, yeah. And it doesn't cost a damn penny. And its not a problem. And its not like they're going to sleep the rest of their life away and not become productive citizens, because that's really the question. That's the question, you know, the question isn't do I let them sleep? The question is, are you gonna have them get off their ass and become a productive citizen? [. . .] I think that's very interesting language. That's the language of euphemism. "You're letting them sleep" really means "Are they going to become productive citizens?"

Not only does Sylvia emphasize the need to sleep safely, but she reveals the constant vigilance against violence, arrest, theft, and other factors those living on the street and without houses continually face. Lily, a white lesbian woman in her mid 40s and an activist and former HIV outreach worker referred to it as "living on the edge":

Yeah, I'm thinking about street workers and off-street workers. I think everything is magnified with street workers because they're living on the edge in a lot of ways. They don't have any money. Women who work off street can afford to take a three-day vacation and go away for awhile. Women who are working the street don't really have that luxury. Women who are working the street also are often in unstable working, uh living situations, so they're living with abusive partners or they're living in an abusive family, dysfunctional families, so there are no calm, safe places in their lives for them to go to.

Working on the street exposes women who exchange sex to violence, and because street-based sex work is illegal, there are added aspects of secrecy and risk. The existence, threat, and experience of violence impact an individual's physical, emotional, and psychological health. Women who exchange sex for money or drugs often struggle with psychological problems because of their violent experiences on the street, in relationships, and from clients. My participants discussed the violence they had experienced as a result of exchanging sex for money or drugs. Most mentioned they had several experiences with violent men, and one refused to talk about those experiences. The social service agents and the activists focused primarily on the women's safety as a central need. For example, as Joan, a white, 43-year-old, bisexual woman and an activist with a sex worker rights organization, stated:

I think it's dangerous. I think it's very dangerous because no one might see them get into a car and so this guy has, and we know unfortunately from history that men and women in private, men get wild. Every six seconds a woman's abused by her spouse in this country. We're putting women in an isolated setting with a guy she doesn't know. I think it's very dangerous. Very dangerous for her. That's the biggest problem I see. And I think psychologically to be in that kind of a survival mentality that you have that kind of anxiety and you know you could be killed or beat up continually every time you get in a car. These women are going to have, its like going to war. They're going to be emotionally, psychologically, just ravaged. So its rough, I think it's very dangerous.

The woman's safety and exposure to danger is the primary concern, along with the secondary affects of remaining vigilant in order to protect oneself from possible assaults. Isolation can create conditions that allow for the violence to occur. Joan's metaphor of "going to war" and "survival mentality" speaks to the psychosocial impact this isolation breeds. Sandy, a 46-year-old, white heterosexual woman, described what affected her level of control over exchanging sex:

Sandy: If I had the money in my hand already, if I had all the money in my hand, if I was in an area where I could, uh, know that I could get out at any time, I'd be a little bit more in control because I knew I would be safer in those areas and I'd have a place to run to. If I was in the places that normally I wanted to go to. Because once I got out of the car . . . You know what I mean? That was the way I knew that I could have more control over being in a safe area or safe places. Because I knew that if I could control the situation, and I knew there was more money to come, I'd be more controlling because I knew I could control the money flow, I could get more money.
Jill: What about your use of drugs? Did that ever affect your level of control?
Sandy: Oh yes.
Jill: How?
Sandy: Like I said, money. Number one, if I was really high, I would lose a level of control because I just . . . Whatever you want, just do it, let's get out of it, you know. Even though it wasn't a safe area but he wanted to park there, I would allow it because I would be real nervous, but I just wanted to get it out and get done. So my drug use has had . . . yes.

Rosalie, an Hispanic, 43-year-old heterosexual case manager at a women's facility, emphasized this relationship between drug use and control:

Oh yeah, there's a fair number. And I hear some of the women who don't do it, who don't use drugs, that say that she doesn't do the drugs because she likes to be able to know what's going on. She wants to be able to control everything, and know that if something's wrong that she's gonna know that something's wrong and she can get out of the situation. You know, if she's high, she can't do that.

Donna, a 47-year-old, white, heterosexual woman, discussed this relationship explicitly:

Donna: I'm doing better now because—and I don't get high before I go to work . . . anymore.
Jill: Oh, you don't?
Donna: No, no. Um, I never liked getting high with tricks. I don't like being not in complete control, you know? And tricks have always told me I'm mean [laughs]. Because, to me . . . I hop in, I hop out. I'm not trying to be your girlfriend, we're not going sightseeing, this ain't a layaway plan, come on, da da da da [laughs]. Come on, let's do this, let's go.

Several women cited the fear of violence as the reason they no longer exchanged sex for money or drugs. When I asked Tiffany, a white, 33-year-old heterosexual woman, what she thought about women who exchange sex for money or drugs, she said:

Tiffany: I used to do it.
Jill: Yeah, what do you think of women who do it?
Tiffany: That they need to stop. Before they end up dead. Like I did a couple of times, but I took the knife on them instead.

Brenda, a white, 48-year-old lesbian woman said:

I had to jump out of a car one time. This is when I totally quit doing prostitution. I jumped out of the car, and this pimp wanted me, and I wouldn't let him get me, so I got in the car with these two guys, and they wouldn't let me out. Well, I reached through the bucket seat and went out of the car backwards, and this leg got all twisted, my head was out like this [gestures toward head].

Laura, a 36-year-old, white, heterosexual woman, talks about her experience with violence, as well as why she did not report it to authorities:

Jill: Have you been in violent situations?
Laura: Yes.

Jill: Can you tell me about that?
Laura: There was one about a year ago, right here in Nemez, right in front of the Nemez Inn.
Jill: Mmm hmm.
Laura: Right out there at the bus stop I got my ass beat, two big 'ol black eyes, and I basically got raped. That's why I wanna quit, before I end up dead.
[. . .]
Jill: Did you call the police when they did that?
Laura: No, no. I would have went to jail for prostitution.

In addition to the violence these women are subjected to, the women's health was also a primary concern of the public figures I interviewed. As Chelley, an Hispanic heterosexual female in her late 40s who worked in community outreach for a mental health organization, said:

> Their health is one of them. Because of the substance they use and because of the trade, of catching something [. . .] Not being able to take care of themselves when they're down. [. . .] Because maybe they're using substance [and] it doesn't help them to keep up, to do what they need to do. So it brings them down when they're in a spot where they can't help themselves at the moment.

Chelley emphasizes the women's health and its impact on substance use and the diseases that might be passed from person to person through sexual contact. The substance use can also prevent the women from taking care of themselves and "do what they need to do," which then puts them in a place where they cannot "help themselves".

Sandy explicitly outlined the relationship between using drugs and taking care of one's health in relationship to wearing condoms and protecting oneself from sexually transmitted infections:

Jill: And did [using drugs] affect whether you wore condoms or not?
Sandy: Yes. Oh, most definitely.
Jill: How?
Sandy: Because I wanted to get back to the dope house. I wanted to get back to the dope faster. I wanted to get the money faster. I didn't care. Let's do it. If they didn't have a condom, they weren't [going to] give me the money. I had to have the $20, I was going to have to buy the condoms or I was gonna . . . No. Let's just do it.

Officer Eugene Matthews confirmed these sentiments:

Officer Eugene Matthews: I mean, health issues have always kinda bugged me because, I mean, it's such a time bomb out there, you know? It

Systemic Violence Perpetuates Victim Status 111

would be worth—I mean, I would like to interview some of these girls and say, "Look, you know, you're carrying this around, you know." But they don't—I mean, they don't care. I mean, I have talked with them in my cases, but I mean, it would be really interesting to do a study, you know, to find out . . . because there are so many of them that are carrying this crap around and they're just infecting everybody, and the guys are infecting them with this stuff, and it's just like . . . It's almost like Russian roulette of disease. [. . .] I think they walk around and many of them don't even know they have it. *Casa Segura* is doing some work in that area and had some statistics which are confidential because obviously the girls, you know . . . But, you know, *Casa Segura* has given us some indication that, you know, I think, when it comes down to it, like 60% of the girls are carriers. A through Z. You know, you name one or the other. AIDS. They've got. . . . You know, a lot of them with substance-abuse problems have things like hepatitis and other diseases. And you know, they're not probably careful or . . .

Jill: Do they use condoms?

Officer Eugene Matthews: Some of them actually carry condoms with them. That's one thing that some of them will say: "Well, I've got a condom." But I don't know that there's any . . . I don't know that they would even push the issue if it comes down to it. I mean, I know some of them would probably, but I don't think that there's any . . . much consideration given to that area. [. . .] I think that some of them . . . It could be collection of . . . some of them who have low intelligence don't understand the ramifications of their activity. Some of them don't care because the only thing they're looking at smoking rock. And others, they got it, they know it, they're carrying it, they don't care. So I just think there's just not a whole lot of responsibility in the whole trade.

Officer Matthews places the emphasis on the woman as a potential "carrier," making her responsible for using a condom. The woman somehow makes others unsafe, exposing them to diseases, when she is just as likely to be exposed to infections. The men purchasing sex are barely considered, when they, too, could be held responsible for using a condom, both protecting themselves and the women selling sex.

In addition to the risks the women faced when not using condoms with clients, Lily, an activist and HIV educator, discussed the difficulties women faced in using condoms with their primary partners:

> The majority of people who had sex for drugs or money used condoms at least part of the time in those relationships, in those transactions. They almost never used them with their primary partners. And I think

I have a sense that that's probably true for a lot of the sex workers that I've talked to over the years whether they were street workers or not, that there was something about, there's a line for them that's very clear. This is a person with whom I have unprotected sex because I trust them and they're an intimate relationship and they're very important in my life and then there's everybody else that I have sex with and I use protection with them.

Dr. Annie Shepherd, a 51-year-old white heterosexual woman and a psychology professor, reiterated the difficulties with using a condom based on the differences in relationships:

Jill: Do the women use condoms?
Dr. Veronica Alvarez: Not all women. We find that, through our research, condom use is always—and the literature says—condom use is always difficult to increase. But we find that . . .
Jill: Difficult to increase?
Dr. Veronica Alvarez: Yeah. Greater condom use. We do have some increases in condom use, but we also found that women tend not to use condoms with their primary partner. For a number of reasons. One is that the partner . . . If a woman would bring up the desire to use condoms, the partner would be suspicious and would accuse her of having done something. So with a primary partner, it's very difficult. And we're finding in our data that some women have 2, 3, 4 partners.
Jill: Primary partners?
Dr. Veronica Alvarez: Um, yeah. No. Two primary and 2 or 3 random partners. So they may not use with a primary. They may not also use with a secondary because the secondary is the one that provides this and this and that. But with a third and fourth, she's using condoms. So it's based on the relationship.

And yet Dr. Alvarez draws attention to the language of "empowerment" and women's responsibility to negotiate safe sex:

If I can, I even try to stay away from some of . . . language that's very acceptable, like we're trying to empower women. I mean, most people understand the word "empowerment," so I'll use that with federal officials. But to me, when we're really working with women and girls, a lot of times empowerment is really translated into an empowerment on a continuum that's developed by the males, a kind of a male way of looking at the world; it's not a very feminist approach. For instance, when we talk about trading sex for money or drugs, and we talk about in our intervention programs we need to teach women to negotiate safe sex, well, that's sort of a male concept of what women should learn to do. And while maybe we should, and if women want to learn how to negotiate safer sex, that's great and we can teach them that. But, in a way, that came from kind of a spot in history where women are always then the ones that are supposed to be the social organizers of the family and the communicators and the more verbal person and the one to orchestrate or help, and to me, that's really putting an agenda on women that may not be fair. And so empowerment in that particular sense, in that example, is really still limiting, because you're trying to empower them on a particular continuum that perhaps they did not choose and that was really placed upon them and not with them.

In making this statement, Dr. Shepherd draws attention to the gendered system that largely holds women responsible for condom use. This responsibility is primarily laid at the feet of people who exchange sex for money, even

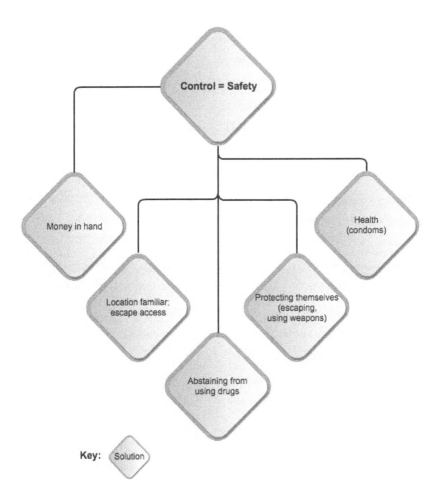

Figure 5.1 Control = Safety.

114 Street Sex Workers' Discourse

to the extent that in some locations, carrying more than a specified number of condoms can be grounds for arrest for prostitution.[5] These issues need further examination: Why is this responsibility placed on the woman? Why is the individual woman responsible for protecting herself from violence, which, in part serves to blame her if she cannot "negotiate" condom use? The woman's body is the site of control and change, and the responsibility is placed upon her for safeguarding both herself and the public at large. Figure 5.1 represents aspects of control that led to increased feelings of safety based on my participants' experiences.

Philosopher Marilyn Frye's birdcage metaphor is apparent when Sylvia, an Hispanic lesbian woman in her late 30s and a director at a mental health organization, discusses this violence: "People are cruel to anyone who has a mental health or substance use problem. Women who [. . .] exchange sex for drugs or money to survive the circumstances of their poverty or addiction or they got some other thing too traumatic, they are frequently victims of violence." The circumstances of victimization, such as poverty, addiction, or other trauma can lead to exchanging sex, which then can lead to subsequent violence.

For the most part, there is no mention that these women *should* be able to live free from this violence. The underlying belief that exchanging sex leads to violence and perhaps death is a given—not even questioned—and therefore a deterrent. The belief—if you engage in "risky" activities, be prepared for violence or death—then implies it is your responsibility to take of yourself in these situations. There is very little, if any, external protection.[6]

"THEY KNOW WHAT THEY ARE": STIGMA'S ROLE IN PERPETUATING THE VICTIM

> Prostitutes, like I say, for the most part, you know, they know what they are, they know that you know what they are, and there'll be a regular, you know, two-way conversation there that you'll get, you know, they'll be honest with you to a degree.
> —Officer Eugene Matthews, a white heterosexual man in his late 30s and a lieutenant in the Nemez Police Department

When I asked Laura, a 36-year-old, white, heterosexual woman, how she felt about the public perception of exchanging sex, she said: "How do I feel about the public thinking about me doing it [exchanging sex]? Like I said before, it makes me feel dirty. I don't like other people looking at me thinking I'm a prostitute or a whore. I don't like the way that they feel or the things that they say, but at the time I'm doing it, it's like I don't care." Donna, a 47-year-old, white, heterosexual woman, also shared these concerns:

Donna: You know there's a part of me that is embarrassed. I don't want people seeing me out there like that. You know, before it didn't bother me, but it does now.
Jill: What is the difference?
Donna: I am older. Because I know I am better than that and I'm so much selling myself short I think.

And yet some of my participants argued the public perception is wrong. When responding to my question about the public perception, Julie, a white, 42-year-old heterosexual woman, said: "I know a lot of people look at it in a bad way, and they're wrong. They're wrong because each individual in life has their own lifestyle. And they're going to live their own lifestyle the way they want to. [. . .] They look down on us. They look down on women. They think it's dirty, disgusting. But you think about it, it's the oldest profession in the world."

Like other areas of work, hierarchies exist in prostitution, and women who exchange sex for money or drugs have the lowest status and are the objects of the most stigma within the sex industry. Many have been excluded from social support networks such as their families. In a study conducted over a twelve-month period in which 150 sex workers were interviewed in North Philadelphia, Sociologists Judith Porter and Louis Bonilla (2000) found most white women did not have family or a support system of friends, and they also rarely spoke about their children. The African-American women were more likely than the white women to have contact with their relatives and sometimes lived with them. Most of the women had children and spoke of them living with their own mothers (p. 112).[7]

Sociologist Adele Weiner (1996) reports on a study conducted in the five boroughs of New York that began in 1989 and resulted in data collected from 1,963 female prostitutes. She found many prostitutes were excluded from their families and communities. In general, they are more vulnerable to the loss of social services and the removal of their children and termination of parental rights. As Sociologist Wendy Chapkis (1997) argues, "[T]hose who are most visibly and obviously selling sexual services carry the heaviest burden of the 'whore's stigma'" (p. 103). This stigma may make it impossible for these women to return to more "legitimate" areas of work and lifestyles. As Sociologist Gail Pheterson (1990) points out: "Prostitution for women is considered not merely a temporal activity (as it is for men who are clients and often for men who are sex workers), but rather a heavily stigmatized social status which in most societies remains fixed regardless of change in behavior" (p. 399). All of these issues perpetuate the lowered social status of sex workers both within the hierarchy of sex work and in society as a whole.

Stigma is clearly recognized in the language used to talk about these activities. Many of my participants argued the term *prostitute* is derogatory and ultimately dehumanizes the subject being referenced. As Joan, a white, 43-year-old, bisexual woman and an activist with a sex worker rights organization, stated:

> I think that whenever you call somebody a prostitute, you take them down a notch from everybody else. It makes them easier to disregard and ignore, and it makes them easier to rape and kill and beat up because they're somehow less than human, when in fact they are people who have addiction problems and other issues going on and that's what we need to deal with to help these women.

Chelley, an Hispanic heterosexual female in her late 40s who worked in community outreach for a mental health organization, stated "I don't like the word *prostitute*." When asked why, she said "I don't know, it bothers me. I like sex worker better." Sylvia, an Hispanic lesbian woman in her late 30s and a director at a mental health organization, related the word *prostitute* to ignorance in general. She said: "People are very ignorant. I mean they still call these women *prostitutes*. I find that to be one of the most derogatory words in the United States. Absolutely. Just offensive to me." The neighborhood association leaders, police officers, and most of the participants used the term *prostitute* to talk about women who exchange sex for money.

Some of my public figure participants emphasized these women should *not* be referred to as *sex workers* because it invokes a different concept of socioeconomic class and choice. This distinction was not consistent among all participants. Many simply referred to them as *sex workers* in general. But, at times, activists and social service agents made a distinction, only using the term *sex workers* when discussing women who worked in a higher socioeconomic bracket, identified as choosing this work as an occupation, and were largely considered by the public to be call-girls or escorts. Lily, a white lesbian woman in her mid 40s and an activist and former HIV outreach worker, who primarily referred to the women as *sex workers*, critiqued this idea. She argued the term *sex worker* offered legitimacy to these actions that many people did not want to acknowledge. In response to my questioning how others in her field refer to these women, Lily stated:

> Often prostitute. Very rarely sex worker, because most of the people I worked with didn't want to offer any legitimacy to what the women were doing and so by calling it work you remove a lot of the stigma from that and they didn't want to do that. They wanted to acknowledge that the women were doing something they shouldn't be doing.

Here a distinction is made between legitimacy rather than class. If one identifies these women as *sex workers*, the name provides a legitimacy that does not exist when the term *prostitute* is used, and yet Sylvia argued the term *sex work* implies an empowered choice the women who are working on the street are not necessarily making. Figure 5.2 offers a visual representation of some of the problems and solutions directly related to the language surrounding street-based sex work. Language awareness becomes a solution that both humanizes those participating in street-based sex work as well as works to influence perceptions about these practices with those less familiar with street economies.

The women did not directly address issues of stigma except when they talked about the language used to identify women who exchange sex for money or drugs. Most of the women stated they did not like the words *prostitute* and *whore*, among others—especially when used in reference to themselves. My participants would agree with the social service agent who said using this term takes the subject of the conversation "down a notch from everybody else." Defining a person based on this one action alone, and one many people believe is morally wrong and contemptible, serves to perpetuate stigma because the action, rather than the humanity of the individual, is emphasized.

Like its affect on violence, isolation also decreases a woman's authority and control. Due to the social stigma and criminal status of prostitution, many women are afraid to reach out for help or information. Most women who exchange sex do not identify as members of a profession, view their involvement in the sex trade as a temporary activity, and therefore are less likely to devote time and energy to organizing. Oftentimes these women and men do not find their work rewarding, even financially (Weitzer 2000, p. 4). In my findings, their exchanges are not viewed as a "workplace" but

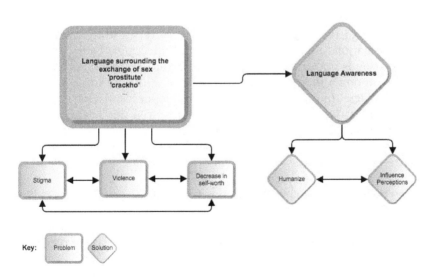

Figure 5.2 Language as a problem and solution.

more as a way of life "every so often." Therefore, the concept of "organizing" was not mentioned or even considered.

Stigma and the resulting isolation were primary concerns of activists and social service agents because they ultimately resulted in increased danger for the women. As Lily, an activist said:

> I think the stigma involved is really huge because it keeps them from getting custody of their children, it takes power away from them in their intimate relationships because that can be used against them. You're a whore, you sell sex. [. . .] I think that it extends into sex workers' abilities to work safely. [. . .] I think that crimes against sex workers are not taken seriously because its like well, what can you expect so that if they are robbed or beaten or otherwise injured there's really not a, there's a sense that they deserved it somehow because they were not good women, they were not following the rules.

Within this example a woman's power is decreased due to the stigma affecting her relationships and ultimately her safety. Lily also argues the stigma and resulting lack of power encourages the general population to further victimize sex workers because they place themselves in dangerous situations and are not "good" women who "follow the rules." This statement implies people who follow the rules should not be victims of crime, and if they are victims, then the police and society should take these crimes seriously. And yet if one does not "follow the rules," one cannot expect to avoid criminal activity and require criminals be held accountable for their actions.

She went on to say: "I think it all comes back to the stigma. The isolation is also associated with stigma. But isolation is *huge*. Women who can't, it's not safe for women to work in networks." Lily also relates stigma directly to an individual's health: "Try to work healthily. Stay healthy, get information about sexually transmitted infections. Even getting that information is not easy for people to do. If they go to a clinic they don't like to put down they are a sex worker because they're stigmatized there as well." Here, the stigma keeps the women from identifying or claiming the activities that may put them at increased risk for health problems. And because they may be hesitant to claim this identity or action, they are not given the information they need to better protect their health. Figure 5.3, Stigma's Related Problems, outlines some of the problems that emerged among my participants.

In many ways the material conditions of women involved in street-based sex work create an influential and fixed birdcage that is difficult to pull apart and dismantle. I include Philosopher Marilyn Frye's description of the cage [in Chapter 2] for two reasons: as a demonstration of the interrelated and interlocking nature of existing power structures, and secondly, to place attention directly on these structures as the central problem.

Systemic Violence Perpetuates Victim Status 119

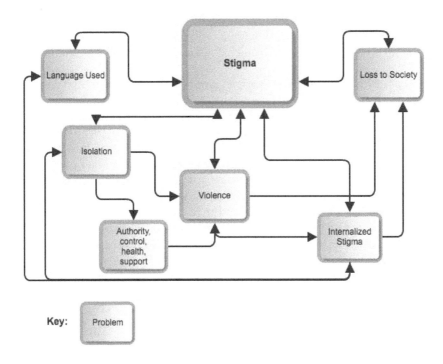

Figure 5.3 Problems related to stigma.

SYSTEMIC ISSUES: IMPEDIMENTS TO "CHANGE"

> I think always that it's important to tie the types of behaviors that our communities find distasteful back to the structural elements that contribute to these behaviors.
> —Sylvia, an Hispanic lesbian woman in her late 30s and a director at a mental health organization

Due to their lack of job skills or other resources needed to find and keep a job and their common addiction to drugs, many people continue to work as prostitutes because there are very few alternatives (Porter and Bonilla 2010, p. 116). Addiction to substances can then perpetuate a cycle wherein individuals who trade sex for drugs or money have even fewer alternatives for making a living outside of prostitution and therefore continue to exchange sex not only to make a living but also to support their habits.

All of my research sites emphasized the role of services in one's ability to "change." And yet the women, in general, found it difficult to access these services, and for the most part, the public figures agreed the necessary

120 *Street Sex Workers' Discourse*

services were not available. One inconsistency occurred when speaking with the police officers, who held different opinions about the availability of services. As Officer Eric Johnson, a white heterosexual man in his mid-40s and the supervisor of the Nemez Police Department vice unit, argues:

> It's the "goody two shoe" people, what I call it, think that you can go over and give them some money and you've helped them out. Well, all you've done is made yourself feel better because whatever money they get is going for that drug habit, so all you're doing is enabling them to continue on with their drug habit. So I mean, and that's why places like *Casa Segura*, where they bring them in, they tell them that ok, we want to see them now, or we want to see you Tuesday, and they get them in there, they start building self-esteem. They have them, they found several that are very good artists and they can draw pictures there. They start developing some skills to let these people realize that they have some other self-worth than just doing this. And then they just don't dump them back on the street. They help try to get them into treatment centers, they get them off their drug habits, but once again, how serious is the person? I mean, that's what they hear is I want off this, until tomorrow when the boyfriend's calling them saying "Hey," you know, then they're back with him, they don't show back up at the program and we end up with them again on the sweep.

Officer Eric Johnson clearly places the responsibility on the women, arguing they have access to services through *Casa Segura*, but prefer to go with the boyfriend because of their "drug habits." The choice is outlined as the program versus drugs and subsequence arrests. Officer Eugene Matthews, a white heterosexual man in his late 30s and a lieutenant in the Nemez Police Department, describes the scenario as one of addiction and lifestyle:

> You will often hear the excuses they'll give, you know, like "I gotta find a place to live," "I've gotta feed my children," "I've gotta . . ." you know, all these kind of things, which I think are fairly lame excuses, because there's a network of social organizations out there. Basically, when it comes down to it, they have an addiction or they have a lifestyle that they are into and . . . Um, you know, I don't believe that they are . . . Some of them—there is a segment that is really trapped in that, but there are outlets, and these organizations like *Casa Segura* actually provide training for them, they provide . . . There are some housing options for them. They've taken them—in some of these programs, I understand they've relocated outside of areas that they've been operating in. Because a lot of them have zone restrictions that they've got slapped with, you know, and so it's . . . There's a number of social options for them. And outside of that, a lot of them could just get jobs

Systemic Violence Perpetuates Victim Status 121

and, you know, by their own means, they could probably exist, if they chose to make that decision.

Officer Eugene Matthews argues there is a "network" of services available to them, and in spite of the fact that the women say they need help, they choose an "addiction" or "lifestyle." Contrary to these opinions, none of the social service agents stated there were adequate resources available to meet the need. Officer Jennifer Castillo, an Hispanic 34-year-old heterosexual female who worked for the Nemez Police Department as an undercover officer also offered this contrary perspective:

> I don't think there's enough resources out there for them, quite honestly. I don't know how good of a job *Casa Segura* does when they do contact them. Um, I know the police don't have really any services, I mean, just the officer that's arresting them, you know? I'm no longer gonna be doing that in the vice unit, so I don't know who's gonna be the arresting officer. [. . .] So I can guarantee they're not gonna have the same relationship that I've had with the girls, you know, because it's probably gonna be a male officer and, you know, it's . . . To me, I'm more, I guess, I want to help these girls more because I'm female and they're female, and I know what they can do or possibly do, you know, that this isn't worth it. But I don't think the police . . . I think we could probably do something for them, more so than what we're doing. You know, I don't know.

In addition to the lack of resources, locating and accessing the appropriate services is challenging as well. As Kristina, a 34-year-old Hispanic heterosexual woman and outreach coordinator for a mental health organization, explained:

> When I first got into *Casa Segura* and in this particular type of program, I was really kind of appalled at all the obstacles that you run into. Because, I mean, there's so much criteria and hoops that you have to jump through to get a woman into some type of treatment. Oh, well, you know, they have to have these specific drug issues. Or they cannot be on public healthcare assistance. Okay, they can be on public healthcare assistance. I mean, every facility has different criteria that you have to meet, and just jumping through that myself sometimes is difficult, you know, trying to place somebody can be difficult. I think, again, you know . . . Oh no, does this individual have kids? Well, we can't take that individual because we don't house children; we're not, you know, licensed to house children. They can't have severe medical issues, you know, we're not licensed to do that. They cannot be pregnant when they enter. I mean, there's just a bunch of hoops that you

have to jump through, and I think that makes it difficult to provide services. [. . .] And, you know, a lot of 'em don't have any other means of income. They don't have, um—again, it's kind of a cycle: Let's say you get popped [arrested] for, you know, some small charge. You know, you go to . . . felony, um, you get out. You're trying to establish employment . . . set up in a specific way, it's really kinda hard to—I mean, you've already gotten labeled. You've gotten the charge, you've gotten the felony, you've been to prison; right there is a huge label. And I think it's difficult. It's difficult to get out of that situation, and society doesn't make it easy for you. For me, um, I see those that really wanna make a change; they really want to . . . They want to get out of this, they want to do something else, they want to go to school, I mean, they want to have an apartment.

Combining the difficulty in locating services with lack of knowledge and possible criminal charges creates an even more challenging environment for "change."

Sylvia, a director at a mental health organization, echoed these sentiments:

There's very few resources for women in Nemez period. It doesn't matter what the issue is: domestic violence, there's like no beds available, there's no housing for the homeless, if you can get housing there's so many restrictions on it its very, very frustrating and there's a waiting list a mile long. There are limited number of beds available at the detoxification center for women, which is in my opinion a crime, but who am I? Yeah, there are very few women's resources. Extremely few.

Dr. Veronica Alvarez, a 48-year-old heterosexual Latina woman and Project Director of an HIV-prevention program talked about her experience trying to locate services for a client:

Dr. Veronica Alvarez: I can say that I think that there is a lack of expertise and services that provide women . . . For example, if you look at the number of beds for women in detox, there are a limited number of beds; and if we try to get a woman into detox and they say "The beds are full," what do you mean? How many beds do you have? And we can't get that information. We hung up and had someone else call with a different voice and ask for a detox bed for a man.
Jill: For a man?
Dr. Veronica Alvarez: For a man. They have the bed for a man. And then also with shelters: If you try to get a woman into a shelter, women who are single, who are not . . . domestic violence, what does that mean? I mean, women have suffered domestic violence for a lifetime, and they don't happen to be coming out of that right now,

but there's no place for them. Or they have to go into a religious-based thing, which forces them to attend certain services and get up at a certain hour, perform this and that. I don't think that's . . . I mean, I think that's fine because maybe there are women who want to do that, but I don't think that's the majority of women and I don't think that there are alternatives to that. Or women have to be tied to children to find a bed, shelter, transition house. I think that there's a lot lacking in services for women. Women's identity continues to be tied to the role as mother and caretaker, and at the same time, they're judged for that or for seeking out services as mother or caretaker. So I don't know.

In addition to locating and accessing available services, Valarie, an Hispanic heterosexual female in her mid 30s and a program manager at a behavioral health agency, outlines some of the barriers the women face because of the trauma and criminal status many of them have experienced:

Well, a lot of them, like I said, have gone through so much trauma. A lot of them think that they really aren't worth it and they believe it. I guess when speaking of helping them stop using, when speaking of helping them, most of them don't want to exchange [exchange sex for money], you know? I know very few women that'll tell you, "Yeah, I exchange because I like it." Most people feel that they really have to continue doing it; they don't have any other option. Most of them really think that that's all they're worth and that's the only thing they can do because they feel that they can't really achieve anything else. It's the easiest. And they find themselves with no way out. When it comes to looking for a job, when it comes to looking for housing, again, everything comes back and haunts them. If they have a felony, it's really hard to get housing. If they don't have money, it's really hard to get an ID or a birth certificate to get a job. If they're looking for a job, it's really difficult for people not to look at the background and judge them by it. Just giving them that belief that they are worth it I think is really difficult. That's what makes our job very difficult.

Later in our interview, in response to my question about who's problem (women on the street exchanging sex for money) it is, Valarie responded:

Valarie: [laughs] I don't know if I could call it a problem, but more of just a representation of how our society leads a lot of our women to just not be able to access going to school or getting an education or getting a job. You know, I think our system makes it very difficult to get back on your feet. Like I said, if you don't have a license, you can't get a birth certificate. If you don't have a birth certificate, you can't get a social security card. You know, it's just

... It's just a trap. So I think a lot of times, even though a lot of us want to say we're helping, it's really difficult.

Jill: What do you mean it's a trap?

Valarie: It's a trap. I mean if we want these women to finish school or we want these women to get a job, we're not really making it any easier for them. It's a lot easier to just give up and go back on the streets, if I'm not going to be able to get the money to get the license, to get the birth certificate, to get the social security card, you know? [. . .] It's just a representation of society in general. It's reality. . . . It's almost like we bank on these people continuing to use [drugs]. We bank on these people continuing to get arrested, you know? For some people, it creates jobs, you know? I mean, we called the paramedics not long ago on this person that had OD'd [overdosed on a substance], and finally, they were okay by the time they got here; and one of us said, "Well, if you're feeling okay, then we shouldn't waste the paramedic's time," and the paramedic said, "Oh no, she's not wasting our time. Money is money" [laughs]. And we're like "What?" He said, "Yeah, we're offering a service, and business is business." So if that's how the paramedics see it, I wonder how the Nemez Police Department sees it, you know? [. . .] I think the issue is just the way the system works in general. I mean if the system is not all on the same page, then we're never going to achieve anything. I mean if we're trying to help them get a job or whatever, and the system is out there not making it any easier for them, where are they gonna get this money from, you know? Or how? I mean, we can't say one thing and do another. [. . .] It doesn't mean other women haven't been able to jump through the system, through the hoops and barriers of the system. But it is difficult. It does make it a whole lot more difficult. I mean, if some people are saying, "Yeah, you should get your own job so you're not on food stamps," or you're not on, you know, whichever it may be . . . on the welfare system, then make it a little easier. For some women, it becomes a lot easier just to apply for social security. It's a lot easier than actually going through the whole system and trying to get a job which they really don't have skills for, you know? [. . .] Again, I think it's back to the system. If it's [prostitution] illegal, it creates more money. This is my personal take: If it was legal, I really don't think that it would change, because the people that are doing it are going to whether it's legal or illegal. The only thing is, again, we wouldn't have this whole system, like I said, arresting women for three hours, letting them out, charging them or having people owe money. It becomes just this invisible . . . It doesn't make any sense. [. . .] And then for most of 'em, it's like, "Well, why am I even gonna go there if it's just gonna take too much work to

> become legitimate again? Why even bother?" For me, it's just—
> I mean, it's obvious: They need our women to just stay where
> they're at right now because it's creating jobs. I mean, it would
> be like me sitting here and being like, "Yeah, I wanna work here
> for 20 years," you know? Because anyone in these fields should
> really be in these jobs to end this job, you know? I mean, not . . .
> It just doesn't make any sense.

A certain amount of individual responsibility is required in order for a person to achieve a life she can feel good about, but when systemic issues related to poverty and violence are at the root of many of the choices this individual has made, it is unfair to simply place the total responsibility on her shoulders and expect her to change. These women are often fighting constant battles—which they frequently lose—to do the right thing for themselves and their loved ones in the face of nearly insurmountable challenges. Hence, the hero status ascribed to the one who changes her life by those who know all too well how difficult it is to kick the drugs, alcohol, and life on the street. Can a strong woman make a choice to escape the sex and drug lifestyle? Yes. Will she be successful? The odds are very much against it, no matter how determined she might be, because there are so many countervailing forces working against her. The ideology of personal choice and responsibility serves to further isolate the individual who has already been wronged by the injustices of society.

The series continues: An individual experiences pain, wants to escape, turns to drugs, and exchanges sex for money or drugs; Society places the responsibility for this circumstance on the individual and looks to the individual for the source of change; The individual struggles to change; Systemic support for this change is lacking or nonexistent; Perhaps the cycle of drug use and exchanging sex continue; Punitive measures and social service agencies are created to empower these women to "change"; If the individual changes, the individual and support systems are praised; Society does not address the origins of the abuse and violence and they are therefore allowed to continue; More individuals experience pain and begin the sex and drug cycle. The cycles of personal responsibility and societal indifference and ignorance are mutually reinforced and maintained.

SYSTEMIC VIOLENCE AND RESPONSIBILITY

> If you say, what would you call yourself, they might say 'prostitute,' but if you sit there and talk to them for a little while, they're like, 'Hey bitch, I survived this or that and the other thing.' I think they see themselves as people that have opportunity and either feel really bad because they think they threw it all away, they have shame and guilt, or they see themselves as people that have value but they've been abused,

neglected, and misused. I think they see themselves as people that have something to give back to the community but don't feel worthy.
—Sylvia, an Hispanic lesbian woman in her late 30s, and a director at a mental health organization

Within each of my interviews with women who exchange sex for money or drugs some concept of "help" was discussed, whether in the context of assistance from social service agencies, from family, or even in reference to sex work itself.[8] For instance, when I asked Karen, a 49-year-old, white, heterosexual woman who had immigrated to the United States, the question "What do you call it when people exchange sex for money or drugs?" she replied with a laugh "Ummm, getting help with my money". Examining my participants' perspectives of "help" did not yield easy answers, and yet this analysis did reveal insights that can be applied to the current system of criminalization and social service assistance in the United States.

"Help" is a concept that can be understood as a transaction between a giver and a receiver. This transaction creates a power differential because the giver provides something the receiver needs, a lack she cannot fill on her own, whether it involves homelessness, hunger, or sickness. The giver, or one who has access to providing this help, has more power, particularly in terms of resources or access to resources, than the receiver. In many cases, the helper then sets the terms for the help provided, including where, when, how, how much, and in what format such assistance is given.

To need, ask for, or open oneself up to receiving help implies this lack, as stated above, but it can also imply membership in a group of individuals who cannot meet their own needs, such as those who are experiencing homelessness, addiction or poverty. These groups can be viewed pejoratively by those who inhabit both insider and outsider status. In my findings, membership in the "prostitute" group occurred on a continuum, as the speaker defined herself in relation to the group—as a member or not—even within the same conversation.

For example, as the women shifted their subject positions in their interviews with me, the pronouns they used blurred as well. When my participants described the public perception of women who exchange sex, they referred to the women who are in need of help as "them". Ava, a white, 23-year-old heterosexual woman, exemplified this position when she said, "I think [the community] should try to help them." When these statements were made, it was clear the speaker did not identify with either population, but as an outsider—both outside the "women in need" category as well as outside the "community." And when the women discussed their own perceptions of street work and their reasons for participating in the interview, they bridged the divide between someone who participates in street-based sex work and the community by expressing their desires to help others through their own experiences, knowledge, and empathy—as Olivia, a 43-year-old Hispanic heterosexual woman, said: "I wish I could help them."

These ideas of getting and providing help are grounded in a system that views exchanging sex as immoral and illegal. The women I interviewed argue the public perception needs to be changed and the community needs to be more involved in addressing these difficult issues. But as long as these core beliefs of immorality and illegality exist, it is extremely difficult for the one who is acting in illegal and immoral ways to identify what she needs systemically, and it becomes even more difficult to identify as one who needs that help because her position is devalued by the moral and legal systems. She can ask for this help, but she's most likely to believe and experience she *won't* get it, largely because of her position in this system as someone who does not *deserve* it. Asking for this help becomes even more difficult if she believes that her actions are wrong. And when she is surrounded by a culture that tells her how wrong it is over and over again, she must almost identify as *amoral*, in contrast to either moral or immoral, in order to preserve her sense of dignity and self as a valuable person.

As I came to better understand my participants and their lives, the choices available to them emerged more clearly. If only certain choices are available within the material conditions surrounding one's life, then one must make a choice, which then leads to other possible choices. And what are the influences and pressures that lead to making particular choices? And how do these choices become less intellectual and more concrete in terms of where one lives, how one chooses to work through difficult emotions, one's addiction, one's lack of community, one's access to resources, and what choices stem from those conditions? For example, as I read through the interviews, a part of me was right back there in my kitchen sitting with Lisa, a 47year-old, Hispanic heterosexual woman, and listening to her stories. Feeling so much awe for her, wanting to be her friend—to see the world through her eyes. And understanding, a bit better, her material reality of living in a hotel room with her son who was just released from prison, while her second son, a four-year-old, was unlocateable to her because he had been placed in the adoption system without her permission. How does one inhabit this reality? And how does that reality influence and constrain one's choices? How are the results of those choices concretized—not only in the hotel room, but in her mind that knows only a hotel room is available and that it is a better choice than being on the street and exchanging sex for money or other gain? The concrete material options are housed in the influential and fixed material that exist and are made available based on one's moment to moment choices as well as what systemic opportunities exist.

What options or choices are available to the women, and how do they, in turn, view these options or choices? As was stated explicitly through all three sites of research—the primary option is for the women to take personal responsibility for their actions and situations and to make a change. And this change largely occurs through substance abuse treatment and aid from social service agencies. How this treatment is accessed is a point of contention. Although substance abuse treatment and social service agencies may be available, a primary obstacle is making the decision to create a different and "better" life for themselves, taking the necessary steps to achieve this change, and then maintaining this change. And all of the above must be achieved in a society quite inhospitable to people living in these conditions—the conditions society itself has often created.

A shift in focus must occur from the individual women to an emphasis on the systemic inequalities, poverty, and abuse that compel people to use drugs and exchange sex. Blame and responsibility are placed on the women *after* these choices are made. Rather than focusing solely on substance abuse as an individual problem solved through detoxification and rehabilitation, the community must take responsibility for the environment in which these choices are seen as the only viable option. Although individuals have to take responsibility for their actions and lives, the role overarching systems play in creating this violence and abuse that leads to drug abuse must also be addressed.

Left to their own devices, which often involves "criminal" behavior to create a habitable life, individuals go to jail or are arrested and then need more social services or low-income housing because there are no jobs available that pay a living wage. Perhaps then the person having difficulty navigating a system in which she seems to be nothing but bound for failure becomes more dependent on public systems. Her inability to support herself financially, physically, emotionally and psychically, can then lead to actions, perhaps, of denial or escape, that perpetuates the cycles.

Figure 5.4 offers a visual representation of the two ideological collages and their related problems and solutions. The social service agencies are designed to "help" these people—whether through halfway houses or low-income housing, mental health counseling, etc., and so resources are funneled through these agencies—whether public monies of tax dollars or private foundation monies—which seem to be largely designed for rehabilitation rather than prevention.

All three of my research sites—the newspaper articles, public figures, and the women themselves—place the responsibility for these women's choices and their current situations on the women themselves. All three layers place the responsibility on the individual—both in choosing to exchange sex and choosing to end the cycle of sex and drug use. *And yet this focus on the individual does not prevent these situations from occurring in the first place.* Society allows for and even creates conditions that violate children, women, and men, and this violation increases as people move away from "legitimate" employment into cycles of drug use and addiction. After participating in these cycles of abuse, violence, and escape, society then asks these individuals to take responsibility for themselves, change their lives, and create better ones. The individual is responsible for this change when she is now in a situation where she perhaps has lost her family, her children, her friends, her home, her job, and virtually every other form of support that might help her make such a difficult transformation.

Systemic Violence Perpetuates Victim Status 129

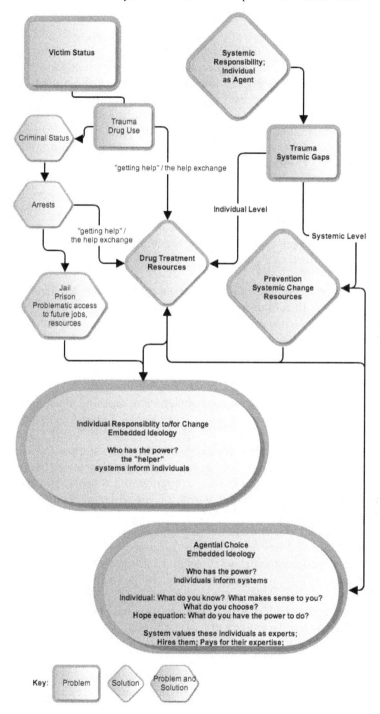

Figure 5.4 Victim status versus agential choice.

WIRES OF OPPRESSION

As has been explored throughout, the material conditions surrounding street-based sex work combine to create increased oppression and violence. As Lerum et al. (2012) argue "Policies that increase the already intense criminalisation of sex workers disproportionately scrutinise and punish the most disenfranchised, increase the economic and social marginalisation of both the providers and the purchasers of commercial sex, and create new ways to penalise men, women, and transgender people of colour and immigrants" (p. 88). These conditions simultaneously co-construct individuals as both victims and those who do not *matter* as much as others.

Based on their status as marginalized and their practices in street-based economies, these individuals have virtually no protection against violence, rape, and even death. The research that outlines the extreme violence people involved in street-based sex work encounter and live with on a daily basis are too numerous to mention. As Shannon et al. (2009a) argue:

> the extremely high prevalence of rape experienced by female sex workers over the 18 month follow-up period points to the immediate need to scale up violence prevention strategies, including increasing support for female sex workers accessing legal and victim services and improving the monitoring of and legal responses to violence against female sex workers. (p. 7)

Romero-Dazaa et al. (2005) found that victims of rape and abuse are seen as the ones at fault for their victimization. They include Lopez-Jones's argument:

> Attacks on sex workers are common not because prostitution is an intrinsically violent job, but because violent men are more likely to get away with physical attacks on a woman who is a prostitute. Prostitute women ... being sexual outlaws have been denied many of the human, civil, and legal rights available (at least in theory) to other women. This lack of social power is key to understanding the violence prostitute women face and what can and must be done to end it [...] women and children who try to survive through prostitution are ... criminalized and accused of "attracting" violence. In this way, the victim, rather than the attacker, is blamed for the violence she suffers ... When sex workers report violence the police often dismiss the attack as "part of the job," accuse the woman of "asking for it," or even threaten her with arrest. (qtd. in Romero-Dazaa et al. 2005, p. 158)

Valera et al. (2001) cite The Council on Prostitution as estimating that "female prostitutes are raped approximately once a week" (p. 51). They found that violence is one of the most significant threats to their participants' health. People involved in street-based sex work are raped and killed with almost no attention paid to them unless the killings amount to serial proportions. The International Day to End Violence Against Sex Workers, held annually on December 17,

> was created to call attention to crimes committed against sex workers all over the globe. Originally conceptualized by Annie Sprinkle and initiated by the Sex Workers Outreach Project USA as a memorial and vigil for the victims of the Green River Killer in Seattle Washington, the International Day to End Violence Against Sex Workers has empowered workers from cities around the world to come together and organize against discrimination and remember victims of violence. During the week of December 17th, sex worker rights organizations and their allies stage actions and vigils to raise awareness about violence that is commonly committed against sex workers. The assault, battery, rape and murder of sex workers must end. (SWOP-USA, "International Day to End Violence Against Sex Workers")

Stigma, combined with criminalization, sends a powerful message that these individuals are "throwaways" or not worth anything anyway—a belief that is apparent in the lack of interest in pressing charges against the extensive violence that is committed against them. Current policies and their enforcement create the conditions that allow for this violence to occur. As Shannon et al. (2009a) argue: "In Canada over the past two decades, urban centers have experienced epidemics of violence against street based female sex workers that have been posited to coincide with prohibitive policy changes and enforcement based strategies, such as police crackdowns" (p. 2). At their best, the policies are not solving the problem of prostitution, and at their worst, they create the conditions for violence to occur. These same conditions provide little recourse for those individuals when this violence does occur—sending a message to perpetrators that their actions will not be punished—further perpetuating this cycle where sex workers and people who exchange sex do not matter because the laws that apply to citizens who do not participate in these activities are not upheld.

Systemic changes must be implemented that prevent individuals from being in a position where this "choice" is the only available one. If the spotlight were placed on the system, what responsibilities and choices would be revealed? Rather than constructing the individual worker and her client as those on the margins and thereby responsible for creating change, the discursive and practical emphasis should be placed on redesigning and implementing systems that currently do not successfully provide support for our community members.

6 Creating Agential Choice from Cages of Oppression

> I'm doing it for myself, not because of probation and all that. Because I've tried to do it for everybody else and all I've done is relapse.
> —Brenda

> We live embedded in systems of power-over and are indoctrinated into them, often from birth. In its clearest form, power-over is the power of the prison guard, of the gun, power that is ultimately backed by force. Power-over enables one individual or group to make the decisions that affect others, and to enforce control. [. . .] We are so accustomed to power-over, so steeped in its language and its implicit threats, that we often become aware of its functioning only when we see its extreme manifestations. For we have been shaped in its institutions, so that the insides of our minds resemble the battlefield and the jail.
> —Starhawk, *Truth or Dare*, p. 9

Power is inherent in the concept of agency, and in many situations, the power to take responsibility for change is thrust upon the women who exchange sex for money or drugs. In order to be an agent, one must be inhabiting and enacting her own power. Otherwise, that power is a façade. Starhawk (1990) outlines three types of power: power-over, power-from-within, and power-with. As I included in the epigram above, power-over involves domination and control. *Responsibility to and for Change*, as I have explored in Chapter 4, is grounded in external pressure—as a parent tells a child they need to take responsibility for something and change—and is enacted through a "power-over" dynamic. It is often enforced from outside through punitive measures as occurs in my participants' fear and experiences of arrests and violence. And although an individual can internalize this voice and behavior, she is not necessarily acting as a genuine agent.

Humanities Professor Marilyn Cooper (2011) argues "Actors, or agents, are entities that act; by virtue of their action they necessarily bring about changes. (It should go without saying here that all actions are embodied, including what are thought of as 'mental' actions—speaking, writing, reflecting.)" (p. 424). Without agency, or the power and ability to self-determination, one does not have the power to make an authentic choice. Starhawk links power-from-within "to the mysteries that awaken our deepest abilities and potential" (p. 9) and is based on personal ability and integrity. One enacts this power from a place of trust, love, and strength in oneself. The person is an agent responsible to herself. She takes care of her own needs and perhaps others as well. "Power-over" and "power-from-within" are never entirely separate, but are continuously enacted *upon* and *through* each individual. Choice occurs on a continuum of power based on external and internal motivations, pressures, and goals.

Oftentimes, based on the "help" transaction, a person in authority, whether purposefully or not, maintains a role of authority and operates from a power-over position. I draw on Starhawk's concept of "power-with" as a framework for understanding and co-constructing agential choice. Starhawk defines power-with as

> influence: the power of a strong individual in a group of equals, the power not to command, but to suggest and be listened to, to begin something and see it happen. The source of power-with is the willingness of others to listen to our ideas. We could call that willingness respect, not for a role, but for each unique person. (p. 9–10)

Starhawk uses the concepts of authority and obedience to demonstrate her theory:

> The influence, the respect commanded by an authority is different from the respect we give to an equal. The influence of authorities comes from their roles or positions in a hierarchy. They have a *title*, a named role, which *entitles* them to influence others. Ultimately, their entitlement derives from their power to enforce obedience. [. . .] Power-with is more subtle, more fluid and fragile than authority. It is dependent on personal responsibility, on our own creativity and daring, and on the willingness of others to respond. (p. 10–11)

My term, *agential choice,* comes from within and between and requires each individual has an authentic choice, the ability to make that choice happen, or the belief she can make it happen. Agential choice requires a desire, based on internal and integral values, for one's best interest. It is not based on external morality or obligation, but rather an integration of personal values and ability. Genuine choice requires agential choice—that in which an individual believes and can take responsibility.

As I explored in Chapter 1, Marilyn Cooper's responsible agency "requires one to be aware that everyone acts out of their own space of meaning and that to affirm one's own meanings as absolute truth is to negate the other person" (p. 442). As Cooper argues: "Recognition of an other as someone capable of agency, someone capable of making a difference, is important in persuasion, but rather than creating agency, it is how a rhetor becomes responsible, how a rhetor enables real persuasion" (p. 442). She continues:

Respect for listeners' opinions, being open even to "unreasonable" opinions, to "troublemakers," means being open to them as responsive beings who, like the speaker, will understand or assimilate meanings in their own way. It means recognizing both speaker and listeners as agents in persuasion, as people who are free to change their minds. This recognition defines responsible rhetorical agency. (p. 441)

Agential choice, then, is grounded in responsible rhetorical agency—it can only be created when individuals, especially those in traditional roles of power, recognize others as "agents."

And yet not all agents are as free to act as others, based on the contexts created through both systemic and individual circumstances. My position as a white, forty-something, single parent and woman in the United States is both a product of and a constraint on the actions I can and do take based on my agential choice—or what I believe is in my best interest. My context, both internally and externally, creates, limits and produces my agency. Prostitution, at least within the last 200 years, has been considered a derogatory profession. English and Gender Studies Professor Anne McClintock (1993) emphasizes this perspective is based on more than one's choice to exchange sex:

> Most sex workers insist it is not the exchange of money that demeans them, but the context in which the exchange is made. Depicting all sex workers as slaves only travesties the myriad, different experiences of sex workers around the world. At the same time, it theoretically confused social agency and identity with social context. Sex worker efforts at self-empowerment cannot be reduced to the conditions of stigma and legal disadvantage that entrammel them. (pp. 2–3)

McClintock's distinction is an important one, and one my participants identified as well—their *contextual* agency. They were agents in these choices, and the choices available to them were directly related to the material conditions through which they co-create their lives. One's agency, or ability to make a self-determined authentic choice, although powerful, is constrained by surrounding material conditions. For example, what options are available to a person if she has felony charges for prostitution and drugs, is recovering from drug addiction, has no family or community available, and has just been released from prison? The possibility of "change" is certainly open to her, but what, tangibly, does this change look like? And who is she to trust to help her achieve this change? Or should she be expected to achieve this change on her own? As Anthropologist Susan Dewey (2011) states in her analysis of dancers in *Neon Wasteland* "It is problematic to imply that women compelled for whatever reason to engage in sex work do not make choices designed to improve their lives materially, but it is even more dangerous to argue that they are agents free of coercion by poverty and other limiting circumstances" (p. xvi).

Creating Agential Choice from Cages of Oppression 135

Marilyn Cooper (2011) draws on neuroscientist Walter J. Freeman's theory of neurons and its constructed compatibility to its environment. She explains rather than "passively 'storing a memory,' [. . .] Freeman argues that neurons interact to create a pattern that is not a representation of an odor or color, for example, nor information about an odor or color, but rather a response unique to each sensing individual, shaped by each individual organism's history and shaped anew in every iteration" (p. 427). This pattern is unique to each individual that is "compatible with the history and goals of the organism" (Freeman, qtd. in Cooper, p. 428). These patterns continually shift with the changing experiences of the organism and are similar to Brummett's (1991) mosaics, where an individual orders her world by constructing patterns, or mosaics, that make their experience meaningful while at the same time creating herself as a subject who is positioned by the pattern (p. 84).

Language, questions about specific subjects, and exposure to new information provide opportunities for slight shifts in this mosaic, thereby making the kaleidoscope a helpful image. The creations are continuously *in medias res*, so to speak, or in the middle, which is "the agency in charge, not our awareness [of it], which is constantly trying to catch up with what we do. We perceive the world from inside our boundaries as we engage it and then change ourselves by assimilation" (Freeman qtd. in Cooper, p. 428). Cooper continues:

> The process of assimilation defines an agent as an individual with his or her own intentions or goals; individual agents are determinate, but not determined, in an ongoing becoming driven by the interactions among the components of their nervous system and by their interaction with the surround. They change themselves through these interactions and at the same time instigate changes in others with whom they interact. (p. 428)

Developing an ideology and practice of power-with not only creates and respects agential choice, but can influence material reality. As I asked in the Preface: How do the current perceptions contribute to the constructions of problems and solutions surrounding street-based sex work and therefore influence the material conditions of these people's lives? What happens when we frame the "problem" of street-based sex work differently? And how would this reframing affect the material conditions and outcomes related to individuals' lives? Based on the analysis presented, I outline how agential choice applied to a street-based sex work context can create movement toward necessary systemic rehabilitation and change.

In order to facilitate agential choice and participate in responsible rhetorical agency, the victim status must be reframed and replaced. Secondly, criminalization of prostitution must be reconsidered. The people participating in these exchanges must be at the forefront of this process, which helps to both highlight and address systemic violence and responsibility. And finally, I offer practical applications, concrete examples, and suggestions for responsible rhetorical agency as a foundation of both agential choice and material change.

REPLACING "VICTIM" STATUS WITH AGENTIAL CHOICE

Jill: Who do you trust?
Karen: Myself.
Jill: Yeah? Anyone else?
Karen: Myself mostly.
Jill: Yeah?
Karen: Yeah, myself. You know, I have a lot of faith in me. [. . .] Because I always liked myself, I always respected myself.

In my findings, "victim" status is ascribed to most, if not all, women who exchange sex. Considering someone to be a victim relates the individual to the "scene of the crime," so to speak, where the person became a victim, and, perhaps, a survivor. As a survivor, she is given accolades because she has not allowed the trauma or event to destroy her, but rather, has come through it to the other side. I argue the victim and survivor status not be attributed to women who exchange sex because this status places the attention on her presumed lack of power.

My argument came about, in part, through my own "victim" status. I began this research because I am interested in the relationships between power, sex and sexuality, bodies, and gender. I chose women who work on the street because they seemed the most powerless, and I wanted to better understand their world and how it might be made differently. To be honest, I wanted to "help" them. Throughout my research, I also became involved in different sex worker rights organizations, and joining these organizations in both leadership and membership capacities educated me, while also providing opportunities for me to "give back" to the community that offers me so much—my research, livelihood to a degree, best friends, and passion.

These broad categories of power, sex, the body, and gender are tied to my own experiences. I will never forget the conversation I had with a dear friend of mine. When I talked to her about my trauma and experience of sexual abuse, she looked at me and said, "Oh, so that's why you do the research you do." I was shocked. I wondered what my own abuse, trauma, and violation had to do with my research—the two seemed completely separate. And yet this research has brought my own experiences as a victim viscerally front and center. And as a person who can also be considered a victim, that label or status does nothing for me. I am not a victim. Although I haven't experienced "victimization" in the same ways as my participants,

Creating Agential Choice from Cages of Oppression 137

I know from my own perspective I am not a victim, nor do I want to be referred to as such.

At the risk of too much self-disclosure, I offer an explanation. By referring to me as a victim, a victim of sexual abuse to be precise, the speaker, reader, or listener's attention is placed on the act of abuse—which further disempowers me and keeps me in that place. The experience has colored much of my life and has influenced who I am today—a woman I am proud to be. Rather than focusing on those experiences as a victim, I value myself and all of the experiences in which I have participated that embody various levels of choice. I have integrated those experiences into my personhood—who I am as an agent, mother, scholar, friend, lover, and person. They all contribute to who I am today—with all of the anger, fear, terror, and sadness that corresponds with those events. And yet calling me a victim or a survivor places the attention and the power on that event, rather than on the person I was, am, and continue to create. The victim status shifts the focus from my own agency and power as a woman, an individual, a creative force—which is where I reside. My power is most fully realized when it is viewed as creative, owned by me, and agential—as it contributes to me becoming more of an agent in my own experiences, growth, perceptions, and creativity.

If the "victim" status is not appropriate, then how do we talk about these issues? For one, a "status" is not ascribed to an individual for each event that is or is not based on her own power and choice. Is it even possible for an event to exist that can be solely ascribed to one's own power and choice? Of course not. Life is an intrinsic web of people, systems, chance, and many powers beyond our knowledge and certainly our control. I might have become a victim when leaving the house this morning if I were robbed while walking to my car. And after the robbery, I become a survivor, because I have come through the event to the other side. And yet I am the same person walking out the door whether I am robbed or not, albeit altered in certain ways. There are many systems in place that have buffered and buffeted me, contributing to where I sit at the moment. I have many personal attributes that have contributed as well. And there is chance, fate, the universe, god, the goddess, and those other individuals and experiences that each contribute to the layers upon layers of me-ness that make me what I call *me*—too many to name or categorize. Perhaps an individual should choose when he or she wants to claim the victim or survivor status—for example, I am a survivor of a hurricane—I lived through it and it contributes to who I am today. My participants did not use the word *victim* to refer to themselves or others—not once. I do not mean to imply they did not feel like or consider themselves to be victims, but they did not name themselves or others as such.

The victim and even survivor status reduces an individual's power because it contributes to the appearance she is less of an agent and more someone who has and may continue to be victimized. Considering the "prostitute" as primarily a victim can actually *create* the conditions for violence because the individual is viewed as having less power than others who do not share this status. Further, these individuals then require power from outside of themselves, or "help." This "helping" mentality also does a disservice to these individuals, as I have argued in the previous chapter, because their internal strength, power, intellect, and perseverance is often not recognized or valued at a great cost to them individually and to society as a whole. What is lost to society when this victim/needing-help/less-than status is ascribed to so many? Most importantly, the value of each individual is lost—which is and always has been present. As Research Coordinator at Framework Housing Association Rachel Harding and Criminologist Paul

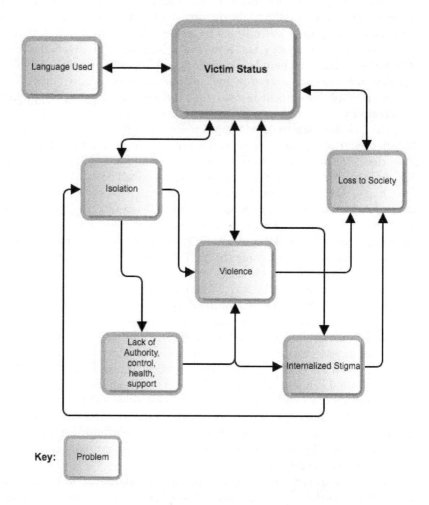

Figure 6.1 Victim status reinforces problems.

Creating Agential Choice from Cages of Oppression   139

Hamilton argue: "Ultimately, that abused and vulnerable homeless women should *choose* to sex work has tended to be overlooked in official discourse. Yet, this is a much needed debate: government policy will remain peripheral unless it is understood that the rhetoric of victimhood is frequently ignored by the women it seeks to assist" (2009, p. 1133). These individuals have power, expertise, and knowledge, and others can learn from them on both individual and systemic levels. Understanding every individual is capable of agential choice shifts the kaleidoscope and subsequently changes the view. This kaleidoscopic shift creates space for different kinds of identities and practices to emerge that integrate empowered choice and agency.

Wendy Babcock, a former sex worker and activist who took her life on August 9, 2011, is an example of an individual who has helped others make this kaleidoscopic shift as well as worked to make sex worker safety a material condition in Toronto. Tonya Gulliver (2011), in her article written to honor her close friend Wendy Babcock, mentioned Wendy had "won the first Public Health Champion award from the City of Toronto in 2008 for her activist work including 'co-initiating a partnership with the Toronto Police Services to ensure sex workers can report incidents of assault without fear of persecution or prosecution, and being a member of the advisory group to the Special Victims Unit'" ("Mourning the passing of Wendy Babcock"; City of Toronto, 2010). This activist work is an example of a practical, concrete action that helps solve the problem of violence and manifests agential choice.

Figure 6.1 provides a visual representation of the "victim" status and the problems reinforced based on this status alone. Language reflects beliefs and values, and this language can even hold one's beliefs hostage to some degree when the concepts are not questioned and examined. Holding these ideas and practices up to the mirror creates space for material change.

AGENCY AND DECRIMINALIZATION

The criminalization, decriminalization, and legalization of prostitution have been debated in numerous formats around myriad issues. Worldwide, there are varieties of systems that range from legalization, which subjects the activity to various levels of government control, to decriminalization, which makes the activity no longer subject to criminal charges. In the case of prostitution, scholars argue criminalization often increases harm to people participating in these actions because they are forced to negotiate quickly due to their fear of arrest and cannot take the precautions necessary, such as screening clients or hiring a bodyguard, to help ensure safety. For example, Lutnick and Cohan (2009) explore the relationship between criminalization of sex work and HIV prevention from sex workers' perspectives and found "The majority [of sex workers] voiced a preference for removing statutes that criminalize sex work in order to facilitate a social and political environment where they had legal rights and could seek help when they were victims of violence" (p. 38). Studies such as this one begin to examine how the wires of the bird cage come together to oppress and can be designed differently to provide greater safety, health, freedom, and support for individuals who exchange sex. As English and Gender Studies Professor Anne McClintock (1993) argues:

> Most sex workers insist that the laws punish rather than protect them. Why, they ask, should men be punished for paying them, but not punished for raping or robbing them? Far from protecting women, abolitionist laws only deepen the dangers. Where prostitution remains criminalized, sex workers cannot alert the police to the existence of dangerous clients, of slave-brothels, of violent pimps, or battery or rape, for by coming forward they implicate themselves in a criminal trade, and immediately face—under different legal systems—summary arrest, jail, exorbitant fines, deportation, loss of custody of their children, confiscation of their property, eviction from their homes, and possible arrest of their loved ones. (p. 3)

Some residents advocate for the decriminalization of consensual, adult prostitution in the interests of freedom, human rights, and safety. For example, in October 2004, *The New York Times* reported on a "Bid to Decriminalize Prostitution in Berkeley" (Marshall 2004). This ordinance, although defeated, received support from nearly four out of ten Berkeley voters and would have shown the city's support for the repeal of prostitution laws, direct the City Council to lobby in favor of repealing these laws, and ask that enforcing existing prostitution laws remain the lowest priority of the Berkeley Police Department (Sex Workers Outreach Project, "Why You Should Vote Yes on Measure Q"). In November 2008, residents in San Francisco voted on Proposition K, a ballot measure that would have decriminalized prostitution in the city. Again, the measure failed, but was supported by 41 percent (2009, Smart Voter, "Proposition K").

As an alternative to blanket criminalization, Sociologist Ronald Weitzer (2012), in *Legalizing Prostitution*, argues "because prostitution manifests itself in fundamentally different ways on the street and indoor venues" a two-track policy would address some of the problems of criminalization. His policy would: "(1) target resources toward the reduction of street prostitution and (2) relax enforcement against indoor actors who are operating consensually" (p. 53). Weitzer creates these two tiers because of the difficulties associated with street prostitution, arguing it is not a harmless vice because it adversely affects the quality of life for some communities and, as he rightly argues, "is a multifaceted *social problem* whose harms are not reducible to its illegality" (p.58). As he states: "The push factors that lead individuals into street prostitution (e.g., poverty, unemployment, running away from abusive parents) will not be alleviated if street-level transactions are simply decriminalized" (p. 58). While his assessment is correct, continued criminalization of street-level sex work can actually lead to greater harms. Weitzer argues street prostitution be treated as a social problem rather than a "narrow law enforcement problem" in order to reduce its prevalence. Inherent to his design is that resources be diverted from control of indoor prostitution to street-level prostitution, with the priority being to protect prostitutes from violence and assist them in leaving the streets (p. 57). Although decriminalizing indoor prostitution would increase autonomy, it does not necessarily follow that the special needs he mentions as specifically related to street-based sex work (drug addiction, sexual trauma, social stigma, arrest records, and physical and mental health problems) would be alleviated through this two-tier system. Maintaining tiers within sex work, especially in relationship to illegal (street-based) and legal (indoor), although meant to curb some of the problems the neighborhoods experience, further marginalizes those on the street as victims and therefore not fully "choosing" this work.

Sociologist Wendy Chapkis (1997) calls for decriminalization of all consensual sexual activity, explaining:

> The state should not be in the position of criminalizing adult sexual behavior whether in the context of loving relationships, recreational encounters, or commercial transactions. Instead, our collective resources should be devoted to teaching respect for sexual diversity and creating conditions under which consent can be made more meaningful. (p. 213–14)

Criminalization of prostitution, on the whole, does not lead to reduction in the behavior and oftentimes creates circumstances that make people who exchange sex more vulnerable to violence. And although decriminalization would not end social stigma, a criminal record creates additional hardship because it often negatively impacts one's ability to obtain employment and housing. The financial resources required to enforce and house those convicted of these crimes are also high. Currently, the State of Texas is rethinking its policy (State of Texas, 2003) of making repeat offenders subject to felony charges. In the article "Texas rethinks law making repeat prostitution a felony," (2012) author Mike Ward states:

> But now, with more than 350 prostitutes—most from Houston and Dallas—occupying bunks in the state prison system, and dozens more serving time for drug and theft charges related to the sex trade, questions are being raised about whether the enhanced criminal charge is a waste of money. For about one-fourth the cost, such nonviolent, low-level criminals could be rehabilitated in community-based programs aimed at curing their addictions to alcohol and drugs.

Although the focus here is still on the "rehabilitation" of "low-level criminals," it is obvious criminalization is not a deterrent or a solution.

Recently there have been significant challenges and victories won by sex workers at state and local levels. These challenges to existing laws criminalizing prostitution are based on safety, liberty, and equal representation. For example, in 2007 a group run by and for people involved in street-based sex work in Vancouver wanted to address the intense violence and marginalization they experience and therefore joined together to challenge the laws that criminalize adult prostitution. Upon filing a constitutional challenge to the laws, the case was dismissed in part because the judge found the group did not have "public interest standing" to bring the case to court, meaning the organization could not challenge the laws because it was not at risk of being charged under the laws in question. Therefore, the law of standing, or the question of under what circumstances a court can grant "public interest standing," became the central issue. West Coast Legal Education and Action Fund (LEAF), a Canadian organization that "works to achieve equality by changing historic patterns of discrimination against women through BC based equality rights litigation, law reform, and public legal education,"[1] together with their coalition partners, argued:

> that representative groups like the Sex Workers United Against Violence Society (SWUAV) should be allowed to bring forward important constitutional cases on behalf of those who do not have effective access to justice on their own. [. . . They] argued that the test for public interest standing must be interpreted in a manner that is consistent with the principles of substantive equality and contextualized by an understanding of the barriers marginalized communities face in accessing the courts. (SCC decision affirms equal access 2012)

In the *SWUAV v. Attorney General of Canada* case, Canada's Supreme Court unanimously ruled "a former sex worker and an organization run by and for street-based sex workers should be granted public interest standing to challenge the laws related to adult prostitution" (Bennett 2012). As the ruling states:

> being a witness and a party are two very different things. In this case, the record shows that there were no sex workers in the Downtown Eastside neighbourhood of Vancouver willing to bring a comprehensive challenge forward. They feared loss of privacy and safety and increased violence by clients. Also, their spouses, friends, family members and/ or members of their community may not know that they are or were involved in sex work or that they are or were drug users. They have children that they fear will be removed by child protection authorities. Finally, bringing such challenge, they fear, may limit their current or future education or employment opportunities (Affidavit of Jill

Creating Agential Choice from Cages of Oppression 143

Chettiar, September 26, 2008, at paras. 16–18 (A.R., vol. IV, at pp. 184–85). (Qtd. in Bennett 2012).

The conditions of loss of privacy and safety as well as increased violence from clients are real threats that have been systemically acknowledged as deterrents to one's ability to gain "public interest standing" in its most narrow definition, thereby allowing for the system to further marginalize those individuals from speaking on their own behalf. Like many aspects of systemic policy and legislation, multiple layers exist. Criminalization of prostitution was initially challenged to address the effects it has on the violence and marginalization of people involved in street-based sex work. This argument has not yet been heard, because the issue was sidetracked by questioning the organization's ability to even have this issue heard by the courts. Through this ruling, rhetorical and material representation was addressed, thereby making space for marginalized individuals to inform the courts and subsequent legislation.

Likewise, Louisiana's Solicitation of a Crime Against Nature (SCAN), which dates back to the nineteenth century, was "founded on moral disapproval of what kinds of sex acts are acceptable. The statute criminalizes sexual conduct considered contrary to the laws of nature because it is non procreative and historically associated with homosexuality" (Center for Constitutional Rights "Louisiana's Crime Against Nature Law"). Women With a Vision (WWAV) has been working on this legislation for years and outlines the initial problem as follows:

> In Louisiana, allegations of solicitation of oral or anal sex in exchange for compensation can be prosecuted either under the SCAN statute or under the prostitution statute. Though the conduct alleged is identical, for decades a SCAN conviction has resulted in harsher sentences and higher fines—as well as mandatory registration as a sex offender for periods of 15 years to life. The new law equalizes the penalties for SCAN and prostitution going forward, though not retroactively. (WWAV 2011)

The mandate that those convicted register as sex offenders further marginalized them because this status is so public and associated with "force, lack of consent, or children" (Center for Constitutional Rights). For example, as the Center for Constitutional Rights points out:

> For individuals convicted under the statute, sex offender registration has a devastating effect on every aspect of their lives, including their access to housing, employment, social services, and shelter in the event of an emergency or natural disaster.
> Registration is required annually for between 15 years and life. You must carry a state ID with the words "SEX OFFENDER" in bright

orange capital letters. If you fail to pay annual registration fees, you are subject to prison time or a $500 fine.

You must mail neighbors postcards notifying them of your name, address, description, and your Crime Against Nature conviction—which requires that you spend additional hundreds of dollars every time you move. Your name, address and photograph will appear on a sex offender website, and you may be required to publish your name and Crime Against Nature by Solicitation conviction in the local newspaper. You must disclose the fact that you are registered as a sex offender to your landlord, employer, school, parks department, community centers, and place of worship.

Many individuals have been denied access to homeless shelters and drug treatment because such facilities do not accept those labeled as sex offenders. And in the case of an evacuation in a natural disaster or other emergency, you will not be allowed to stay with your children or family in a publicly-run emergency shelter, and you must present yourself as a registered sex offender in all emergency situations.

SCAN exemplifies the extreme level of marginalization that can occur based on criminalization of certain sexual acts in exchange for money. And as Haywood points out, it also reveals how this level of criminalization greatly decreases an individual's ability to obtain the basic necessities for living.

Recent legislation eliminating the mandatory sex offender registration requirement for individuals convicted of Louisiana's Solicitation of a Crime Against Nature (SCAN) was signed into law on June 28, 2011. This legislation also allowed police to target people of color and transgender individuals disproportionally. As Deon Haywood, Executive Director of WWAV, explained:

> For over two decades now, people—largely low-income women of color, including transgender women—have been branded with this scarlet letter simply because they were convicted under this archaic, discriminatory law [...] For the women I work with, and for LGBT young people, this has created an almost insurmountable barrier to much-needed housing, employment, treatment, and services. At long last, the legislature has equalized penalties for the two offenses going forward. But we will continue to fight for justice for all those still living under the penalties of the past. There is still serious work to be done. (Ibid.)

The Center for Constitutional Rights substantiates this claim:

> In Orleans Parish, almost 40 percent of registered sex offenders are on the registry because they were convicted under the Crime Against Nature statute—despite the fact that their convictions did not involve

Creating Agential Choice from Cages of Oppression   145

any force, lack of consent or children. Furthermore, 75 percent of those registered are women, and 79 percent of them are African American. ("Louisiana's Crime Against Nature Law")

As Jordan Flaherty, a journalist and community organizer, has revealed:

> New Orleans' Black and transgender community members and advocates complain of rampant and systemic harassment and discrimination from the city's police force, including sexual violence and arrest without cause. Activists hope that public outrage at recent revelations of widespread police violence and corruption will offer an opportunity to make changes in police behavior and practice. (Flaherty 2010b)[2]

Andrea Ritchie, co-counsel for WWAV and expert on US policing of LGBT people, emphasizes the importance of community groups and action in this struggle for individual rights:

> The grassroots and national leadership of Women with a Vision in tirelessly raising this issue for the past three years is nothing short of heroic. [. . .] This victory is a product of collaboration between community groups, legal advocacy organizations and legislators seeking justice on behalf of the women and LGBT youth suffering from the discriminatory effects of SCAN—it is clear that community organizing can make real change. (Flaherty 2011b)

Like the issues raised about criminalization by my participants, these examples reveal the difficulties placed on individuals due to criminal law and its repercussions. They exemplify how laws can be used to target individuals who may already be marginalized based on their identity as a person of color, transgender/transsexual individual, or anyone presumed to be a person who participates in street-based sex work. These cases simultaneously reveal how, through great energy, persistence, and resources, individuals can systemically challenge and change legislation and its impact on surrounding material conditions.[3]

AGENTIAL CHOICE MEANS CHANGE IS NOT NECESSARY

The belief that change is *not* necessary is a basis for agential choice because it resides in responsible rhetorical agency. In other words, social service agents do not assume they know better than their clients. Chelley, an Hispanic heterosexual female in her late 40s who worked in community outreach for a mental health organization, responded to my question, "Do you think they should change?":

No, if they don't want to, no. I don't think you should force a person. Because its not going to work anyway. So if they're happy where they're at, let them be. As long as they are able to survive ok for themselves and they're not putting themselves in really bad harm, you know what I mean?

Dr. Veronica Alvarez, a 48-year-old heterosexual Latina woman and Project Director of an HIV-prevention program reiterates this belief:

Because I don't think everyone wants to change, nor do they need to change. People need to be able to do what they want to do and make those decisions. But I think that there are a lot of women who have been put into a corner and have not had that option. So that there need to be services that give women a respite and that are, again, respectful, feminist-oriented, and provide avenues for women to explore who they are, who they want to be, what they want to do, and provide linkages for them to integrate them as they want to be integrated. And help them, give them the tools to help them determine that, not be corralled into things because someone says that this is what they need to do.

Joan, a white, 43-year-old, bisexual woman and an activist with a sex worker rights organization, said:

I don't know what the answer is. I really don't, and I also think some people choose to live in ways that we don't understand. And its not our job to help them not live that way if that's what they choose either. But you can't help but think that if we didn't have the rampant poverty in this neighborhood and in Nemez and people could get a living wage and support their kids without a PhD, maybe they wouldn't be there.

Two activists explicitly show how this attitude is the basis for agential choice. Valarie, an Hispanic heterosexual female in her mid 30s and a program manager at a behavioral health agency, responded to my question about her role within the system:

I guess it would be advocating for these women, understanding where they're coming from, and trying to the best of our ability to put ourselves in their place first of all, and teaching them, you know, not everyone out there is out to get you and we are only here, again, to help you get wherever it is that you may want to get, even if it's not very far or even if I don't agree with it. So I think, more than anything, it's just giving them the right—the right to be who they want to be and giving them the right to speak up.

Approaching the situation with the assumption that "change" is not required or necessary can be the first step toward achieving agential choice in a street-based sex work context.

AGENTIAL CHOICE AND CHOOSING SEX WORK

If change is not necessary, is it possible to choose sex work from a place of agential choice? As I try to answer this question, I think back to what I believed about sex work when I started this research. I do not remember explicitly, but I am fairly certain I believed it was "wrong". I certainly understood people did it for particular reasons and didn't blame them for making these choices, but I believed most would not exchange sex if they had other viable options. I'm fairly certain all sex workers also fell into one category for me. I wasn't nearly as familiar with the different types of sex work that existed, but I assumed people who exchange sex for money would rather be doing other things if they paid equally as well. I was wrong. There are many, many gradations of personal preference when it comes to sex work, similar to so many other professions. There are people who choose this work as a profession because they love it, and there are those who choose it because they can make money in a short amount of time. This choice then makes it possible for them to spend more time with their children or on other pursuits.

I have learned choice must be the focus as well as the solution. And one can only make a choice when she is coming to that decision from a position of power. There are many gradations of power that constrain our choices. Let's take, for example, my occupation as a teacher. If I hate my job, hate going to work, and only do it for the money, then that is a choice I am making, but I would be happier if I were making this choice from a place of passion or love for the job rather than simply for money. If I love painting but cannot make my living as a painter, then I am not choosing to teach from the same empowered place in which I would reside if I were choosing to paint. If I were able to earn the same amount of money as a painter, then I would love my job and be choosing it as a passion and a livelihood. And if my partner forced me to be a teacher, and I knew I would be emotionally or physically abused if I didn't continue my job, that would be a less empowered choice. And if I were living on the street and I could trade teaching for food, and that was the only thing I could do, I would continue to teach, but it would be an even less empowered choice. These levels of empowerment relate to the degree to which I feel like an agent in my life. I choose what I eat, where I live, where I work, and what I do for a living. And each of these choices are made continuously and add to my own power and feeling of power over and within my life. The more I make choices due to outside forces (what others may think, livelihood, a gun held to my head) the less of an agent I become. And as I continue to make those choices to achieve the desired outcome at the expense of my agenthood, the less powerful I feel. I may even begin to feel badly about myself because I am not in control of my choices and am pushed around by others' expectations or contextual circumstances—I am not making choices from my center based on my greatest good. And the more I feel badly about myself, the more difficult it becomes to find agential power within me—which is required for authentic choice.

It is not immoral or wrong to exchange sex for money or other gain. It *is* harmful to make choices based on external factors or needs that do not align with an individual's best interest. This same stance would apply whether the choice was to teach (my chosen profession) or to exchange sex. It is not immoral or wrong to teach, it is harmful to choose to teach if I am not choosing it as an empowered agent of my own life. Many sex workers choose to exchange sex as empowered agents. The issue is not about exchanging sex— it is about being in a position where one can make empowered choices. That is the goal and problem I am far more interested in addressing.

Most of the women on the street I met and spent time with were not making the decision to exchange sex from a position of agential choice. They were making these choices based on incredibly powerful external needs, whether it be for food and shelter, to care for one's children, or to satisfy an addiction. All of these external needs demanded attention and powerfully influenced the choices they made. But the women were often not choosing to exchange sex as agents in control of their lives.

This philosophical exploration is not new, as empowerment is integral to many programs. And yet emphasizing this point, and defining this lack of agential choice as central in the debates about exchanging sex should be the priority. When this problem is named and defined, then different solutions become apparent. For example, criminalization of prostitution does not lead to one's empowerment and ability to make agential choices. Although it is possible to create an environment where a person is required to abstain from drugs for an extended period of time, which can then encourage her to choose a drug-free life, criminalization also causes problems that reduces one's agential power or choice such as fines, a criminal record that can make it more difficult to find employment or housing, and separation from families and children.

A person who exchanges sex for money is not necessarily exploited by others or making a choice without power. Most of the women I interviewed did not choose to exchange sex from an empowered position, and they often believed it was wrong, immoral, and/or physically disgusting. It makes sense if someone believes something is wrong and she engages in that activity, she will not feel good about her choice. And given that exchanging sex can be an extremely intimate activity, it also stands to reason she would not feel good about her body when she engages in these activities. She may feel good about her choice to feed her family, but having to choose to participate in an activity one does not feel good about does not add to one's agential power for that and future choices. The cycle then continues, for in addition to making a choice she does not feel good about, having made that choice leads to decreased feelings of self-worth and power over one's life. And if she believes exchanging sex is immoral and wrong, then it is likely she will feel even worse about herself as a result of participating in this activity. Social stigma and criminalization serve to intensify these feelings.

Creating Agential Choice from Cages of Oppression 149

A person who believes exchanging sex for money, or sex work, is a viable choice (meaning not immoral or wrong) would not have these same feelings of shame and disgust toward her body or her choice. Even if this person was forced to choose to exchange sex based on external forces, this choice would not be as difficult to face emotionally because the derogatory personal beliefs and values about the activity would not be present. There were examples of people among my participants who found a source of power in these choices. For instance, when I asked Karen, a 49-year-old, white, heterosexual woman who had immigrated to the United States what her reasons were for exchanging sex for money, she said:

> Putting money in my pocket. You know, it made me feel better about me. That I was kind of, my independence, my self-esteem, basically, and that I had a choice. You know, if I was in that frame of mind with all the issues that I was dealing with, and I wanted to escape for awhile, well, yeah, I'd use it for drugs. But if it was like I want to treat myself to snow cones, I had a craving for those (laugh), yeah, I wanted some of them (laugh), you know?

Likewise, Lily, a white, lesbian woman in her mid 40s and an activist and former HIV outreach worker, found:

> When I was doing work with street-working sex workers, the philosophy of the program I was working for was these poor women had nothing else to do but sell their bodies for drugs and that's why they're doing this, and if they weren't addicted then they wouldn't be doing sex work because its disgusting and degrading. And that's what I heard from a lot of women, that they hated it. But I also heard from women that this was a source of power for them, that this was a source of pride, they were good at it, they had people coming in for a convention once a year and that person would call them and say "Hey, I'm renting a hotel room," and they would spend the week with that person.

Jill: This is with street workers?
Lily: Yeah, street workers. And I had women tell me "The only place in my life that I can say no to a man is in my relationship with a client." You know, they couldn't say that in their families, they couldn't say that in their primary relationships. And I started to think that illegalizing sex work and stigmatizing sex workers was probably not the best way to empower any women [laughs].

Research Coordinator at Framework Housing Association, Rachel Harding and Criminologist Paul Hamilton discuss the role respect for a person's choices plays in developing a trusting relationship:

Respecting a woman's decision to sex work, however diminished her ability to choose for herself might be, is crucial in demonstrating a non-judgemental attitude towards vulnerable women. Therefore, it is the construction of a professional relationship of trust between a support worker and a homeless woman (who has or continues to sex work) that is key to beginning the work of housing and support provision, and thus to minimize the risk with which they are faced. (Harding and Hamilton 2009, p. 1132)

The ultimate goal is to create a society where agential choice is a reality and where people can freely choose between lots of options. These choices begin, as Cooper explains, in responsible rhetorical agency, or that which occurs when one "recognize[s] both speakers and listeners as agents in persuasion [and] as people who are free to change their minds" (p. 441). There are people who choose sex work over other forms of employment or labor. One cannot separate those on the street from the debate about sex work and its criminalization or legalization. Yes, street-based sex work must be considered within its own context, but it should not inform, wholly, the debate on criminalization and legalization of sex work. Sex work is about individual expression and sexual desire, who can participate in these activities, under what circumstances, and with who, and who has the power to decide. Sex workers embody an array of conflicting themes because they are marginalized, glorified, awed, and hated. Just as it is impossible to put lawyers in a conditional box about their work, the same is true when making encompassing claims about sex work.

PRACTICAL APPLICATIONS: OPPORTUNITIES FOR AGENTIAL CHOICE

An ideology and discourse of agential choice is imperative, especially in light of increasingly difficult economic situations where resources for public health are steadily decreasing. But what does an ideology and discourse of agential choice look like? The role of agency begins in one's own awareness of language and the construction of problems and solutions, as one example. This awareness shifts both the viewer as well as what is viewed, and the viewer plays an active role in making meaning. A shift in the kaleidoscope of meaning creates space for new understandings—a new collage—and therefore the realization of material change. I present the following examples that offer myriad perspectives on agential choice that can be facilitated in a sex-work context. Within these examples, opportunities for agential choice exist—meaning the woman is ultimately in control of her goals and choices. Because each one represents different aspects, I let them largely speak for themselves. The agency of the woman who is exchanging sex is central, and the speaker, or public figure, makes space for that agency

Creating Agential Choice from Cages of Oppression 151

and the woman's ability to make her own best choices. Empowered with the knowledge and respect these individuals and organizations place in the woman, she is better able to make an agential choice based on her own goals and priorities. When a social service agent, for example, respects the individual's knowledge and experiences, trusting she is making the best choice for herself, the agent not only creates space for agential choice based on the individual's goals and priorities, she also learns from those working in street economies. The relationship is mutually beneficial.

RETHINKING "VICTIM" STATUS

"I think these women are amazing."

Dr. Veronica Alvarez: I think people have images of who these women are in their mind. And the reality is that they're no different than us; they're exactly like us. And they have the same hopes and dreams and the same fears, except perhaps they haven't had opportunities that some of us have had, that set us on a different path. [. . .] I think that the public perception is not a positive one. These women have been traumatized, and they've been rejected and made invisible in certain rooms.
Jill: Anything else you'd say about what the public thinks?
Dr. Veronica Alvarez: The public judges, immediately judges the worth of a person without knowing the person.
Jill: Judges how?
Dr. Veronica Alvarez: Again, puritanical notions and judges a woman based on what she's had to go through to survive.
[. . .]
Jill: How does your organization view these women?
Dr. Veronica Alvarez: They view these women with great respect. They're welcome here. They're treated as knowledgeable about their own lives and as having life experience that can educate us.
Jill: What do you think—well, let me ask this first: How do you see these women?
Dr. Veronica Alvarez: I think these women are amazing. I love to see these women, like in the groups that I've had, when they come in and . . . There's a paper that I've drafted up, which I have, which I need to push to completion. But I talk about the beauty of these women, where they may come in and are coming from really difficult places. But when there's a purpose and a place where they're respected, they take on, you know, they flower. The reading groups, for example: The women each had a copy of the book, they had their notebook and papers and pen, and they'd come to the groups. They'd begin to call the groups all sorts of things: my

class, my teachers, this and that. But they'd come to groups early. They'd be sitting in the waiting room with their—and walking out in public with their books and, you know, coming to work, coming to women's groups where we talk about things, where we read and we challenged notions of what reading and literacy are . . . by taking . . . making a very public group activity where everyone read whatever they wanted, and we read orally together as a community and paused the reading because the more important stories are our own. Then they would discuss in class and share, and I think that was novel for women to be with other women in ways that are not competitive and not based on survival. And I just think they're amazing.

Dr. Alvarez, a 48-year-old heterosexual Latina woman and the Project Director of an HIV-prevention program, emphasizes that these women are respected and viewed as a source of knowledge. These individuals participate in activities that take a tremendous amount of courage. They upset gender roles and prescriptive ideas about women's sexuality. Sex workers charge money to participate in sexual activities that have been historically, legally, and psychologically demanded to be given for "free."[4] Transgender and other marginalized individuals find the courage to live in a culture where hate-crime laws have been developed in response to the crimes that target them based solely on their gender and sexuality. Simply interacting with society exposes one to violence. This perspective practiced by Dr. Alvarez and her colleagues lays the groundwork for agential choice.

This lived, daily courage does not necessarily translate into self-esteem. In response to my question, how do these women see themselves, Dr. Veronica Alvarez replied:

Dr. Veronica Alvarez: I think that when they come in, they may not see themselves very positively. Very low self-esteem. They believe what they've heard from what's been told to them and [how] they've been treated, and they think that they're deserving of that. And I think that when they're in groups where they're treated respectfully and encouraged to contribute and allowed to interact with the curriculum . . . The curriculum also is designed to be responsive to different learning styles, and so the information is presented [in] different ways . . . we interact with it differently, and it doesn't isolate anyone because they don't get it. And I think that they see themselves as . . . We encourage the women to ask questions when they have them. They ask questions in groups. They can submit questions in a suggestion box, and we do that deliberately because we want them to pose questions to others, not take things for granted. Push and ask questions and demand.

Creating Agential Choice from Cages of Oppression   153

Jill: What do you think the differences are between the public perception, the way your area views it, you view it, and the women view it? What are the differences?

Dr. Veronica Alvarez: I think one of the biggest differences is doing away with classifications of individuals and status, and accepting that everyone is knowledgeable about their own lives. I think that the public is handicapped if they can't do that; and that women, because of the lives they have experienced, the way they've been treated, it's very difficult for women to believe otherwise, when that's all they've been told and if they've only been treated a certain way.

Two aspects of Dr. Alvarez's statement lend themselves explicitly to agential choice: first, accepting everyone is knowledgeable about their lives. Here, the trust is placed on the individual, believing she knows herself best and the social service agent can not speak for or tell her what is right for her. And secondly, the *public* is handicapped if they cannot recognize this knowledge. Dr. Alvarez places the responsibility for this trust and respect squarely on the public's shoulders. They/we are handicapped—meaning there is a lack of integral ability—if we do not recognize these basic human aspects.

Another example arose when Dr. Alvarez and I discussed condom use. Chapter 5 explores the responsibility that is placed on the women to use condoms as well as the difficulties some women encounter in trying to employ their use. In the example that follows, Dr. Alvarez reveals how a discussion about condom use can be grounded in one's own agential choice to take care of one's body and overall health:

[W]e promote condom use. For those women who aren't able to convince their partners to use condoms, we talk about and demonstrate the female condom. And we also discuss and demonstrate and have the women, they actually do the demonstration on putting on a condom or the female condom on models, and also using dental dams, so that it's not just for heterosexual women, but all women. [. . .] [Our program tries] to provide information and opportunities for women to engage with information and topics. And provide testing and give women tools to make decisions that are more informed, and then they can determine what is important to them in their lives, but that they have information. [. . .] Yeah, when I say information, it's more to connect women to access resources and ways of accessing information and those resources. For their health. [. . .] The nurse makes charts up when she has a 1-on-1. Our women get first numbers. We can take up to 6 women a day and the first 16, and they go in a group and that's to create a different dynamic about "This is about our health, and we're happy to be here because we want to make sure we confront whatever it is." Yeah, it's really very different than when you see the other clients at the clinic. [. . .] It's a healthy way of looking at it. And also, we're trying to, as we've done in the curriculum, do away with some of the shame associated with talking about STDs or being screened for STDs, and saying "This is a healthy approach. If we have something, we just need to take care of it like we do anything else." And expect that our healthcare provider will be respectful and not judgmental. And if they are [judgmental], then they need to turn it back on them and let whoever know and not subject ourselves to that.

Dr. Veronica Alvarez emphasizes her organization's role in providing information and education while supporting the women to make their own decisions. An ideology of "taking care of ourselves" rather than shame permeates the discussions. The women are also encouraged to expect an atmosphere of respect for the individual from the provider. These strategies encourage women to move from a belief she has little power over her sexual health to someone who views herself as an agent who makes decisions about her health that serve her best interests.

Dr. Julie Everett, a 36-year-old lesbian woman and a medical doctor in the HIV/STI division at the county health department, outlines her and the clinic's role in providing an environment for agential choice:

> [HIV prevention program] clients come to our clinic and they've already talked with our nurse, who goes to The Shelter [a live-in facility for women], wherever they are hanging out, to sort of talk about sexual health. And so by the time women come to the clinic, they're pretty much on board about "You know, I really want to know what's going on with my body." So it's not just like a cold thing, you know, "I'm in crisis." So people are really coming in to get checked out. So this was a woman, a middle-aged woman, who had done sex work on and off for probably the last six or seven years, substance-involved, who I don't know exactly how she got to the rehab center—that didn't come up—but, again, wanted to . . . just sort of framed it around health, wanted to come in and make sure things were okay. And that's what we tried to do, and that was sort of directly from our nurse. She was like, "Yeah, I think it's a good time. I wanna get checked out." So essentially, she came in, was self-identified as someone who was trading sex for drugs on and off for awhile, had a boyfriend who was sort of an on-and-off partner, lived in Nemez, involved with, um, actually interestingly dual stimulants. You know, we often see people who are really involved with crack or cocaine or really involved with meth [methamphetamine], and we often don't see people sort of blending them. But she had sort of blended those, which I thought was interesting. And we offered her a variety of tests—some of them she had already had with our nurse—and

we just talked about sort of general health stuff, too, because I like to . . . With women through [this organization]—and others, too, if it comes up—but just talking about taking care of your body in a variety of different ways: When was the last time you had a Pap test? Are you interested in birth control? Do you have a regular doctor? Would you like a regular doctor? Do you have other medical issues? So trying to do some wraparound healthcare for her, too, because she'd been out of medical care for a long time.

In concert with taking control of one's health, Dr. Julie Everett also advocates strongly for providers to listen and provide nonjudgmental care:

Jill: When you say "culturally responsible and appropriate care," what do you mean by that in terms of providers?

Dr. Julie Everett: Providers—so providers often think that they know exactly what people need; however, they very often don't listen to what people are really telling them or not telling them, and doing frank, open exploration to try to get to some of the issues that people really want to talk about, and a lot of the time, that has to do with issues of sexual health or sexual activity or needle use or a whole variety of things. So, culturally responsive when it's in the context of LGBT [Lesbian, Gay, Bisexual, Transgender/Transsexual] communities and health has some specific things that I like to focus on. When working with sex workers or people who identify as such, it has some other things. And the basis is in nonjudgmental care. [. . .] And if, for whatever reason, that they're unwilling to do so, to please do the kind thing and make a good referral. Because patients way too often have been literally abused by their providers, by the things that they're told or the way they're made to feel or a variety of things. [. . .] So sort of talking with our staff around, again, these issues of sensitivity: "Are you really meeting the patient where they need to be met?" You know, those sorts of things. Not making assumptions about individuals who—whether they identify as a sex worker or they've disclosed some things that would suggest that they are, to make assumptions about their sexual practice, their health, their life, that sort of thing. So that's difficult to do when you're dealing with people who, even though they do sexual health work, come in with preconceived notions of what a sex worker is, what a prostitute is, that sort of thing. [. . .] Ideally, the goal would be to provide people with services that allow them to make healthy choices, you know? So whether it's coming in for treatment to make them physically feel better or it's coming into the needle exchange for clean needles, that sort of thing, it's providing the opportunity for people to achieve health.

This example places the responsibility on the providers to listen and provide services without assuming they know what is best for their clients. The emphasis is on education as well as asking the woman questions, emphasizing her role in making decisions about her health. Respect for the woman, her choices, and her life is paramount.

"Addressing the underlying issues."

Tracy Sherlock (2011) describes an example of agential choice through access to resources. Emily Grant, the woman featured in the article, was provided housing two years prior while she was still using drugs. Part of a three-year study that provides supplemental rent money and access to support services from the Assertive Community Treatment (ACT) team,[5] Emily found an apartment in Vancouver and was housed within five days of joining the program. She has since stopped using crack cocaine and is on methadone for her heroin addiction. The rent is paid for by both the participants and the program. The participants can also choose to meet with professionals provided by the program, including psychiatrists, addiction counselors, and employment counselors. Greg Richmond, the associate director at RainCity Housing and Support Society, said: "One of the really cool things is all the choice that's involved. It's a bit radical, but we have apartments in Marpole, the west end, the east side and we let them choose [. . .] Having a home is huge—for us it's the foundation of a good life." Richmond reported 80 per cent of the participants were doing well.

Lily, a white lesbian woman in her mid 40s and an activist and former HIV outreach worker, described a similar situation in terms of "addressing the underlying issues":

> The difference is the philosophy that says "Your problems are due to the fact that you're doing sex work and you're doing drugs" versus, "You're doing sex work and you're doing drugs because you have other problems that haven't been addressed." Do you see the difference? So I think that if your coping mechanism is drugs, and you're getting money for your drugs by doing sex work that you don't want to be doing, ok, me telling you not to do sex work isn't going to help, me telling you not to do drugs isn't going to help. Addressing the underlying issues that will make you want to numb the shit out of yourself for twenty-four/seven, then maybe we can, rather than simply taking your coping mechanisms and saying, "No you don't get to have that anymore." Let me give you another coping mechanism, and then maybe we can kind of step you away from the things that are hurting you. And maybe sex work isn't hurting. Maybe that's not a problem for you. And I don't feel that I have the right to define that for someone.

Creating Agential Choice from Cages of Oppression 157

The above examples address the individual's needs rather than focusing on the more typically problematic behaviors such as drug use or exchanging sex for money. An individual's choice is also valued and trusted—where she lives and if she participates in programs. The individual is the focus and she creates the solution with external support.

Agential Choice is a Process.

Like other researchers have argued, when a person wants to leave the sex trade, it is a process, not an event.[6] I question the ideology of personal choice that becomes apparent when this process is viewed as a "success," as is the case in Sociologist Rochelle Dalla's (2006) study of 43 "street-level prostituted women" with particular emphasis on "sex-industry exit attempts" (p. 276). Dalla closes her article with the final statement:

> It is likely that each time a woman attempts to exit, she becomes a little stronger, a little more confident, and a little more committed to making a permanent lifestyle change. Certainly, to some degree, development of these attributes qualifies as "success." Even though she may return to the sex industry after attempting to leave, perhaps her next exit will be her last. (p. 290)

All of the emphasis is placed on the individual's choices and abilities to become strong, confident, and committed. Although Dalla does acknowledge the role services play in realizing a life outside of the sex trade, I question the construction of this success and failure model as being housed primarily within the individual. Simultaneously, I argue for an honoring of agential choice, whereby the individual's genuine choice and power is contextualized within a framework of material conditions that may not provide the support needed to realize and sustain a different, perhaps more "chosen," lifestyle. Rather than viewing exiting as a process, with the "exit" as the final goal and "success", the emphasis must be placed on the process of realizing agential choice. As Deon Haywood, Executive Director of Women With a Vision states: "harm reduction as a method of treatment is based on recovery by degree rather than a complete reversal in terms of lifestyle change" (Piano 2006, p. 207).

One of my participants, Evelyn, a 60-year-old heterosexual white woman and the director of a mental health counseling agency, discussed her opinion about the primary role of services:

> I think that the primary role of services is education. It's really critical that they [clients of the organization] understand what they're doing, some level of insight into what motivates their behavior, and what the consequences could be, both to their health and their safety and

socially. If we can do that, we could put a dent in this. You're not gonna stop this, because people have to live, and until we can create a venue in the society where there's options for people, where there's money, where there's jobs, where there's some sense of hope, you're gonna turn this around in very few people, because once they leave the program, all those basic things are still there. So if you can send them out knowing that they're homeless but with a better idea about how to move through things, then you've done something. Because then when it comes time to make a choice, they're gonna make a different or better choice. It may appear to be the same choice, but there's gonna be something different about it. I mean, just an example: One time, my husband, when he worked for a small agency, he had this client. The client finished treatment and went out and we never saw him again. Well, about maybe almost 10 years later, he saw my husband and he said that when he left treatment, he didn't stop using and he hadn't stopped using until a couple years before we saw him. So there were years where he finished treatment and he used and used and used. But he said, "I never forgot the things you told me. And it made a difference." So when the time came that he was going to stop, he had that background; he had those memories of the things he'd been taught. And I don't know that we can do anything more than that. Just give them a sense that there's a safe place for them—they can come back any time they want—that they've been respected and treated fairly, and they've gotten the information necessary to try to move in a different direction in their life, when they're ready to do that.

I do not argue that the emphasis here is not also on "change" and one's ability to make that change, although Evelyn points out the systemic obstacles as well as the respect she has for the choices each individual makes. She places the primary responsibility on the system, acknowledging that "choosing" to change is influenced beyond one's individual desire and is heavily grounded in one's ability to meet her basic needs. Rather than focusing on the outcome as the choice the client makes to "stop using" and maintain that abstinence, Evelyn focuses on her own responsibilities, as well as the system's, to educate and provide services.

Sociologist Brené Brown (2010) offers a description of hope grounded in agential choice rather than external pressure. Drawing on the work of C. R. Snyder, she defines hope as:

> a thought process made up of what Snyder calls a trilogy of goals, pathways, and agency. In very simple terms, hope happens when
> - We have the ability to set realistic goals (*I know where I want to go*).
> - We are able to figure out how to achieve those goals, including the ability to stay flexible and develop alternative routes (*I know how*

to get there, I'm persistent, and I can tolerate disappointment and try again).
- We believe in ourselves (*I can do this!*). (p. 65)

All of the above are grounded in personal choice and power—knowing where one wants to go, how to get there, and believing in the ability to achieve that goal. If an individual is able to identity what her goals are, can figure out how to get there, and believes she can achieve them, she is acting from a position of agential choice.

CONCLUSION: SYSTEMIC OPPORTUNITIES FOR STREET-BASED SEX WORK AND SOCIETY

Language has power and influences our beliefs, actions, and material reality. Language and its subsequent effects on belief systems and actions ultimately influence what choices, options, and paths are and are not available to an individual, which can then further constrain or create opportunities for action and change. The way the problems and solutions are defined directly affects how resources are distributed, and individuals and systems are intricately intertwined. Learning from individuals creates space to better understand and change these systems for the betterment of the individuals they serve.

Many calls for change focus on working toward equality of men and women, empowering the workforce, decriminalizing prostitution, forming unity among activists, and creating rehabilitation programs. Sociologist Wendy Chapkis (1997) outlines her goals for change as follows:

- A fundamental redistribution of wealth and power between women and men, as well as among women and men. Gross economic disparity between classes, races, sexes, and nations produces conditions of economic coercion and desperation that undermine meaningful "choice." No woman should be forced to engage in prostitution—or any other form of productive or reproductive labor—against her will.
- An organized and empowered workforce. A feminist prostitution politics that honors labor would evaluate policies on the basis of whether they serve the interests of workers rather than employers or clients. Prostitutes, as all others who labor for a living, should be guaranteed full workers' rights and benefits. (pp. 213–14)

Others focus on education and drug rehabilitation. For example, in their article on prostitutes and AIDS medical doctor Judith Cohen, public health expert Priscilla Alexander, and medical doctor Constance Wofsy (1988) write:

160 *Street Sex Workers' Discourse*

We recommend local, state, and federal funds be allocated for education programs directed at prostitutes—particularly street prostitutes, because of the higher prevalence of intravenous drug use at that level of the industry. We also recommend funding be provided for increased drug and alcohol treatment slots for women, especially women with

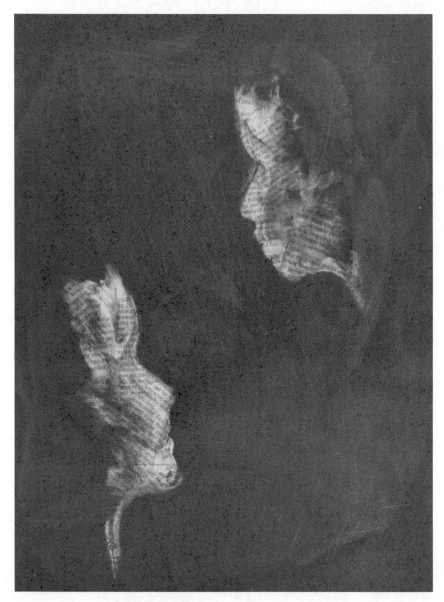

Figure 6.2   *Profiles*. Illustration by Kristine Richardson.

children, and for job training and other transitional programs for those who no longer want to work as prostitutes. (p. 20)

The criminalization and stigma associated with both drug use and exchanging sex reinforces the cycle of violence and pain. Arresting women in order to provide them with access to substance abuse treatment is not the best course of action and should not be the priority. Although currently prostitution is illegal, rather than further penalizing those participating in these activities, the focus should be on addressing systemic violence and individuals needs.

ALTERNATIVE WAYS OF SPEAKING AND THINKING ABOUT THE EXCHANGE OF SEX FOR MONEY OR DRUGS—SYSTEMIC VIOLENCE AND INJUSTICE

In order to envision alternative ways of speaking and thinking about exchanging sex for money or drugs, society's responsibility for systemic violence and injustice must be addressed. English Professor John D. Ramage (2006) explores "the Imperative to Create Uncertainty" and argues the ability "to deliberately and regularly challenge [one's] assumptions about the meanings of things and to remain open to contrary interpretations" is challenging at the very least, and yet, "the costs associated with a failure to modify our interpretations are too high not to try" (p. 150). One way to take responsibility for these interpretations lies in language awareness and choice, which then impact how the problems and solutions are constructed and understood. The ideologies of personal responsibility and societal indifference and ignorance are also established in this language. I offer the following suggestions as a way to begin modifying the discourse and ideologies surrounding the exchange of sex for money or drugs.

- **Agency and Language.** Because the term *prostitute* has historically offered less agency and is considered derogatory by those in and outside the sex industry both on and off the street, using this word reduces individuals to one activity in which they participate. This term could be compared to people being identified as murderers, thieves, etc., where one negative behavior is emphasized over all others. This same categorization occurs when people are referred to as teachers, pilots, and technicians, for example, and yet the assumption is although the person is being defined by their occupation, their lives are not limited to this one activity or behavior. When a person is primarily identified by a negative, and specifically illegal, behavior, this activity tends to overshadow the "personhood" of the individual. Therefore, the words *prostitute* and *whore* should not be used to talk about women, men, and transgendered individuals who participate in these

activities. *Rather, a description of the actions should be used. Even more importantly, the person participating in these activities should be asked how they identify and prefer to be identified by others.*
- **Sex Workers at the Forefront.** Consider the women, men, and transgender individuals who sell sex experts—working with legislators, neighborhood association leaders, social service agents, etc.—to resolve community conflicts, share resources, and address individual needs. Sex workers must be at the forefront of these organizations to help define the needs and how best to meet them. They *are* the experts and can help provide the best "solutions" about criminalization, drug policy, homelessness, personal responsibility, as well as systemic change and how these systems impact their positions and agential choice in the community. Their lives, perspectives, and how they understand the material conditions in which they live can inform laypeople about these systems in direct and tangible ways. *Sex workers must be valued for their expertise and therefore compensated for their contributions to help improve current material conditions.*
- **Decriminalization, Anti-Criminalization, and other Policy Alternatives.** Numerous experts have argued for a change in laws against prostitution. As Shannon et al. (2009a) argue, their findings "provide new evidence to support global calls for the removal of criminal sanctions targeting sex workers, including statements by UNAIDS, and further support the need for systematic evaluations of the effects of legal strategies on health outcomes among female sex workers and clients" (pp. 5–6). As Emi Koyama (2012) argues in her blog post:

  We need an anti-criminalization movement, not decriminalization movement. An anti-criminalization movement is not just about sexual freedom or "right to choose," although it supports these ideas too. More fundamentally, it is about fighting for social and economic justice in the face of pervasive state violence against communities of color, immigrants, street youth, drug users, and others.

  Sex workers and individuals involved in street-based sex work must be at the forefront and involved at all levels of this policy revision.
- **Rights-Based rather than Law Enforcement/Prosecution-Based Approach.** Although Lerum et al. (2012) are speaking primarily about the Trafficking in Persons [TIP] report as well as other related trafficking legislation, this same argument should be applied to the criminalization of prostitution and related crimes in general: "A related concern around the organisation of the TIP system is its emphasis on criminal justice outcomes (e.g. higher arrest rates) rather than human rights outcomes (e.g. Increasing access to safe living and working conditions) as a measure of success."[7] In addition to paying attention to the categories and realities of race, gender, age, and sexuality as material

conditions that directly impact one's relationship to criminalization policies, overall, a rights-based approach is necessary to obtain safety and protection as opposed to a prosecution-based approach that responds after the crime has been committed. The law-enforcement/prosecution approach may act as a deterrent, but unless human-rights based preventions and solutions are in place, the conditions that often drive those to become involved in these activities persist and little material change occurs. And finally, the law-enforcement/prosecution based approach, in many cases, causes and increases harms to those it is purportedly working to "help."[8] As Lerum et al. recognize: "We now face a unique opportunity—afforded by a global mandate of the United Nations—to begin systematically implementing human rights principles into research, activism, and policies regarding both sex work and human trafficking" (p. 102). *Rather than a criminal justice approach, we must emphasize a human rights based approach where progress is measured not in the number of arrests made, but rather in the number of bodies housed, protected, and valued based on the unique experience and expertise of each.*

- **Systemic Value of Material Bodies.** Much of the emphasis surrounding street-based sex work is on the individual body—the woman's body, sex worker's body, woman of color's body, transgender/transsexual body—as a site of control. This body is the site of potential HIV, drug use, violence—both in acting and being acted upon. And as much attention as is paid to these individuals and their bodies, they do not appear to "matter" very much. Therefore, I would reverse the emphasis and ask which systems and systemic principals revere, protect, and value myriad forms of bodies? Simultaneously, responsibility must be placed where it is due—at the feet of the persons who commit the violence and the society that breeds and facilitates these actions. *Place the emphasis and responsibility for systemic value and support for bodies and individuals of all kinds.*
- **Gendered and Racial Examinations of Power and Status.** Many of the material conditions related to the woman's health and safety are based on her own power, her body, as the site that must be protected *by her.* Whether this protection occurs in negotiating condom use or preventing violence, the responsibility lies primarily within the individual woman, even to the extent that she is, in part, "blamed" for being a victim of violence (physical, sexual, even death) because of her choices. Alternatives must place esteem on valuing the individual and redirecting violence. For example, what if using a condom was a sign of status for men, both in protecting themselves and their partners? Likewise with violence: what if a central value was respect for women, all individuals, and most especially those who are marginalized? And when these standards are not present, the individuals not upholding these values are placed under the microscope rather than

those persons they choose to violate. *Studying and understanding gendered and racial practices, stereotypes, and values implemented in power and status and their implications for marginalized individuals, in particular, is imperative.*
- **Future Research Directions.** As an individual who has been researching "sex work" for almost a decade, I am grateful for the many people who have pointed out the mistakes I have made. Case in point, the title of this book, as I mentioned in the Preface. I advocate that individuals who exchange sex for money not be identified as street sex workers or street-based sex workers unless that is how they identify themselves. Laura Agustín (2005b) illustrates in much of her research, but particularly in her ethnographic material from Spain, "the variety of people involved [in the sex trade] and their myriad connections to the fabric of everyday life" (p. 626). She argues for a broader perspective on research, including: "economic (links from other industries and role of the informal sector); class and ethnic segmentations; sexual subcultures; gender performance; homosociality; the accumulations of social and cultural capital; the shaping of urban, suburban, and rural spaces" (Ibid.). More openness and examination of these stigmatized actions must be employed. In addition to these suggestions, it is important that researchers not fall into preconceived ideas about the power individuals may or may not have, such as the stereotypical belief that people who exchange sex are "less powerful" than those who purchase it. Simultaneously, the victim/exploiter roles must also be examined rather than blindly perpetuated. And finally, placing systems and policies at the center of research, rather than the individuals who are perceived to exist "outside" them, is paramount. *Close examination of the structural inequalities built into rhetorical, physical, economic, and ideological systems, among others, must be rigorously identified and analyzed. These same structural entities are also responsible for maintaining the silence of marginalized communities and individuals, and research that explores this relationship as well as where crevices might exist for disruption are imperative. And although ideology is always present in any research project, governmental funding must strive to support research that makes these ideologies transparent and guards against them with sound, rigorous, peer-reviewed methods.*
- **Develop Mutually Reinforcing Processes.** Consider the "help" transaction and its inherent power relationships; rather than providing the receiver with both the morality and resources owned by the giver, develop mutually reinforcing processes, exchanges, that sustain and uplift all participants. *Most importantly, involve the people involved in street economies in the creation and facilitation of mutually reinforcing processes of exchanges (for both givers and receivers in the transactions) that respond directly to all individuals' needs.*

- **Harm Reduction and Communication.** Shannon et al. (2008) argue

  The narratives of sex workers document the adverse impacts of local policing strategies and enforcement of the "communicating" provision: pushing women to work in dark and deserted areas, alleys and industrial settings, severely limiting women's means of self-protection with clients and acting as a direct structural barrier to HIV prevention practices. (p. 917)

  Communication and community is integral to safety, and criminalization of prostitution is often an obstacle to this harm-reduction practice. As Lazarus et al. (2011) find:

  By living together in women-only spaces, women described getting to know each other on a more personal level than they were able to while working on the street. These peer support mechanisms also acted as informal safety strategies with women looking out for each other. [. . .] By developing peer support mechanisms in their living environment, women were then able to carry those relationships out to the streets when working. As women got to know and trust each other, they more freely exchanged information about bad dates and were more likely to work together in groups. (p. 1064)

  Likewise, as INCITE! Women of Color Against Violence (2011) find:

  Additionally, demands for increased penalties for prostitution-related offenses expose young people, including LGBTQ [lesbian, gay, bisexual, transgender/transsexual, questioning] youth, who work in non-exploitative peer networks, to significant jail time for sharing resources and engaging in practices aimed at increasing safety and survival. They also drive the entire industry further underground, and the young people we reach further away from help.

  As Shannon et al. found: "gender-focused harm reduction and violence prevention targeting sex workers was largely absent" (pp. 911–12). The criminalization of prostitution, lack of harm reduction strategies for individuals in street-based sex work, and criminalization of communication and support networks combine to create devastating effects. *Not only are harm-reduction strategies imperative for survival, but encouraging individuals to communicate, trust, and value each other should be integral to policies that work to find solutions to problems leading to and stemming from street-based economies.*
- **Participate in Responsible Rhetorical Agency as a Foundation of Agential Choice.** An ideology of agential choice is the foundation of

all of the above suggestions. Everyone can practice responsible rhetorical agency in every moment of their lives. Enacting a power-with framework creates an equality of voices based on agential choice, and this practice is especially important when people inhabit a traditional role of authority. The answers to the problems surrounding street-based sex work are not clear, understood, or known. There is a tremendous amount that those considered to be less powerful can and do contribute. Listening to their language, values, goals, and experiences—even when difficult—while making room for agential choice is the beginning and the goal.

Examining quotidian rhetoric and its relationship to the material conditions of a construct such as street-based sex work contributes to scholars' understanding of rhetoric and rhetorical and ideological analysis because the connections between discourse, underlying beliefs, and assumptions and the related material conditions are made more apparent. For example, all of the above suggestions in the conclusion are directly related to what was contained and revealed in the interviews and corresponding analysis of specific material conditions. Understanding how language and material conditions mutually shape and influence each other makes these relationships more apparent, which can then impact how change can be applied and realized. Examining the language of individuals whose lives are co-created by these materials conditions—valuing their expertise in an ethnographic context—not only contributes to these conditions made differently, but to how individuals shape and are shaped by discourse and can in turn teach scholars of rhetoric more about their craft and analysis.

Criminalization, morality, victim status, and access to services are interconnected, complex practices that require further research grounded in the agential choice of participants. Changing the discourse and ideology from one of *responsibility to and for change* to one of *agential choice grounded in responsible rhetorical agency* can create material change and integrate the personhood of all participants more fully into the dialogue.

Appendix A

PARTICIPANTS

Anna is a 43- year-old, white heterosexual woman who had lived in her apartment for the past five years. Anna had spent years exchanging sex for money in Nemez, but at the time of the interview was exchanging with only one "regular" client she had known for eleven years. As a young wife, Anna had been training to be a medical secretary with only three months until graduation when her third child was born. When her husband died unexpectedly, his mother, who owned the house they were living in, told her she had to move out. She moved in with a friend and didn't have the education to get a job or home of her own. She ended up giving her mother custody of her children, and they lived with her mother until they were 18. Anna struggled with depression and got involved in a series of abusive relationships. During this time period, she was also using drugs, exchanging sex for money, and ended up homeless. Anna had never been arrested for prostitution.

When I interviewed her, Anna was searching for a new place to live. Originally from Pennsylvania, she had lived in Nemez for about half of her life. The grandmother of eight children, she spent time at *Casa Segura*, but had spent less time there recently because she was helping to take care of her grandkids. In the past she had worked in construction and food service. She wasn't currently working, but was looking for a job. Anna had never gone back to school, but she had aspirations of finishing. As she said early in our interview, "Like that gentleman there says [referring to her partner who was sitting in the kitchen], it's never too late, Anna, it's never too late." She hopes to go back to school and work with computers.

Ava is a white, 23-year-old heterosexual woman who had lived in Nemez for one year. Her mother is white, and her father is Sioux Indian. Her father went to two years of trade school, and her mom completed high school. Her parents had met in a bar and got pregnant with her. When I asked her what her parents did, she said: "My dad is actually now a police officer. He just became one within the past couple years (laugh). It took him a long time to grow up. And my mom, she likes to . . . be a professional alcoholic."

Ava lived with her mom until she was 11, when she was removed due to her mother's alcoholism. The state called her father and told him if he didn't take her, she would be in foster care, so she went to live with her dad. She was resistant to her father, who had trouble handling her, and so her aunt stepped in and offered to adopt her. They adopted her when she was 14, but they "couldn't handle her either," and so another aunt and uncle took her in. When she was 15 and living in the northwest she had "been involved in some crap [. . .] and was in a juvenile facility for awhile." The first time Ava exchanged sex for money was to buy Christmas presents. She was 14. [Ava did not explain this event in any detail.] Ava had never been arrested for prostitution.

At the time of the interview she had been living in an apartment for one month. She was not working, but she was looking for a waitressing job. Her boyfriend currently paid all of the bills. She had been released one year before from prison for selling drugs and stealing cars. While in prison, she earned her GED and was enrolled in the local community college. She had been in prison for one year. Prior to prison she worked in a casino selling drugs and sex. Ava was introduced to using and selling drugs by her former boyfriend. She exchanged sex for money again when she was released from prison because she was homeless.

Her goal was to continue her education, get her felonies expunged, and become a social worker to work with juveniles. She said: "And since I was enrolled in college when I got into all my trouble, my judge said in the courtroom that if I went back to school and could prove for a year that I was passing, he would expunge my felonies." Ava has a four-year-old son who was living with his father. She was working on getting visitation with him.

Brenda is a white, 48-year-old lesbian woman who had lived in Nemez for 44 years. She lived by herself in a trailer and was on disability from a work accident. She was on probation and had been sober for approximately two years except for a brief relapse three weeks before our interview.

Brenda was removed from her parents when she was eleven because her father was abusive. Her mother gave them up to the state. She started using drugs when she was eleven to "escape from getting beat." She was moved to a foster home and later a group home. At fourteen she was sleeping with the housemother of the group home. The home was shut down by the state, and at fifteen she was on her own. She had completed eleventh grade.

Later she earned her GED and attended the local community college and a local technical school. She ended up dropping out at 23 because she couldn't keep up with the other kids.

She started exchanging sex when she was 15.

Brenda: See when I started prostituting, I did it because I was only 15 and I was doing it to survive . . . to make money so I could have a place to live. Because I was working at Wendy's two hours a day.

That wasn't enough to pay rent and stuff. And I wasn't into drugs then. And then, once you start doing it, it just kind of falls into place, like, you have to do the drugs to be able to do the prostitution. And I used to have a 500 a day habit. Never did heroin, but I've done every other drug that they made.
[. . .]

Jill: Did you have friends then that did it that weren't involved with drugs?

Brenda: No because everybody I met was doing drugs.

Jill: So you were pretty rare, at 15, to be doing it and not being involved in drugs.

Brenda: Yeah, but it only took me about a year, and I was into doing coke [cocaine] and meth [methamphetamine] and downers [drugs that are depressants].

Jill: What do you think led you to the drugs?

Brenda: Prostitution. Because you get so sick of always having to go out to make money, and having guys on top of you. And its like it just turns you into doing drugs. Because its easier to do it when you're high. And I see a lot of women, that's why they get high, and then they go out and pick up the guys.

Her old sister taught her how to do prostitution. She said: "Yeah, how to survive. Because she was the only one there for me—my family wasn't."

Brenda had worked in landscaping and construction on and off. As she became addicted to drugs, she continued to exchange sex to supplement her income to support her drug habit. Brenda had been arrested four times for prostitution. Five years prior to our interview, Brenda relapsed again after the state took her daughter from her. Her daughter was five at the time, and Brenda put her up for adoption. Brenda had been in and out of rehabilitation centers, her last one occurring after her daughter was removed.

Denise is a 43-year-old, white, heterosexual woman who had lived in Nemez almost two years. As the interview progressed, she explained her family had Cherokee Indian in them, "like five different blood lines in us, but I always tell everybody I'm white."

Denise had finished eighth grade and had children at a young age, so she dropped out of school. She said: "I have a learning disability that really is a struggle for me, that I get really humiliated, and I won't even say anything; I'll just sit there and look at the people, you know, because it humiliates me. But other than that, I haven't had a desire to go back." Her father was an alcoholic who was physically abusive. She was in and out of foster homes because her mother had medical issues. Her older sister got married when she was 13 so she could take care of her brothers and sisters. As Denise said: "She got married so she could take care of us kids so the state wouldn't have us no longer. She got married to her husband and fought for us kids, and three of us got to go live with her. The other two didn't." At the time of this transition, Denise was eight years old.

Her parents had lived out west all of their lives, and Denise has just recently moved to Nemez. She wasn't sure of her parents' education levels, but she knew her father had served in the military in World War II, and her mom was a housewife all her life. Denise had been taking care of both of her parents, who had chronic illnesses, and when her sisters and brothers wouldn't help her with them, she moved out of the state. At the time of the interview her parents were both in medical facilities because of their health conditions.

Denise wasn't working at the time because she was disabled, caused by foot surgery, which led to a staph infection, a subsequent bone infection, and then partial amputation of her foot. She had received disability since that operation and it was enough for her to live on. Denise had never been arrested for prostitution.

Donna is a 47-year-old, white, heterosexual woman who had lived in Nemez for 20 years. Donna identified as half Italian and half Cherokee, but because that was complicated, she told people she was white. Donna's father had been in the Navy and they moved around a lot when she was growing up. Her mother stayed at home and later worked at a factory. Donna's father had been adopted and they didn't know much about his family, and she believed that was where her addiction came from. She said: "Because no one in my family is an addict. I'm the only one." She said she came from "a very dysfunctional family," but she was raised with a lot of values and morals.

She went on:

> I did come from a pretty good family, you know? So being out here in this world, it's been real hard for me because I do have conscience, I do have a heart, I do believe in certain things. I know I'm better than a prostitute. I'm not just putting prostitution down, but I know that I'm a good person. And it's been real hard to be a drug addict and a prostitute because I still have a lot of values and I do have a conscience. [. . .] And this last month that I started prostituting again, it's been really hard for me. Especially because of my age, my medical conditions and issues. I don't walk with my head down. I'm not ashamed. I'm not proud, but I'm not ashamed. Because I take care of me. And if that's what I have to do at the time, that's what I do.

Donna got married when she was 16 and had a baby. She said: "I was living with my parents until I was 16. I got married when I was 16. I had my first daughter exactly one month after I turned 17. My high school sweetheart is who I married. I did not love him. I wanted to get away from my father. That's why I got pregnant and got away."

The first time Donna exchanged sex for money was for her kids. She was 21 and living in her car with her kids. Her husband had left her, leaving a note saying "he didn't want the responsibility of me and my kids anymore." As she said:

> I was 21. I had to make a $1,000 a night or I couldn't come in. And anyway, I brought my kids out there and he [her boyfriend] ended up molesting my kids. I was police-escorted away from him. From that day on, everybody in Nemez, when I started prostituting for drugs, everybody in Nemez knows that that's something that I will . . . I'd flip, 'cause, you know, this man, I made a $1,000 a night and he was hurting my children.

Donna called her parents and told them she was "prostituting" and they came and got her and took her home. She had been raped several times while working on the street. When she returned to her home, she was drinking alcohol and smoking pot. Donna explained:

> And, um, my mother and father didn't know how to handle it. I didn't know how to handle it. I thought I had "prostitute," "dirty whore" written across my forehead, you know? It really messed me up, and I really got . . . I got raped a couple times really, really bad while I was out there on the street. And my parents didn't know how to handle it, and they ended up taking my kids to CPS.

In terms of her drug use, she said:

> I was using pot . . . I was doing a lot of alcohol for quite a few years. When I started doing cocaine, I started right off with the needles. Yeah, and I quit everything else. That was it, you know? And I shot dope for 13 years. I started doing heroin and coke, and, um, I OD'd [overdosed] on coke [cocaine] really bad. I was dead for three and a half minutes; they brought me back.

Donna moved to Nemez because her parents had retired there. As she said: "I'm stuck here. For the last ten years, I've been going to prison, probation, parole, so I haven't been able to leave." Donna wasn't using as much crack as she had in the past:

> But I'm kind of glad because I don't want to be . . . It's like I'm smoking again, but I don't want to be out in that world again, and I see myself slowly slipping there because of the prostitution thing. And I know what that'll eventually do to me, with my emotions. That's why I think I started going to the Women Restored Program, and I'm still going to my one-on-one counseling. I don't have to do none of this stuff;

nobody's making me anymore. But I feel I have to have some kind of ... something to keep my stability or my mind focused, so I don't go all the way back out there, you know? (sigh) Well, it's something that I'm not really wanting to do.

Jill: Prostitution?
Donna: Yeah. And I don't want to be back to where I'm on the street and in a hotel (crying). I don't want to go back. No. [...] But I'm too old, I'm too tired, you know, I'm really tired. And my personality is so angry. I'm going to end up getting killed out there (laugh) because I just don't ... you know, like fuck you. I'm just ... and if somebody tried to come up and rob me, I'm going to kill them, because you're not taking from me. I'd rather die first. And, um, so that kind of mentality is not healthy, you know. [...] It's just ... I'm tired. I'm tired of my addiction, and I'm so tired of people saying, "Well, you know, you can stop, you can stop, go to meetings, da da da." I've done everything with my addiction. I've been to seven rehabs, prison four times. I've been SMI [Severely Mentally Ill], I've been on ... I've been through it all, and I'm still using. You know, what part haven't I gotten? I don't know. I don't even know why I use anymore. I don't enjoy it. I do not—I've got to where I want to be alone when I get high, I isolate really bad. I mean, it's hard for me—like all these people out here make me nervous [laughs], you know what I mean? I just ... When I'm walking down the street, it's hard because people are staring. I've isolated to really extreme, and it's not good. And ... so right now, I'm kind of like lost, you know? I really don't know where I'm at right now. And it's hard. It's hard. But there's that one little piece of me that was raised right and believes right and has hope, and that's the part, I guess, that keeps fighting. But even that part's getting tired, you know?

Donna completed tenth grade when she left school to get married. She later earned her GED when she was in prison, graduating the valedictorian of her class the same year her daughter graduated from high school. Donna had two prostitution charges, and the majority of her arrests were for drugs. She had been to prison four times in Nemez for possession and sale of drugs.

At the time of our interview, she was living with a man who had been her neighbor prior to her last prison term. She said:

I realized I had no friends, I had nobody, and that's where I ended up. And he let me stay there, and I've been there a couple months now, and he knows not to come at me sexually, he knows, it's not happening. I think he's scared of me a little bit [laughs]. Because I'm very quiet and I'm very . . . I'm not a bad ass, but I can hold my own.

She talked about her current status:

> Reality is, I've been an addict for 35 years. I've been prostituting 25. And it's like . . . I really don't believe I'm going to go to school and have a career at this late state of age, okay? I really—I mean, you can say, "Oh, you can do it." Well, me, knowing me . . . I'm still battling my addiction, and I have been. And I really don't see it happening.

Donna loved animals and had worked as a veterinarian technician. She explained:

> And I loved that job. I wanted to work. I wanted to be a part of society, you know? And it was good for a while, but I know now that I can't—I've got a bone degenerative disease in my spine, and I got a lot of things going on. I'm just not . . . I'm not going to be able to function, and I know it, and I finally admitted it and said, "Okay, look. Let's get back on medication, let's get your head together. You're still battling this addiction. Let's just go from here." And I can't just sit around. I don't want to prostitute the rest of my life, you know? So I'm going to try to do what I can.

Eve is a 23-year-old African-American heterosexual woman who had lived in Nemez her whole life. She was living in an apartment and working for a temporary agency approximately once a week. Prior to her temp job she had worked as a housekeeper for a hotel. She had completed eleventh grade and was working on getting her GED. She was born with a disability and was currently receiving social security. She had two boys and wanted to get more education in writing and reading. She had never been arrested for prostitution, but she had been arrested for trespassing while she was waiting for a car to pick her up.

Julie is a white, 42-year-old heterosexual woman who had lived in Nemez since she was 13 years old. She moved to Nemez when her mother got remarried to her stepdad. Her father was in the Navy, and her mother worked as a dental assistant. Her parents are both white, and she wasn't sure what their education had been. Julie dropped out of school at eighth grade and mentioned she had a learning disability, making it hard for her to spell and count.

Julie was first introduced to drugs at thirteen by her brother and his girlfriend and had used them, as she said, "all my life." Julie had first exchanged sex for money when she was fifteen years old.

On the day of our interview, Julie hadn't used crack in three days. When I asked her why she quit, she said: "I got tired of waking up broke. I got tired of no food. I got tired of no cigarettes, no nothing, in case I didn't get called up [for work] the next day."

When I asked her if it was hard for her to not use drugs, she said:

> It's all up here, it's all up here in your head, you know what I'm saying? Its just like, it's just like if you turn around and you do something and you really, really want something in life, you want something or I don't know how long, you know what I mean? You turn around and you use your head. You know it? I can't think of the word I'm trying to say.

Jill: Like determination?
Julie: Determination. You've got to put your foot down and say, you know what? Is this what you're gonna do? Are these the consequences you want to deal with? Do you want to become broke with no food, money, or nothing? You know? It gets old.

At the time of the interview she was working daily jobs at the labor hall (a temporary labor agency), which paid between $5 and $7 per hour. When she went to find work at the labor hall, Julie had to get up at 4 am and walk four miles to the labor hall and then wait until 8 am to see if there would be work. Julie had been working at the labor hall for about three years. Prior to looking for work on a daily basis at the labor hall, Julie was in prison, and prior to prison, she had worked at a fast-food chain as a cook and cashier. Julie had spent three and a half years in prison for possession of crack. Prior to prison she had been to jail many times for exchanging sex for money—she estimated forty or fifty times.

If Julie didn't work through the labor hall, she spent most of her days at *Casa Segura* where she participated in educational and health classes and had access to computers. Julie had been involved in the programs offered at the women's center since its inception, so she was very familiar with it and was often a resource for other participants.

Julie said it was hard for her to get a full-time job because she had some medical issues and she was currently homeless. She was interested in getting more education because she wanted to work with kids in a daycare, but being homeless made it difficult to get dressed up every day for a full-time job.

Karen is a 49-year-old, white, heterosexual woman who had immigrated to the United States twenty years before with her first husband. Karen was raised in a wealthy family. Her mothers' parents were very wealthy, and Karen had always lived in nice homes and had all of her needs met. As she said, "Yeah. I was spoiled then. I was. Then I come to Nemez, I got off the plane, and I thought "Oh my goodness. What have I done to myself?" (laugh)

Karen first exchanged sex for money when she was in her mid-forties. She was homeless, divorced, and an immigrant unable to work. She had lost her children and was living on the street.

Karen was never arrested for prostitution. She was arrested for cashing a check for someone she didn't know, which turned out to be stolen. It was a misdemeanor charge that resulted in jail, six months in a "halfway house," and three years on probation.

Karen used marijuana when she was seventeen with her brother, but she had never used cocaine until she met her second husband, Jay. Prior to meeting her husband and coming to America, she had worked selling fabric and in interior design in her home country, working up to manager at a design store. She also worked selling fabrics in America for several years. She graduated from high school and completed one year of business college.

Having come to the US with her husband, Karen was a legal resident alien since 1989. Her husband died from a massive heart attack when she was six months pregnant with their son. They had a business selling magazines through the mail, but no medical or life insurance. Shortly after her husband's death, the bank "pulled out from the mail-order business." Karen's late husband's mother helped support her initially. Karen had planned to return to her home country when she met and married one of her husband's best friends. She stayed in the US and had her second child 11-and-a-half months after her first with her second husband. She remained a resident alien because she didn't want to give up her home citizenship.

For seven years Karen had been dealing with immigration proceedings. She went back to her home country in 1998 and returned 14 months later, not knowing she would no longer qualify as a legal resident alien, but rather only have visitor status. As she said: "So about six years later, I get to the actual court proceeding. Things get put off and put off and put off. I couldn't get [state provided medical insurance], couldn't get food stamps. I was on the street because I'd just gone through a divorce. The kids were taken from me because of my ex-husband telling lies about me."

When she and her second husband divorced, Karen was investigated by child protective services and lost custody of her children in spite of the fact her ex-husband had 27 arrests for cocaine use. He was wealthy, well connected with the police and prison life, and she suspected he bribed the caseworker before and during the custody proceedings. As she said: "Because in the CPS case, there was not one thing I could do right. Nobody explained anything to me. They'd just jump in my shit when I'd do something wrong. I mean, I'd visit with my kids. I'd say things in front of—we had supervised visits, which is life—I was the one that raised my kids! My husband was never, ever there. He was always downstairs doing the dope. Always, and I knew what was going on. She [the case worker] got a new car while my case was going on. And I'm on the street, and I have to live with all this stuff and deal with myself at the same time. [. . .] So that's where me earning a little bit of extra money, that's where that came in, because I couldn't get

176 Appendix A

anything, you know? I couldn't find work, couldn't get the food stamps, couldn't get [healthcare] [. . .] because I was doing the immigration thing. So that lasted for, like, about seven years."

Karen had just started working for a telemarketing company at the time of our interview. She had been living in a "halfway house" for six months and had just completed a thirty-day intensive program with a social service agency. She found a job prior to completing her intensive program, which was extremely unusual, and she felt good about her progress. As she said, "After going through immigration for so long, I'm *really* enjoying the fact that I'm going to work."

Laura is a 36-year-old, white, heterosexual woman who had lived in Nemez for four years after moving from the northern United States where she was born and raised. Laura's father had worked in a machine shop and her mother "didn't do nothing . . . She just did prostitution." Laura's father had passed away during a heart transplant almost twenty years before, shortly before her 17th birthday. When he died, she said she "kinda just gave it up."

Laura had worked in prostitution both in Nemez and up north where had had lived previously. She first used drugs when she was 28. Her ex-husband was a "crackhead" and got her involved with drugs after she lost her job at the factory. He was selling crack and she "ended up doing the sex thing." She first exchanged sex when she was 30 because she needed money for herself and her kids. Her husband didn't know about her participation in prostitution, but when he found out, "he was pissed right off." Laura didn't stop though, and "then after awhile, after he got used to it, because of the money and stuff involved in it, he's like, 'Go ahead and do it.'" Laura had never been arrested for prostitution.

Laura was the mother of three who wasn't able to care for them anymore "because of the prostitution and drugs." She said the drugs were bad up north, but in Nemez, "the drugs really got bad. I mean, it's so easy to find them here." She and her husband moved to Nemez because he thought it would be easier to find jobs. They both "got into the crack really bad" and he left and took their two daughters back up north. He left Laura and their son in Nemez. She ended up giving her son up for adoption because of the drugs. Her daughters were living with their grandmother because their father was in prison for molesting her oldest daughter.

At the time of the interview, Laura had worked on and off for three years pulling up and recycling carpet and carpet padding in Nemez. She had worked at a factory when she lived up north. In addition to recycling carpet, Laura was still occasionally exchanging sex for money, although she did not enjoy it. As she said:

> But when I need money . . . I mean, I look at people like that, I can't really put nobody else down because I do it myself. I don't like putting

myself in that situation to have sex with people for money or drugs, but sometimes I have to. And I look at other people and I might call them a 'ho. And that's wrong for me to do when I'm doing the same thing."

Jill: Okay. Yeah. What's wrong?
Laura: (crying) Just thinking about it. I don't like being dirty like that.
Jill: Yeah? Is that how you feel about it?
Laura: Yeah. It is dirty.
Jill: What makes you feel that way?
Laura: Having sex with other guys, giving blow jobs with other guys, just trying to make money to survive. It feels gross. Really gross.

Linda is a 58-year-old white, Jewish heterosexual woman. Her parents were both white and Jewish as well.

Linda met her husband at 17 and married him at 20. They ran a business together; her husband was the owner/chef and she was the waitress/assistant. As she said:

> And I thought I was happily married to him. I mean, we lived in a nice house; we had a successful business, two cute kids; but the truth of the matter is he was always abusive; I just didn't realize it. I didn't realize it. I guess I was raised with abuse and I was very young when I met him. He was young and handsome, and I was young and beautiful, and the money and food and sex was good, so I thought I was happily married. [. . .] I mean, he used to hit me and strangle me. His five favorite names for me were "whore," "bitch," "nag," "fat ass," and "dummy." And that was in my 20s.

Prior to having children, Linda had attended a couple of years of junior college. Her parents had both been to college as well.

Later in their marriage Linda had a miscarriage. Their business burned down twice, and she began battling depression.

When her kids were 10 and 8, Linda tried to divorce him. Linda remembers: "And he said, 'I will never give you your kids, any money, or any property, so forget it.' And I was scared of him. I had no parents to go home to; I didn't know what to do, so I dropped the divorce proceedings. But it was never a good marriage after that—not really."

After her son graduated and her daughter was almost 16, she left her husband and moved to Florida. Later her husband visited her there and she got pregnant with her third child. Over the next several years, her husband was able to gain custody of their third child. She ended up in Arizona living in and out of shelters. It was at this point she met several men that paid her to have sex with them. They would either pay her rent or buy her food or clothes. Linda never used drugs and did not abuse substances. As she said: My ex-husband and I never had a drinking or drug problem. It was an income tax problem, and it was adultery, it was abuse. She exchanged sex for money for approximately three years in order to support herself. She did not become financially stable until she was able to receive social security. Linda had never been arrested for prostitution.

Lisa is a 47-year-old, Hispanic heterosexual woman who had just started a substance abuse program and was between places at the time of our interview. She was born in Nemez and had lived there her whole life. Her mother was Native American and her father was born in Mexico but grew up in the United States. Her father committed suicide, and Lisa was given up for adoption when she was two years old. She lived with her adoptive parents, who were from Mexico, until she was thirteen, started getting into trouble, and was taken away by the state. She left school during seventh grade when she ran away from home and ended up in juvenile detention. Lisa said:

> I ran away from home. I was in a foster home, and I was just real rebellious, you know what I mean? My parents, they didn't have a right to tell me what to do you, you know, I just had that attitude, and so I ran away and then I went to juvenile. Then I got out of juvenile, and that's when I met my husband, which was, I lied to him and told him I was 18. He was 21 and I ended up getting pregnant. I got married and that didn't work either.

Lisa had her first son at 14.

Lisa started drinking when she was eight years old and smoking pot at 12 or 13. She started doing heroin at 27 or 28, when a boyfriend was using it. She was a heroin addict for 17 years. Lisa had been arrested "probably 30 times" for prostitution.

Lisa first exchanged sex for money when she was "about 24." She said:

> I was in a bar and I met this gentleman in there and . . . we went out to . . . we went out, you know, and at the end he asked if I needed any money, if I needed anything, and I said "No," and he gave me some money. And he told me to call him, and I started calling him and that was my first john. [. . .] See, I wasn't on drugs. I mean, I would drink and I smoked pot, okay? But I wasn't like shooting heroin, doing crystal, or smoking that shitty-ass crack shit that just blows, you know, the mind.

Jill: So when you started, you were just doing it for fun?
Lisa: Yeah. Like I said, I met him at a club, we'd go out dancing. My sister was watching the baby, watching my son, and I was out having fun. I'd call this guy up and he'd come and see me, pick me up, and we'd go out, you know? It was like that. [. . .] I still don't see nothing wrong with it if it's a consenting adult.

During our interview, Lisa's son called her, who, she later explained, had just gotten out of prison a few days before. She was very excited to see him. He had been in prison for 11 years and was now in a rehabilitation program.

Lisa also had a four-year-old son she was trying to locate. He had been put up for adoption shortly after she wouldn't "go testify against the big cartel person." She wouldn't cooperate with the police, and she believed they put her son up for adoption. Lisa recounts the story:

So I go and I gave them four clean drops [urine test where no drugs are found in one's urine] for my baby to go see him at CPS [child protective services]. He was a preemie [premature]. [. . .] I gave four drops for CPS so I could see my child. [. . .] And my drops were clean and I was trying really hard. [. . .] My baby was given up for adoption. All of a sudden, they can't find him. I've taken letters. I've taken letters, cards, and you know, called this person, called that person. [. . .] I shouldn't have been on drugs, and I shouldn't done a lot of things, but everything happens for a reason, Jill, and I guess I was just the chosen one to go through this so maybe I could help somebody so they wouldn't have to, or something. I don't know why.

For the three months prior to our interview, she had been doing part-time work with a friend who owns his own roofing business. She earned her GED when she was nineteen. She was interested in getting more education, but was primarily concerned about looking for a home and trying to get situated financially.

Lourdes is a 31-year-old Hispanic heterosexual woman who had lived in Nemez all her life. Her mother is Hispanic and was from Nemez and her father is Mexican and was from Mexico. Her parents had gone through sixth grade. Her mother, being a slow learner, was put in classes like sewing. She soon got bored and just stopped going.

Lourdes was not working when we met. Four years before she had worked as a teacher's aide at an elementary school.

She started using drugs at 18 and used them on and off for months at a time. She had gone to school until tenth grade, and when she started "hanging out with the wrong crowd" she "just stopped." She wanted to get her GED, especially because she was currently receiving supplemental social security income (SSI) and had "extra time on [her] hands." She had been diagnosed with depression. Her SSI was not enough to live on, but she lived with her boyfriend, who worked, so they made it work.

Lourdes had six kids, two who were being raised by her sister, three raised by the state, and one who had died. Her older daughters, 10 and 13, lived with her sister. The state had her younger three, who were 4, 2, and 1. All of the three younger kids were taken at birth because she was "using drugs very heavily." She sees her older kids as much as she wants, usually on a daily basis. She was also able to have them on the weekends.

At the time of our interview, Lourdes hadn't exchanged sex for a year. When I asked her what caused her to stop exchanging, she said: The thing is, I was actually doing it while I was pregnant from my one-year-old and I was living in a very bad environment, and I was just really badly hooked on drugs. Her current boyfriend was in jail at the time she was exchanging sex. He is the father of her four-year-old. When he got out, a year prior to the interview, he took her out of that environment and things "totally changed" for her. She had never been arrested for prostitution.

Olivia, a 52-year-old Hispanic heterosexual woman, was in her fourth week of living in transitional housing at the time of our interview. Prior to living in the transitional housing, she had been homeless for a "couple years." She got pneumonia living on the streets and was hospitalized, and a social service agent found her and was able to get her a spot in transitional housing. She had planted a garden, was making decorations for her one-room apartment, and was energetic and happy. She said: "Now it's like the real me, I just burst with energy, like I love me. I didn't love me then; I love me now."

Olivia had lived in Nemez all of her life. Her mother, a homemaker, was from Mexico, and her father, who painted cars, was from Nemez. She wasn't sure what level of education her parents had, and Olivia had gone through tenth grade. She left school at 16 to help her mother with her brother's seven kids, who her mother had adopted when he went to prison. Later she got her GED and went back to the local community college. She went for a couple of years but had to stop because she had young children. She was excited about the opportunity to get more education so she could help people in one-on-one counseling. She said: "Something like that, because you know what? I would know what I'm talking about. And my personality, the way I handle . . . people would listen to what I say. People would feel what I'm saying, and I know that I would be good. Something like that, I would really, really love something like that."

Olivia first used marijuana at 13, and she started using crack socially at 15. By 19 she was using it "hard core." She said: "I've done it like almost every single day for 33 years." Olivia first exchanged sex for money in 2000. Prior to that she was "cooking" the crack for friends and was able to keep the "cuttings," which sustained her drug usage. Her husband died, she went on a smoking binge, and she left the house and found new friends on the street. Her husband had supported her before his death. She soon spent all of her savings and ended up living on the streets. And then she started exchanging sex for money. She had been arrested "three or four times" for prostitution. She wasn't working at the time of our interview, but in the past she had worked as a childcare provider.

Sandy is a 46-year-old, white heterosexual woman. She lived at Carlie's Place (a shelter for people experiencing homelessness as well as offering substance abuse treatment programs) at the time of our interview. She had lived at Carlie's Place for five months, and prior to that was living on the street. She had lived in Nemez for 20 years.

Her parents were educated and "well off." Her dad was an ex-police officer and her mom worked at the post office. They had met while they were in the Marines. Sandy had five brothers and sisters and five of the six had alcohol and drug problems. Her father was an alcoholic, had multiple affairs, and had two children outside of his marriage to her mother.

Sandy started doing drugs recreationally in high school and had used drugs for approximately 30 years. She started drinking in middle school and smoked marijuana and used cocaine recreationally in high school. She began experimenting with "speed" during college. She and her friends also did "acid" and "mushrooms." She married her husband in 1987 and they "partied together," which largely consisted of using cocaine. Her husband didn't use as much cocaine as she did, and he wasn't aware of how heavy her use was. Then they were introduced to crack cocaine. She had been maintaining her drug use, going home to her family, and showing up for work. By 1996 she was heavy into her addiction. She had missed a lot of work, had been warned she would be rehired, but she had to have a better attendance record. It was at this point she started disappearing for a couple of days at a time. In 1997, on her 37th birthday, she was asked to resign or she would be terminated.

I asked her if they knew she had a problem with drugs. She replied:

> Well, he knew there was a problem now, didn't he? [laughs] He never asked me, never offered any type of help, and . . . because I worked very closely with police officers because being a campus monitor. Later, when I ran into them—I would run into them—and they asked me, "Why? You know, what happened, Sandy?" and I told them, I said, "I got involved with drugs and I couldn't control my addiction." And they got upset, like "Didn't the principal offer you any type of assistance?" Because he should of, you know, because I was a very good worker, you know, and I loved what I did. But no, he never asked, "Do you have a drug problem? Can I help you?" No. So they knew.

Jill: Would you have told them yet?
Sandy: Probably. Because I knew I was out of control. I knew.

Sandy was in her second year of college when she had her daughter and stopped attending. She wanted to get more education, and her dream was to work in education as a certified coach. She also wanted to work in the truancy department. Sandy had worked at numerous jobs in the security field, including as a campus monitor for the school districts, juvenile corrections and in loss-prevention at a large department store, which was her most recent job. She lost her job two years prior when she was injured by a shoplifter. When taken for medical attention, she was given a drug test, which she refused because she had been using crack cocaine daily for over a year. She was terminated due to her refusal to take the test.

Prior to living on the streets, Sandy had been married, had a full-time job, and had children. Ten years prior she "tumbled down." As she said: "So for the last 10 years I have been battling. I had almost two years clean and sober, so we'll say eight years of my life since I left my family in '97, I've battled with this addiction and my own habits." Sandy had been arrested once for prostitution.

Tess is a 41-year-old, white, heterosexual woman who had lived in Nemez for 35 years. Her mother had moved her to Nemez when she was six. She didn't know who her father was because her mother wouldn't tell her. Her mother graduated high school but dropped out of college when she had Tess, and she went back to college after Tess grew up. Tess had completed eleventh grade when her mother kicked her out of the house for "partying" too much. She moved in with her boyfriend and didn't return to school. At the time of our interview, she wanted to attend Vocational Rehabilitation School to become a secretary.

Tess had met her husband in high school, started dating him after high school, and got married around 25. They had used drugs together and had gone through times where they were both trying to quit. He was from a wealthy family, and so they didn't have to work, but ultimately his family told him he had to choose his wife or the money, and "he chose the money." Tess said: "I wasn't done using yet, you know?" They were married for three years and didn't have any kids.

In the past she had worked as a receptionist at a car dealership. Tess had multiple health issues, including asthma, and she was hospitalized when she caught MRSA (methicillin-resistant Staphylococcus aureus). During that stay, shortly before Christmas, her company replaced her, and she was fired. Prior to her job at the dealership, she had been living outside and using drugs.

Tess said her addiction had "pretty much killed [the relationship with her mother]." Tess started using drugs at 15, primarily marijuana, and at 19 started using cocaine. She used cocaine until ten years prior, when she started using crystal meth (crystal methamphetamine). Tess would exchange sex for money or drugs when she needed to get high. Tess had never been arrested for prostitution, but she had been arrested for writing bad checks.

Tess hadn't used drugs in six months when we talked. Prior to that she had been in and out of multiple programs, relapsing in between. After working several programs she was finally given an apartment through a social service agency.

Tiffany is a white, 33-year-old heterosexual woman who was living at Wisdom's Home for Women (a shelter for women experiencing homelessness as well as offering a substance abuse program). At the time of the interview she had lived there for three months. Tiffany had been arrested for prostitution two times. Her third arrest was for outstanding warrants, and she went to jail for two months.

When I asked her what her parents did, she responded, "Nothing. At this point in time, nothing." When I asked her if they had ever worked or gone to school she said, "I'm not sure." She said that her mom had been a secretary at one point. She later said her father had been in the military service. They were both white and had been born and lived in Nemez for most of their lives.

Tiffany was born in a large city a couple of hours outside of Nemez. She was not currently working, but in the past she had done housekeeping for five or six years. She worked right out of high school, and when she got pregnant with her son, she continued to work, but it was difficult juggling both. She had a hard time finding a place for her son to stay that she could afford and was reliable. Later she was interested in nursing school and had tried it, but "my youngest wants me: 'Mommy, mommy, mommy this, mommy that.' And I'm sitting there going, 'I'm never gonna get there. I know I'm never gonna get there at the rate I'm going.'" Tiffany got her GED after eight months in jail, and she tried going to college, but with the kids, "It didn't work." She had trouble getting them into daycare. Another deterrent she experienced was, in her words, "Men." She stopped working when her son was three, and at the time of the interview he was about to turn 12. During those past nine years she had been living on social security, which she received because her father had been in the military. She wasn't sure why she was getting the money—she just knew she had been receiving it since she was born. She said her mom wouldn't tell her why.

Tiffany started exchanging sex at 29, when her daughter was 3 or 4. When I asked her what made her decide to start, she said:

Tiffany: Involved with the men.
Jill: Okay. Tell me about that.
Tiffany: The brothers—or the black guys.
Jill: Okay. So you started, what, dating them?
Tiffany: I dated one and then I met another one. I never got rid of him because he came and parked it in the house. And then I got rid of the first one (laugh). And then he had brought some girl up in the house and said, 'This was my daughter.' And it was raining the night she came, so I figured she could stay there. She started living there. Then he brought some other woman up in there, and those two went out and made him money. [. . .] Making him money, and then he turned around and told me see how much I can make within an hour. I got mad at him. Well, I got mad at him first and told him, 'I ain't doing it because I've got two kids.' I just walked out front and some dude stopped and asked if I was

working. And I said, 'Sure.' And it didn't take me more than 15 minutes to make 80 bucks. That dude gave me—I made more than 80 bucks, but that dude gave me 40, and then somebody else picked me up and gave me what was in his wallet, plus 70 more dollars after we went to the bank. [. . .] But I didn't bring him the whole money back. [. . .] I would never . . . I've always hid my money and brought back like $20, maybe $30 to the people I was with. Because I knew better.

Jill: So what made you decide to do that when he told you?
Tiffany: He didn't tell me. He told me, but then I was pissed off because he was feeding them the crack and he wasn't giving me any more until I made some money. So I figured, "Forget you."

Her boyfriend went to jail and when he got out, she was in jail. She talked about a number of men who protected her and also asked for money and/or crack after she did her "business."

Vicki

Vicki: I am an artist.
Jill: Oh, cool.
Vicki: I draw stationaries and stuff like that for the girls, and I get paid for it.
Jill: Oh, that's awesome.
Vicki: Coffee. Usually I get two bags of coffee, a big box of sugar, and cookies.
Jill: When you're in jail?
Vicki: Mmm hmmm.
Jill: Yeah, that's cool.
Vicki: So that's how I make my money.

Vicki is a 43-year-old Hispanic heterosexual woman who was born and had lived in Nemez all of her life. She had worked at a variety of jobs, primarily in food service, and had been married until the age of 34, when she left her husband, who had introduced her to cocaine and "used to beat [her] up really bad." In her words: "When I left my husband, my kids got taken away through CPS [child protective services], and . . . first I was selling drugs. And I didn't do drugs because I didn't know what the hell it was. I was selling crack. And then this guy introduced me to it, and it was like . . . I was on a high."

Vicki first used marijuana at the age of 8, but didn't start using crack cocaine until 35. It was also at 35 she "started prostitution." She noticed the same girls coming to her house, asked about it, and was told "Oh, those are prostitutes." She asked what they did, and "That's how I learned." Vicki estimated she had been arrested for prostitution about ten times.

Vicki stated early in the interview she had had "pretty much a bad life since I was 16 years old and up." When I asked her what happened at 16, she said, "Well, I got molested when I was a little girl, when I was 8 years old, and I barely told my parents at 21 years old that I got molested at 8. And they said, 'Why didn't you tell us sooner?' and I said, 'Cause they told me I'd get beat up by you guys so I didn't say nothing." Raised by her father, who was a printer, and her mother, who sold Tupperware, both college graduates, Vicki left home at 16 when she was kidnapped by her boyfriend at gunpoint because "he didn't want me to be with anybody else." She got pregnant and ended up leaving high school at 17. Her boyfriend died in a construction accident, and she went to live with her dad, who was divorced from her mom.

At the time of the interview, Vicki had lived in the park for three months. Prior to that she had lived in a house with "drug people," but she left there because the people got evicted. While living in the park, she was exchanging sex two or three times a day, until she made $100, which she used to buy drugs. Prior to this time period, she had exchanged sex 10 times a day, until she ran out of drugs, and then went back out again. Vicki had just gotten a job the day before our interview and was excited about it. As she said, "So I'm getting off the streets, prostitution. I won't be getting out of the park for awhile, until I save up some money." Her boyfriend, who was staying with her in the park, had also recently gotten a job and was going to be starting janitorial work on Monday.

It was clear Vicki was tired of exchanging sex for money. In addition to being concerned about the violence she had encountered, she was tired of "sucking all them dicks and fucking." She was currently "only hook[ing] up twice a day now. I used to do 10 dates, be on crack. I used to have a $1,000 crack habit. A day. I don't do a lot more any more." She still used crack twice a day, and as she said:

> Shoot, I'm proud of myself. I gained like . . . I weigh 160 pounds now. I used to weigh 115. I was so skinny. I used to wear a size 4, and now I wear a size 14. But, you know, I'm proud of myself. Because I used to just date anybody just to get crack. I would not get the money; I wanted the crack. And now I just . . . I'm realizing, you know, I don't need that no more. Because there's more to having a better life than to be out there in the streets trying to get killed and stuff, you know?

She went on to say:

> But I'm very happy about my life now. I'm not happy about living in the park, behind the park, with the choo choo train, because I feel like the choo choo train arch is gonna fall down on me, but you know, its better than . . . I'm glad I got a job. That way I don't have to exchange sex for money anymore. You know, I still got my regulars and I'm gonna keep them because they pay a lot of money.

PUBLIC FIGURES

Adele is a 53-year-old heterosexual, white woman who was the Assistant Program Director at a federal residential re-entry center, or "halfway house." People usually stayed at their center from 15 days to 6 months, and on rare occasions an individual might stay there for 2 to 3 years. At this center the residents were confined but authorized to look for employment. Prior to her position at the re-entry center, Adele had worked with people who had committed sex crimes. Her areas of expertise included crime victims and sex offenders, and she worked in this area for approximately 22 years. Because she worked in a federal re-entry center, she came into contact with women who exchanged sex for money when they had also been convicted of another crime through the federal prosecution system.

Dr. Veronica Alvarez is a 48-year-old heterosexual Latina woman who had lived in Nemez all her life. She was the project director of an HIV-prevention program facilitated through a research institute at a local university. The project was a community-based HIV prevention project that works with women who are in drug treatment or who are actively using substances. As Dr. Alvarez explained:

Veronica Alvarez: Without saying we want the women who are sex workers or who exchange.
Jill: You would say that the focus of your program is on—and I don't remember the exact words that you used, but—risk of HIV.
Veronica Alvarez: High risk, either through drug use or high-risk behaviors.

Veronica Alvarez estimated a high percentage of their participants were women who had exchanged sex for money or other gain. The program goal was to provide a service to the community and then implement participatory action research from that service. They provided curriculum on HIV, STDs, and social relationships. The program collaborated with three different residential drug treatment programs in the community as well as participated in street outreach. Prior to her project director position, she facilitated social support groups with drug-involved women as well as worked with immigrant women and mothers. Dr. Alvarez estimated she had about 20 years of experience working with these women, and her expertise was in culturally appropriate, gender-sensitive curriculum; working with the community, immigrant groups, and women in particular; and HIV and STI prevention.

Officer Castillo is a Hispanic, 34-year-old heterosexual female who had lived in Nemez for 29 years. At the time of the interview she was working for the Nemez Police Department as an undercover officer. She had been an officer for seven years, in the vice unit for two years, and had been working undercover for six years. She had also worked as part of a community team that focused on neighborhood crimes, including prostitution, robberies, and narcotic-related offenses. Her primary role in the vice unit was to investigate prostitution, either in picking up prostitutes or posing as a prostitute, and prostitution was her primary area of expertise.

Chelley is an Hispanic, heterosexual female in her late 40s who worked in community outreach for a mental health organization. She had worked in the field for about seven years and her expertise was in working one-on-one with the clients.

Evelyn is a 60-year-old heterosexual, white woman who had lived in Nemez for 26 years. She was the director of a mental health-counseling agency, and her areas of expertise include women's issues, criminal justice issues, substance abuse, and mental illness. She directed diversion programs (Programs designed for first-time prostitution offenders. Clients could have their criminal charges dismissed based on participation in the program.).

Dr. Julie Everett is a 36-year-old lesbian woman who works as a medical doctor in the HIV/STI division at the county health department, which is charged to care for the sexual health of Leagh County residents. Previously she had worked in healthcare for the homeless at a local community health center. Her areas of expertise include working with underserved populations, specifically lesbian, gay, bisexual, and transgender/transsexual health and working with medical providers around provision of "culturally responsive care" to those populations.

Officer Tom Hixson is a white, 52-year-old heterosexual male who was a former supervisor of the vice unit and had worked in prostitution-related activities for about seven years (including narcotics, undercover, and vice). Officer Hixson talked about prostitution in terms of "both sides" which he explained meant "I've worked with community issues [neighborhood associations, business groups, political entities and working with them in eradication efforts directed at prostitution activity] related to prostitution. I've worked on political operational issues and also worked in an investigative capacity, undercover, and I've had a lot of street experience as both uniformed patrol and just as an investigator with the persons that are engaging in that type of activity."

Officer Eric Johnson is a white, heterosexual man in his mid 40s. At the time of the interview he was the supervisor of the Nemez Police Department vice unit and had worked there about one year. Prior to that role he was a supervisor in the field specializing in domestic violence and DUIs (Driving Under the Influence).

Kristina is a 34-year-old Hispanic heterosexual woman who had lived in Nemez all her life. Kristina was an outreach coordinator for a mental health organization. Her expertise included working with women in the jails and treatment facilities.

Lily is a white, lesbian woman in her mid 40s who describes herself as an activist. She had worked as a research assistant and HIV educator, and her expertise lies in sexuality education, HIV STI (sexually transmitted infections) education, and sexual violence issues. She had education in public health and community education.

Linda is a white, 63-year-old bisexual female who worked as a counselor at a substance abuse and mental health counseling agency. She had worked in the profession for twenty years, and she had also worked in a residential treatment program for substance abuse. She is an expert in sexual addiction, sexual and relationship addiction, trauma, and sexual trauma specifically. 70 percent of her referrals were women on the street who exchange sex for money.

Officer Eugene Matthews is a white, heterosexual man in his late 30s and a lieutenant in the Nemez Police Department. Prior to that role he had been a vice supervisor for about four and a half years. Earlier in his career he had worked in narcotics. He had worked approximately ten years with street prostitution, and he considered his areas of expertise to be street prostitution and "related crimes or organizations." He had also policed the adult entertainment and sex industries. According to Officer Matthews, vice includes the adult entertainment industry, escort services, street prostitution, alcohol-related investigations, and illegal gambling. He estimated 70 percent of the time he spent in vice he dealt with street prostitution.

Joan is a 43-year-old, white, bisexual woman who had lived in Nemez most of her life. She is an activist with a sex worker rights organization that advocates for sex workers. As a teenager she had been a sex worker and became an activist in later years. She also taught classes at a local university.

Rosalie is an Hispanic, 43-year-old, heterosexual woman who had lived in Nemez all her life and was a case manager at a homeless facility that serves women without children. The facility included transitional housing as well as a drop-in center. She had worked in the social work field for 13 years and worked primarily in substance-abuse prevention, gang prevention, and community development. Her areas of expertise include counseling on substance abuse and substance abuse issues. She sees her role as providing safety, comfort, and resources to the women who participate in their program.

Appendix A 189

Russell is a white, heterosexual man in his 30s who had lived in Nemez for the past 9 years. He was a neighborhood association leader and had been actively involved with the neighborhood association since he moved to Nemez. Russell had been involved in several neighborhood grants and had worked with the Nemez police department on various neighborhood issues. Even though he had lived there for nine years, he was still considered to be relatively "new" to the neighborhood and didn't know the history like families who had lived there for three and four generations.

Sarah is a white, bisexual, 25-year-old woman who works with non-profit groups that provide support services to sex workers. She worked as a consultant on specific projects, HIV/AIDS education, STD (sexually transmitted diseases) prevention, helping people find shelter, clothes, and food, and education for sex workers, including groups working with prison exit, or re-entry into society, groups, as well as organizations that politically advocate for sex workers. One of her key roles was in developing political tools for sex workers to advocate for themselves. She had worked in the sex industry for 8 years, 7 of which she was active in sex worker organizing.

Dr. Annie Shepherd is a 51-year-old white, heterosexual woman and a psychology professor. She had lived in Nemez for 28 years and had worked for a non-profit organization working with substance users and women who trade sex for money or drugs. She had also worked on a street outreach research project. She was affiliated with a local university and directed several research projects. Her areas of expertise are substance abuse; women and HIV prevention; co-occurring disorders, such as trauma, abuse, and violence; and the development of gender-specific and adolescent-specific outreach, curriculum, and research on HIV and STD (sexually transmitted diseases) prevention. She had worked in these fields for approximately 20 years.

Sue is a white, heterosexual woman in her late 50s and a neighborhood association leader. She spearheaded the formation of the association and had been a member for 20 years at the time of the interview. Over the years she built strong associations with the police department and city leaders and worked to earn their trust and respect as a neighborhood activist and leader.

Sylvia is an Hispanic, lesbian woman in her late 30s and a director at a mental health organization. She was responsible for developing and facilitating community initiatives to affect change in the areas of stigma, abuse, or prevention regarding mental health or drug use. She had also worked extensively in HIV services. Her areas of expertise include community organizing, substance abuse and addiction, mental health, and women's health.

Valarie is an Hispanic, heterosexual female in her mid 30s and a program manager at a behavioral health agency. Previously she had worked in community outreach and education for HIV and STIs (sexually transmitted infections). She had worked in these fields approximately 10 years and her areas of expertise included harm reduction and community support.

Appendix B
Research Process and Layers of Data

Anthropologist Laura Agustín (2005a) argues for researchers to "step out of the supposedly neutral tradition of social research and a familiar feminist discourse of goodness and helping" (p. 79). She writes:

> The recognition of one's own interests does not have to mean abandoning all projects and helping others; one might seek instead an approach that attempts to understand the subjects of one's interests through listening to them, learning about their social and cultural contexts, and resisting the desire to project onto them one's own feelings. Theories of how to help, based more soundly on what subjects say, would be stronger theories. (p. 78)

RESEARCH DESIGN AND PROCESS

One's research design always influences how the reader is able to "hear" the participants' voices as well as what information is conveyed. I provide the following as an introduction to the voices of my participants as well as a context for this study.

I designed this ethnography as an interview and participant-observation study to enable me to both ask questions of and spend time with women who exchange sex for money or drugs and the myriad people who come into contact with them, which I term public figures. These people include those who work within social service or legal organizations, as neighborhood association leaders involved in issues related to women who exchange sex for drugs or money, and people interested in promoting the rights of sex workers, or activists. In addition to my interviews, I spent a great deal of time with my participants as they talked together and participated in activities in social service organizations.

I combined a multi-sited ethnography with critical discourse analysis. Ethnography is a collection of methods—participant-observation, observation, interviewing, and archival research—that is particularly useful when examining events and the perceptions of these events created and represented by many people through multiple communicative interactions. Multi-sited ethnography is appropriate when researching the relationships among people and institutions that exist locally, globally, and internationally. Ethnography can then move from a single-site location to "multiple sites of observation and participation that cross-cut dichotomies such as the 'local' and the 'global,' the 'lifeworld' and the 'system'" (Marcus 1995, p. 95). Anthropologist George E. Marcus argues these ethnographies are "therefore both in and out of the world system" (Ibid.). Like Marcus's theory, I draw on multiple sites for observation, participation, and conversation in order to delineate how individuals use language and how this use reflects the material conditions surrounding street-based sex work.

Within my research I draw on the ethnographic work of Anthropologist Don Kulick and English Professor Elizabeth Britt, who have executed multi-sited ethnography both in and outside their own cultures. I used Kulick as a model because he has proven effective at entering a community in which he was considered an outsider and analyzing sex, gender, and culture related to Travestís, or transgendered prostitutes, in Brazil. Britt undertook an ethnographic study in her own culture and was successful at analyzing notions of normalcy as they relate to infertility. This subject was a difficult one to discuss with her participants, and I draw on her diplomacy and expertise in this delicate area. I also credit English Professor Ralph Cintron, and Anthropologists Emily Martin, Rayna Rapp, and Harry F. Wolcott for aspects of their theories I have incorporated into my work.

The research questions that were the impetus for this research project are as follows:

- What ideologies are embedded in the language about these women as well as these exchanges?
- What are the similarities and differences between these representations?
- How do these differences relate to the material conditions of these women's lives?

My fieldwork began in January 2005 and continued through June 2007. During these 30 months, I volunteered and worked at *Casa Segura*, a social service organization that provides services for women who exchange or have exchanged sex for money or drugs.[1] In January 2007 I became a full-time employee at HealthWise, a social service agency that works with people who are chronically homeless. This position allowed me to gain even more insight about people who are homeless in general and my research population specifically, as many women who exchange sex for money or drugs are chronically homeless.[2]

I learned the political, legal, and social service systems that these women negotiate during my volunteer and subsequent paid positions at these social service organizations. My formal working positions also enabled me to take on additional responsibilities and boosted my credibility—with both those in the office with whom I was working and the women who came to the center as clients.[3] Because I worked at the center, I was also able to participate in outreach and education. This outreach included going off-site to the city jail to talk to women who had been arrested for exchanging sex for drugs or money, to other social service organizations where these women were clients, and to the street where many of these women worked and lived. Although known as an employee of my social service organization, at times on the street I was anonymous, as we weren't allowed to tell people where we worked, only that we were looking for certain people. As I moved from volunteer to employee to researcher, my status as each was known within the organization in which I worked—especially to those who spent a great deal of time at the center.

When I began my volunteer work, I was open about my research interests and status with all of the employees who worked there. The employees at the center knew I was there to help them out while also learning about the organization and the various political and legal systems in place in the city. After my position changed from volunteer to employee, I started spending a great deal of time at the center, both in my paid position and working on my research and dissertation. There were many times I participated in outreach and education as a volunteer in order to learn more about the system, help out the center, and become more familiar with the women who were clients. This strategy of working on my research at the center was successful because I became familiar with the daily workings of the center and was spontaneously asked to participate in different projects. My presence at the center also increased my familiarity with the clients who spent time there. My initial eight to twelve months was a period of learning and understanding the various systems at work.

WOMEN WHO EXCHANGE SEX

The purpose of my interviews with the women was to gain a better understanding of women who exchange sex for drugs or money, the systems in which they are participants, and the language they and others use to describe these women and the systems of which they are a part. My questions and subsequent analysis were somewhat more complicated in these interviews. First, I wanted to better understand how the identities and material conditions of women who exchange sex for money or drugs were represented in the language these women used surrounding this work. In addition to this analysis, my interviews also incorporated questions about my previous analysis of both the newspapers surrounding this work and my interviews with public figures.

I began each interview by focusing most directly on the material conditions of these women's lives and how they identified themselves. This process included asking these women questions about their work, goals, roles in the sex industry, and their understanding of themselves in the community and society at large. I didn't ask these women to focus specifically on the language they use, as I didn't want them to concentrate too much on the words they chose, but rather to have them speak freely. I began each interview asking them about their experiences. Later in the interviews I asked them how they identified themselves in terms of exchanging sex for money or drugs, which was the only direct focus on language until the end of the interview when we discussed the language and my analysis of this language found in the documents and spoken by the public figures when they talked about sex work. At this point the research participant and I struggled with the language in order to better understand each other and how we each understood how others talked about the exchange of sex for drugs or money. At times this was a difficult process, and there were occasions when the participant did not care to reflect on the language with me at all, but overall, it was extremely rewarding. I was then able to utilize these discussions to analyze the language we used to talk about these issues in order to bring the research full circle, as the women were able to comment on both the language used and my analysis of the language and concepts discussed in the public figure interviews.

I interviewed the women formally only one time. I had initial hopes of being able to contact most of the women more than one time for follow-up interviews, but because I was not able to use their real names or contact information, in most cases I was not able to follow up with them. All of the women contributed a great deal, not only in taking the time to participate in the interview, but also by helping me think through how the media and public figures used language to talk about women who exchange sex for drugs or money. Integrating my analysis of the interviews with public figures and newspaper articles in my interviews with the women offered a depth of understanding I couldn't have attained by talking to the women without involving them in this analysis.

My methodology and interviews with the women influenced my analysis of the rhetorics of public figures. In addition to my interviews, I observed classes at social service organizations where the women receive services and visited and participated in neighborhood association meetings where issues related to exchanging sex for money were addressed. These additional sites broadened my perspective beyond the language used in my interviews because I was able to further analyze the language and other communicative interactions that occurred in these situations.[4]

METHODOLOGIES FOR INTERVIEWS WITH WOMEN WHO EXCHANGE SEX

This portion of the interview study began with me speaking to one informant who was familiar with my study and had been active in exchanging sex for drugs or money for many years. After our interview, I asked her for feedback and critique of my interview questions and the project as a whole. This participant offered expertise and insights that contributed to the revision of my interview questions and an enhanced understanding of the project. In subsequent interviews, I asked my research participants for their feedback about the interview itself and my questions in particular, and in this way, was able to integrate this feedback into subsequent interviews. This process did not substantially change my interview questions, but in many cases I did add additional questions based on the suggestions of my earlier participants. These additions integrated my participants more fully into the interview process.

In order to make contact with the women, I created and posted fliers throughout town at key social service organizations where many of them receive services.[5] I paid each of my participants $30 for their participation in a one- to two-hour interview. During our initial conversation, I explained I would pay them thirty dollars for their time and arranged a time and a place to meet them. Because the women were required to contact me, the participants were self-selected and either had access to social services or were in touch with women who had this same access and who had told them about the study. These women were willing to speak out—whether for the money offered as compensation for their time or to share their experiences. Due to Institutional Review Board Human Subjects' requirements, I was not allowed to state how much compensation would be offered on the flier, but only that it would be offered. It is impossible to say how many women did not respond and for what reasons. The promise of compensation also complicates these issues because the women were typically in need of money. I wanted to offer compensation because their time is worthwhile and also as an incentive to participate.

Initially, I had planned on meeting the women at the social service agency where I worked, but management at this location was concerned the women might associate my study with the social service agency and did not want the interviews to take place there. I therefore negotiated a meeting location with each individual. At times, the women would ask me to come to their homes, and we would do the interview there. At other times, we met at a local fast-food restaurant and found a quiet corner where we could talk. I also met participants in the park and at a local library where we could find private locations. I believe the individual nature and casualness of the settings actually made it easier for the women to respond to my questions and talk about their lives than would have been possible at the social service agency where the situation would have been more formal and less intimate.

Because the women I interviewed are a particularly vulnerable population due to their involvement in illegal activities, the Institutional Review Board waived the requirement for my participants to sign a consent form because that form would be the only link between the individual and the research.

Therefore, I obtained recorded verbal consent at the time of the interview by asking them if they understood the study and were willing to participate. I audio taped the consent process along with the interview itself and then used this tape to create transcripts of the interviews. Due to the Institutional Review Board requirements and the vulnerability of these women due to their involvement in illegal activities, I was not able to gain contact information or follow up with my participants after our initial interview.

I asked prescreening questions in order to interview women who had performed sex acts in exchange for money on a regular basis. My initial prescreening questions included asking the respondents how often they currently participate or have participated in this exchange and how long they had been exchanging sex for drugs or money. This eligibility process changed as I began to talk to more women about the process. Initially, in order to be eligible for the study, the woman was to have performed this exchange more than ten times in the past six months. As I talked with the women who called me to schedule interviews, these questions quickly became less relevant. I did not want to make them feel as if they had to "qualify" to participate in the research study. If they had performed these exchanges in the past, I decided to interview them. And within my interviews, all of the women had exchanged sex for money or drugs on a regular basis for a period of at least six months. Based on the goals of my research, it was important to find women who chose to exchange sex for drugs or money as a primary form of livelihood or to support their drug habit. When I decided to no longer ask all of my prescreening questions, I found only one example that wouldn't have fit my pre-existing criteria. For example, during the interview, I quickly learned the woman had exchanged sex for money only one time. Although I continued the interview, I decided I would not include that interview in my data set. And yet as we continued, I found she had exchanged sex for drugs for months at a time with a particular neighbor. These actions fit the initial criteria of exchanging sex for money or drugs, and therefore, I included the interview in my study.

In order to expand my research population, I attempted to find participants who did not access or respond to my flier by asking participants if there were others they would contact on my behalf. This technique allowed me to reach a greater sample of people than those who received services or were currently working and in need of money. When my participants did know of others who might be interested in participating in the study, I asked them to contact these women directly and have them contact me if they were interested in order to maintain their confidentiality.

I interviewed a total of 17 women who contacted me based on my flier or through word of mouth from their friends. (See Appendix A.) When the women responded to my flier, I told them I did not want or need to know their real name at any time during the research process. Because a signature would be the only linkage between the woman's identity and her interview, I was not required to obtain written consent. I read a consent form to the participant and she agreed to the interview on the tape. Therefore, when the women initially contacted me, I told them to give me a made-up name and we would use it in our conversations and meetings. At times the women would give me their real names when they called or left messages, but I never knew their last names and only referred to them by their initials in my transcripts. This process usually worked quite well. I did not have any contact information for these women so as to further protect their identity. I would arrange a meeting place, date, and time with my participant. These meetings usually took place at the public library, their apartments, or a public place like a park where the interviews could remain private. I explained what the interview would entail and then told the participant she would be compensated at the end of the interview. I also made it clear if any questions were uncomfortable or she did not want to answer them for any reason, she was not required to. In only one case did the participant tell me she preferred not to answer a particular question. My participants were also informed they could choose not to participate in the study at any time.

My interviews consisted of both close-ended and open-ended questions, but focused primarily on open-ended questions where the participants would "walk me through" a typical day.[6] I did not have a specific agenda for these interviews. I had specific questions I wanted to ask them about their work and lives, but it was important to me to follow the participant and where she chose to take the interview so she could lead the discussion with her ideas, language, and what was most important to her in light of my questions. In many cases, I would encourage the woman to talk about what was most interesting or pressing to her with respect to the interview and then would find my way back to my questions after she had discussed what was most important to her.

My goals were the same in my interviews with the women who exchanged sex for drugs or money as they were with the public figures. In this way, I was able to hear the language they used to talk about their daily lives and experiences. I did not want my participants to be focusing on the language they used to describe these exchanges and the issues related to exchanging sex for drugs or money, but rather to focus on their lives and let the language emerge from these explanations.

Often, I asked my participants to clarify or expand on a point, and I developed ideas from what my participants mentioned in passing. At times I asked additional questions I thought of after better understanding the experience as a whole. This reflection throughout the interview and my goal of leaving the agenda open helped to move these interviews in directions I could not have foreseen. This meandering approach was not always the most efficient, but the process opened up the interviews to the goals, experiences, and insights of the participants. I was also actively involved in writing my dissertation, the foundation of this book, while completing my interviews with public figures and the women who exchange sex for money or drugs. Participating in these interviews during the writing process allowed me to further reflect on these issues, both while in an interview with a participant, and later when I sat down to transcribe and analyze.

I interviewed my participants over a six-month period during my analysis of the newspaper articles and interviews with public figures. Because I had completed much of the analysis of these two previous sites, I was able to reflect on the representations I was noticing and discuss these representations with the women themselves.

I created a section of questions that asked my participants to reflect on the interview itself. I struggled with the decision about whether to pay these women for their time, as I felt it would be unethical not to compensate them, but one of my concerns was the women might feel as if they were participating in an act for money. During this reflection on the interview, I asked them if they felt like they were performing the interview for money. Although Julie said she felt a bit like a "guinea pig" due to her involvement in this type of research, none of the women said they felt like they were performing for money, and all of the women said they enjoyed the interview because it was helpful to talk about their lives. Within this reflection, I also asked them about the language other people use to talk about street-based sex work and then asked them about how these words made them feel. We then discussed the public perception of street-based sex work and the concerns they believe the general public should have about women who exchange sex for money or drugs. This discussion encouraged them to define the central problems surrounding street-based sex work.

This reflection was extremely rewarding for me as the interviewer because I was able to gain insight into how my participants felt about the interview itself, and I drew on their expertise to influence my subsequent interviews with other women. This meta-level reflection also provided insights into how these women understood street-based sex work and its related problems, which was valuable beyond measure.

I acknowledge most, if not all, of these women knew of my involvement with the social service agency, and all of them knew a social service agency was the vehicle through which the initial contact was made because my fliers were posted there. Due to these factors, I have to assume my stance as a social service agent, rather than a friend, may have influenced their responses, perhaps by stating what they thought they "should" say or what I "expected" to hear. In light of these facts, I do not believe these women were being dishonest with me in our interviews. The social service agency did not provide or deny services based on the actions of these women, and I was no longer directly affiliated with *Casa Segura* at the time of our interviews. As I said, I often interacted with these women outside the interviews, and I knew these women as people experiencing their own ups and downs. Our conversations were relaxed and at times intimate, and I prefaced our conversations with statements about confidentiality.

PUBLIC FIGURES

My second site of analysis focused on my interviews with seventeen people in leadership roles, what I term *public figures*, who are directly involved with street-based sex work in Nemez. These participants include police officers, social service agents, sex worker rights activists, neighborhood association leaders, medical professionals, and academics. The purpose of these interviews was two-fold: to learn more about how the various systems worked in which these women interacted and to analyze the language used by public figures to talk about street-based sex work. My questions were less focused on the language they used and more focused on their positions, the women, the system, and the community. Therefore, I wasn't asking my participants to pay attention to the language they used, but simply to talk about their knowledge of the systems. In fact, in many ways I tried to steer away from my interest in language because I didn't want the speaker to focus too much on her language and therefore be "careful" about her choice of words. I have to assume, because of the interview environment, the participants were already being somewhat careful about the choices they made regarding language. Therefore, I worked to call attention away from this area of study and focused more on the practical situations in which these people worked. At one point in the interview, I asked my participants to reflect on the language they use to identify women who exchange sex for drugs or money, the extent of my direct focus in this area.

My volunteer efforts and work experience enabled me to learn more about the system as a whole, particularly about the workings of the social service institutions in which I was employed and the other organizations with which it was closely connected. In addition to my research, holding these positions made me more aware of the public figures (those people who, in a professional capacity, come into contact with women who exchange sex for drugs or money) who could contribute to my project. In reading local media reports about issues related to sex work, I created a list of police officers; neighborhood association leaders; people who worked for social service agencies, including social workers, medical practitioners, and academics; and local activists who were closely involved with the sex work community. The interview portion of the study began by interviewing two informants—people I knew well who agreed not only to be interviewed, but also to review my questions and offer suggestions and revisions. This process was incredibly useful because these two people were informed about the sex work industry and came from different backgrounds. One person held a position in a social service organization and had been working in that area for nine years, while the other one was a former sex worker and activist who had been working in the field for eight years. Both offered insights about not only my interview questions but also my project as a whole. These initial interviews were valuable in the insights they provided for revisions to my questions prior to interviewing other participants.

200 Appendix B

Depending on my contacts and how I reached a particular participant, I told them about my connections with the social service organizations. If the participant was familiar with the organization, I told them about my position there. If they were not, I would most often tell them I was a student doing research and then mention my role as an employee of this organization within the interview. I would divulge this information within the interview after I had asked questions about social service organizations available to women who exchange sex for drugs or money because I did not want my participant to assume I was familiar with all of the services because I worked with a specific organization. In all cases, I tried to be as open as possible about my role and objectives as a researcher.

I contacted my participants either by phone or e-mail, briefly explained my project, and asked if they would be willing to be interviewed. In addition to explaining my project, I asked them a series of questions in order to clarify if they were appropriate for the research study. I asked how they were involved with street-based sex work, and based on their answers, decided if they were involved fully enough in the industry to be included in the study. To be involved fully meant they had extensive experience with and knowledge about women who exchange sex for drugs or money. If they were only peripherally involved, I asked them if there were others they would suggest I contact that would be more suitable for my study. During the interview I also asked my participants if there were others they felt would be useful for me to interview. In this way, I used a snowball effect, moving from participant to participant based on who the public figures believed would be knowledgeable and interested in my study.

I contacted a total of 35 people and completed a total of 20 interviews, including sixteen women and four men. The sixteen people that did not participate in the interviews either did not respond to my emails or phone calls, referred me to other people who were more appropriate, or were unable to participate due to time conflicts or because they no longer lived in the area. Based on my initial and developing list of contacts, all of the key players who were involved with street-based sex work in Nemez were interviewed. All of my contacts were willing to be involved in the project, and there were no public figures intimately involved in street-based sex work in Nemez unwilling to participate in my study. Of these participants, nine work for social service agencies, four work in various positions within the Nemez Police Department, three are activists, two are involved in neighborhood associations, and two are academic researchers.

NEWSPAPER REPRESENTATIONS OF SEX WORK

Newspaper media create interpretations of marginalized groups that require analysis not only to better understand the stories, but the representations of the people contained within them. These interpretations affect both marginalized and mainstream communities. Like the language found in interviews with my participants, how the problems are constructed directs the solutions realized as well as how material conditions are understood and altered.

I analyzed the newspaper articles printed from 1997–2006, the decade immediately preceding my interviews with the participants in my study. I sought to gain a comprehensive understanding of the rhetorics of street-based sex work as propagated through regional newspapers, a respected and long-standing source of socio-cultural information in the area. I chose to look at newspaper articles because the "mosaics" and "kaleidoscopes" created from these stories largely inform laypersons' opinions of and understandings about sex work. Because newspaper articles inform laypersons' views on sex work, I examined this public discourse as it relates to the material conditions of sex workers' lives—the physical environments surrounding street-based sex work and their effects on the workers' bodies, identities, and spirits. For example, material conditions would include the aspects commonly associated with street-based sex work, such as drug use, poverty, and sexually transmitted diseases, and they would also include how these conditions shape both the experiences of women who exchange sex for money or drugs and the perceptions of them by the general public. I provide a brief overview of the themes that emerged from the articles. Rather than analyzing each article in detail, my goal was to capture a picture of the status of sex work as represented in the local print news media to provide a background against which my analysis of the interviews with public figures and women who exchange sex for money or drugs could be contextualized.

Based on the approximately thirteen hundred pages of text analyzed, I show how this language can influence an individual's perception of street-based sex work in Nemez. Some of the themes that emerge based on the sheer number of particular words and their proximity to other words reveal:

- How problems are framed impacts both the material conditions of my participants' lives and how the solutions to these problems are conceptualized.
- The number of times the words are used, as well as associations made between certain words, creates a powerful message that frames problems and solutions in specific ways that influence the material conditions surrounding street-based sex work.

To deepen my analysis, I engaged in a rhetorical study of the articles in my corpus to reveal how ideological assumptions permeate print journalism that addresses women who exchange sex for money or drugs. Among the total 444 articles analyzed, twelve focused on an in-depth coverage of street-based sex work. In these articles, the overall purpose of each is to examine or discuss street-based sex work in the community. All of these articles were included in the general corpus analysis (explained in more detail below) but were also part of a close rhetorical analysis where I focused on the underlying assumptions and ideological frameworks they contained. Many of the words associated with the material conditions surrounding street-based sex work do not lend themselves well to text searches. Therefore, I rely on my analysis of the articles that focus specifically on street-based sex work in order to explore the language related to these areas.

My initial corpus categorization identified the dominant themes that emerged from a decade's worth of regional newspaper articles addressing some aspect of sex work. Of the six categories (Violence against Sex Workers; Disease; In-Depth Coverage of Street-Based Sex Work; Legal Issues; Arrests; Local Community), only twelve of the articles (In-Depth Coverage of Street-Based Sex Work) within the corpus specifically examined street-based sex work. These articles were all from the three Nemez periodicals described in more detail below and together comprised slightly more than 15,000 words. They include nine full articles (written by newspaper reporters), two letters to the editor, and one editorial written by a newspaper columnist.

CORPUS WORD ANALYSIS

Because there were numerous articles that touched on many different themes, I examined the articles based on the prevalence of certain words and metaphors contained in these articles. Therefore, I created a single text file that contained the full text of each article for all the years searched, resulting in approximately 1,300 pages of source material. Due to the sheer number of pages and words, I chose to use the corpus analysis software *Antconc* 3.2.0 in order to effectively analyze the words contained in the articles.[7] This software enabled me to easily search for particular words and then find them in the initial corpus using the file view/file search capability. I was also able to search for particular groups of words, find words frequently clustered together, and find out how frequently each word and cluster was used within the entire corpus. These capabilities empowered me to search for words I had predefined prior to developing the corpus, while also allowing me to discover which words occurred more frequently than others throughout the entire corpus—including words I had not previously identified. These features enabled me to fine tune my research in directions I hadn't previously considered.

Using *Antconc* made it easy to search how many times particular words are used in general and within specific contexts. I began my search of the text by counting the total number of times particular words were used. These words were chosen from those commonly associated with the material conditions of street-based sex work, which I have outlined in Appendix C. Each word listed also includes close derivatives of that word. For example, when I list the words *sex work*, I also included searches of *sex worker*, *sex worker's*, and *sex workers'*.[8]

These occurrences do not relate directly to sex work in every case—and it is not my intent to argue that as the case, as it would require I examine the context of every use of every word and how it is used within the article as a whole. More important is how often specific terms and phrases are used contextually in articles that discuss or are about sex work, and therefore, what types of general associations are likely to be made when street-based sex work is present.

After my initial analysis, I then searched for clusters of words repeated throughout the entire corpus, or the words commonly found near selected target words. I chose to do cluster searches of the words *prostitution, prostitute,* and *prostitutes,* and began by searching for clusters smaller than five words total, meaning the program only looked for words within five words of the target word.[9] *Antconc* 3.2.0 finds these clusters based on the number of times they occur within the corpus. Therefore, the researcher is not solely responsible for searching for key words. In addition to searching for derivatives of prostitution, I also searched for clusters surrounding all of the words in the above table. Within these searches I increased the cluster size to sixteen in order to validate I found as many associations as possible. The following section provides more detailed information about my analytic methodologies of the newspaper articles.

METHODOLOGIES FOR CODING AND ANALYSIS OF NEWSPAPER REPRESENTATIONS OF STREET-BASED SEX WORK

I examined the three primary newspapers in the Nemez community[10]—*The Nemez Daily, The Nemez Weekly,* and *The State's Daily News.*[11] I analyzed newspaper articles printed in these papers from the ten-year period of 1997–2006[12] in order to offer the most comprehensive viewpoint of how sex work is framed and represented.[13] My initial library search for terms commonly associated with sex work—*sex work, sex worker(s), prostitute(s),* and *prostitution*[14]—led me to read/scan approximately thirteen hundred (1,300) articles. Because my goal was to examine how local sex work, specifically street-based sex work, is represented and discussed in the community, throughout my searches and subsequent analysis I included only the articles specifically mentioning local sex work and issues related to sex work in the community.[15] Within this corpus there were a total of 490 articles that mentioned or were specifically about local sex work. The number of articles written per year ranged from 32 to 71. On average, there were 53 sex work related articles written per year.[16]

If an article dealt with sex work, it was placed in one of three categories: street-based sex work, non-street-based sex work, or illegal sex work in general. This delineation between street and non-street-based sex work is also one many researchers make.[17] The third category, illegal sex work in general, included articles discussing illegal sex work and did not mention street-based sex work specifically.

Within these three categories, 91percent (444) of the articles focused on street-based sex work, 8percent (39) focused on non-street-based sex work, and 1 percent (seven) of the articles focused on the laws and penalties relating to illegal sex work in general. Based on this simple categorization, it is easy to see why the picture most commonly considered by the layperson is *street*-based sex work.

CATEGORY ANALYSIS

After forming these initial categorizations, I divided the articles further according to their individual subject matter. Due to the preponderance (91%) of the articles focused on street-based sex work and my coding of them, I created the following subcategories (listed from least to greatest number of articles): a. historical; b. violence against women who exchange sex for money or drugs; c. disease; d. in-depth coverage of street-based sex work; e. legal cases peripherally involving women who exchange sex for money or drugs; f. arrests; and g. the local community[18] (see Table A.1 for the specific breakdown and number of articles and percentages).[19] These subcategories require additional explanation.

The aforementioned subcategories emerged primarily through the article titles and the focus of each article. For example, "County Syphilis Cases up Third Year in a Row" and "Study is Urged to Check Risks of Border

Table A.1 Categories, Numbers, and Percentages of Articles Found Directly Related to Street-Based Sex Work from 1997–2006

Category	Number of Articles	Percentage of Street-Based Sex Work Articles (444 total)
Historical	7	1.6%
Violence Against Women who Exchange Sex for Money or Drugs	8	1.8%
Disease	8	1.8%
In-Depth Coverage of Street-Based Sex Work	12	2.7%
Legal Cases Peripherally Involving Women who Exchange Sex for Money or Drugs	38	8.6%
Arrests	43	9.7%
Local Community	328	73.9%

HIV" are two articles categorized as being primarily about disease based on the titles and the information they included. Although many articles mentioned diseases in relationship to street-based sex work (HIV/AIDS, sexually transmitted diseases, etc.), the articles didn't focus primarily on the issue of disease and were therefore included in the subcategory that best fit the overall theme of the article, rather than the "disease" category. The previous section provides a snapshot of my analysis. The following outlines each category in more detail.

Historical: The "historical" category includes articles that focus on street-based sex work as it existed in the past. There were seven articles that discussed historical aspects of sex work in Nemez I included. While these articles did not reflect the current status of sex work—they dealt with topics such as legal sex work in Nemez at the turn of the twentieth century—they do reflect how sex work was being reimagined in the public consciousness within periodicals over the past decade. Because these historical considerations and presentations were brought to the public's attention over this period, I included them.

Violence Against Women Who Exchange Sex: In the subcategory "violence against women who exchange sex," each article focuses on a crime that has been committed, such as sexual assaults, robbery, and murder.

Disease: In the "disease" subcategory, each article focuses on disease transmission via sexual contact or intravenous drug use. In these articles, the women are either mentioned peripherally or are central to the article, but ultimately the focus of the article is on a disease in the local community. The subcategory "legal cases peripherally involving women who exchange sex for money or drugs" is simply that. In each article, a legal case is the focus and women who exchange sex for money are mentioned once or twice. This subcategory includes a larger number of articles than was typical for the ten-year period because of a high-profile case spanning two years that mentions a woman who exchanged sex for money almost as an aside. In all of these articles, the women were not the victims of a crime or the focus of an article, but because women who exchange sex for money or drugs are mentioned, I included the articles in my analysis.

In-Depth Coverage of Street-Based Sex Work: The subcategory of "in-depth coverage of street-based sex work" was exactly that. In these articles, the overall purpose of each article is to examine or discuss street-based sex work in the community. All of the articles that focus specifically on street-based sex work were included in the general corpus analysis (explained in more detail below) but were also part of an in-depth analysis where I focused on the underlying assumptions and ideological frameworks contained within these articles. Especially within the subcategory of "in-depth coverage of street-based sex work," a primary focus of the articles is an explanation of street-based sex work within the local community. Therefore, I analyzed all of these articles in depth because sex work was the subject of the article, rather than simply being tangentially related to the subject of the article.

Legal Cases Peripherally Involving Women: I included only the articles that focused on sex work in Nemez and the legal matters related to sex work in the state. Occasionally, some of the articles addressed sex work in other cities, but if the article did not specifically mention sex work in Nemez, I did not include it.

Arrests: I chose not to group articles that focused on arrests of people involved in street-based sex work in the "In-Depth Coverage" category because these articles not only dealt with criminal charges, but also with police tactics, law enforcement regulations, and legal penalties rather than street-based sex work practices in particular. As I reviewed these materials, I determined that analyzing the additional 43 articles that focused on arrests would necessarily and unhelpfully broaden the scope of this project to include many issues not directly related to street-based sex work (e.g., zoning laws, officer deployments, and bench judgments); for this reason I excluded these articles from this part of the project.

Local Community: The subcategory "local community" includes all of the articles that focus on general issues where street-based sex work was mentioned or was one of the central themes of the article but was not *the* central focus. For example, this subcategory includes articles that discuss neighborhood "clean up projects," police politics, letters to the editor, crime, and so forth. Because all of the articles focus on the local community, local conditions, and mention street-based sex work, I chose to identify them simply as "local community." Many of these articles were about specific areas of the local community that the public and/or police were taking an interest in and therefore mentioned street-based sex work along with other "problems" that needed to be or had been addressed in that area.

Non-Street-Based Sex Work: The articles that focused on non-street-based sex work were also further subcategorized according to the following (from least to greatest number of articles): a. other sex work; b. sex work arts; and c. sex work in general (its own category—not included in non-street-based sex work). Table A.2 shows the exact number of articles and percentages for these categories. I offer this subcategory breakdown of the articles related to non-street-based sex work in order to provide the reader with more information about what kind of information this subcategory contains.

Other Sex Work: The "other sex work" subcategory includes articles about aspects of sex work other than street-based sex work. These articles included discussions of topless bars, arrests of escorts, gambling and prostitution at

Table A.2 Categories, Numbers, and Percentages of Articles Found Related to Non-Street-Based Sex Work from 1997–2006

Category	Number of Articles	Percentage of Non-Street-Based Sex Work Articles (46 total)	Percentage of Total Articles (490 total)
Other Sex Work	17	43.6%	3.5%
Sex Work Arts	22	56.4%	4.5%

casinos, etc. This area of sex work is not defined as street-based sex work because rather than one-on-one contact on the street, all of these aspects of sex work involve some sort of advertising, phone calls, and oftentimes management that interacts between the clients and the sex workers.

Sex Work Arts: The "sex work arts" subcategory is a bit more complicated to define. Among the non-street sex work articles, the greatest number of articles falls into the "sex work arts" category. Building on the popularity of similar festivals that have occurred in larger cities such as New York and San Francisco, activists and sex workers in Nemez brought performers to the local community to celebrate, educate, and create awareness about sex work. All of the articles in this subcategory focus on these events in the local community.

After searching, compiling, reading, coding, and categorizing all of the articles according to the themes that emerged, I analyzed these articles as they related to the material conditions of sex workers' lives. For example, material conditions included the aspects commonly associated with street-based sex work, such as drug use and sexually transmitted diseases, and they would also include how these conditions shape both women who exchange sex for money or drugs and the perceptions of them by the general public.

COLLECTING, CODING, AND ANALYSIS

The analysis of the data is never separate from the collection methods. The processes of gathering, analyzing, and understanding are iterative. I interviewed the public figures over a sixteen-month period and the women who exchange sex for money or drugs over a five-month period. Therefore, the interviews, analysis, and writing overlapped. I wrote my analysis of the newspapers and of several interviews with public figures as I continued interviewing both public figures and women who exchange sex for money or drugs. After conducting many of the interviews with the public figures and engaging in preliminary analysis of these interviews, I started interviewing the women who exchange sex for drugs or money. I was then able to incorporate my analysis of both the media and my interviews with public figures into my interviews with the women.

Drawing on the techniques outlined by Anthropologists Emerson, Fretz, and Shaw (1995), I closely read through all of my field notes and transcripts and then adopted a process of "open coding" where I read these documents line-by-line in order to identify and formulate the ideas, themes, or issues suggested by the texts. I coded in this way in order to allow the themes to emerge from the documents rather than searching for predefined categories that would be imposed on the data. This statement does not mean to suggest the categories existed separate from my own questions and concerns regarding the process. Because I had defined my research questions and the study as a whole, in addition to my own interests and concerns, I certainly cannot attempt to remove myself from this equation.

It was through reading, re-reading, categorizing, and re-categorizing these interviews I "found" a coding system that emerged based on reoccurring themes. The problems surrounding street-based sex work largely emerged through my categorization of the women's perceptions of street-based sex work—whether it was their own, reflecting on themselves and street work in general, others who participate in this work, or the public's view of street-based sex work.

Appendix C
Number of Times Terms Included in Newspaper and Participant Interviews Corpora[20]

Term	Number Newspaper Corpus	Number Public Figure Corpus	Women who Exchange Sex Corpus
Total Number of Words	449,742	205,305	213,258
Abuse (in general—drug, physical, sexual)	235	92	28
AIDS	68	14	24
Arrest	451	337	91
Bad	118	80	116
Bar (drinking establishment)	162	14	25
Change	242	92	60
Clean	183	41	88
Community	583	197	13
Crime	1212	78	13
Dirty	20	18	37
Disease	78	40	24
Drug	1061	463	547
Exploit	19	7	0
Gang	137	4	0
Help	522	227	169
Ho	7	6	22
Hooker	38	52	42
Incest	2	0	0
Jail/Prison	657	161	261
"John"	81	96	23
Molest/Molester	27	7	20
Money	301	323	657
Needle	47	21	13
Neighborhood	1226	209	21
Police/Cop	1634	302	182

(continued)

Appendix C

Term	Number Newspaper Corpus	Number Public Figure Corpus	Women who Exchange Sex Corpus
Poor/Poverty	118	41	18
Prostitute	1135	596	214
Rescue (excluding names of organizations)	7	0	4
Resident	665	49	0
Safe/Safety	265	64	16
Save	55	2	27
Sex/Sexy/Sexual	763	967	404
Sexually Transmitted	16	16	1
Sex work	106	433	27
Substance (related directly to use/abuse)	54	83	4
Victim	247	62	0
Violence/Violent	269	73	16
Whore	18	47	35

Appendix D
Interview Materials

1. RECRUITMENT FLIER

Have you ever felt like you wanted or needed to have SEX for Money? or Drugs? or other Personal Gain?

- If so, and if you've done this within the last year, please consider joining my research study.
- I am a student at the University of Arizona and I want to hear your experiences and perspectives on having sex in order to get money, drugs, or other personal gain.
- All information will be held strictly confidential!
- No one will know who you are or what you said—your experiences will only be known to me.
- Your voice will provide information about women who have sex for drugs, money, or other gain—an important perspective that hasn't been heard before.

Please Contact Jill if you're interested or want more information at:
(520) 990-5063

($30.00 for 1-2 hours of your time)

Figure A.1 Recruitment Flier.

2. SAMPLE INTERVIEW GUIDE

Performing Sex Acts for Money, Drugs, or Other Personal Gain

Introduction to Participant: Please also avoid mentioning specific names, especially in relation to illegal behavior. If you do mention names, they will be deleted from the tape and transcript.

I am going to be asking you questions about your life. Many times I'll ask you to walk me through a typical event or interaction. If at any time I ask a question you don't feel comfortable answering, just tell me. You don't have to answer anything you don't want to. I appreciate your honesty and your willingness to talk with me.

General Information:
By what name do you want to be known? First and last.
By what ethnicity do you identify?
How old are you?
Do you live in Tucson?
How long have you lived in Tucson?
Where do you live?
How long have you lived there?
Where are you from?
Parents? Questions regarding parents' economic status.
Education level of parents?
Ethnicity of parents?
Other?

Work Information:
Do you work?
Where?
What is your position?
How long have you been in this position?

Education:
What is the highest level of education you've completed?
Are you interested in gaining more education?
If so, in what area?

Perception
Tell me about a typical day in your life. Walk me through it.
What do you think of women who participate in sex acts for money or drugs?
What do you call this?
What do others call this?
What is the public perception of women who participate in sex acts for money or drugs?

How is your perception different?
Do you have friends who participate in sex acts for money or drugs?
Are their lives similar to yours?
How are they the same or different?

Logistics
How often do you participate in sex acts for money or drugs?
What affects how often you do or do not do this?
How does it work? Walk me through a typical interaction.
What affects how much money or drugs you receive for participating in sex acts?

Material Conditions
Tell me about your social status? Who looks up to you? Who looks down on you? What affects your social status?
Do you choose when you will participate in sex acts for money or drugs?
What else affects this decision?
Do you control where it happens, if condoms are worn, etc.?
Walk me through a typical interaction in terms of who controls or is in charge of what.
Do you compete with others? Who?
When did you first participate in a sex act for money or drugs?
How did this begin?
What do you like about participating in sex acts for money or drugs?
What do you dislike about participating in sex acts for money or drugs?
Have you ever been arrested? How many times?
Walk me through a typical arrest.
Do you use drugs?
What kind?
What do you think about your exposure to HIV and other STDs?
What do you think about the police and other people in the community?
Who are you afraid of? Why?
Who do you trust? Why?

Others
Are there others you think might be interested in talking with me?
Please don't tell me their names.
Why do you think I should talk to this person?
Would you be willing to contact them and have them get in touch with me if they're interested?

Final Questions
Are there other things I should be considering in my research? What am I leaving out or missing?
Do you have any additional questions about my research?

214 *Appendix D*

Anything you'd like to add?

If possible, it would be helpful for me to observe situations where you talk with other women who participate in sex acts for drugs or money and where you or others contact people in order to perform sex acts for money, drugs, etc. These observations are not necessary—only if you are comfortable with the situation. Would it be possible for me to observe any of these situations? I would not take notes on anyone's activities except for yours, and no names will ever be included in my notes.

3. LISTENING TO THE LANGUAGE OF SEX WORKERS—PUBLIC FIGURES.

[Not all questions will be asked for each participant. They will vary based on the individual's position, experience, and expertise.]

Introduction to Participant: Within my study, I am focusing primarily on prostitutes (or their word). My questions will be limited to that area of information. If you aren't referring to this area, please try to let me know, so as to better understand your answers.

Please also avoid mentioning specific names, especially in relation to illegal behavior. If you do mention names, they will be deleted from the tape and transcript.

Work/Position Information:
What type of organization do you work for?
What is your position?
How long have you been in this position?
What other positions have you held that are related to the work you do in this position?
How long were you in these other positions?
What do you consider are your areas of expertise?

Sex Work Questions:

Language
How do you identify people who sell sex or aspects of sex for money?
What are the most common terms you and others in your area use?
Can you tell me about prostitution (or use the words they use) as it relates to your job/role?
Related questions based on specialty.
How does the system work?

Appendix D   215

System
What is your role within the system?
What are the most important issues that need to be addressed and/or dealt with as related to prostitution (again, use the words they use)?
Related questions based on these issues.
What relationship exists between the police and sex workers?
Are there community organizations for sex workers?
What kind of work do they do?

Perception
Who are these women?
How do you describe them?
Age/gender/ethnicity/sexuality/other?
What is the public perception of sex workers?
What is your perception of these women?
Are there primary differences in the two?
If so, based on what?

Logistics
Where do most sex workers work? Are they stable or transient?
What hours do they work?
Do these women have other jobs in addition to sex work?
Do sex workers cross borders to find clients?
How many sex workers are in this city (limited to street prostitutes)?
Do most sex workers have pimps or do they work for themselves?
What percentage would you guess?
If arrested, do police identify if they're underage?
Are you trained in the area of sex/labor trafficking?
Do you know if there are separate laws for forced prostitution?
Do you assume they are choosing to be prostitutes?
If the prostitute is not a legal citizen, do you assume she is choosing to be a prostitute?
How many partners a week do sex workers have?
What do they charge per session?
What do they charge per night?
Do sex workers report STDs/infection?
Where do they go for treatment?
Do sex workers use condoms?
Who are the major clients of sex workers?
Are the clients primarily local?
Where do clients find sex workers?
What do clients pay per session?
What do clients pay per night?
Do clients report sexually transmitted infections?
Where do they go for treatment?

Do clients use condoms?
Other demographics?

Related Organizations and People
I would like to ask you about other organizations and people you work with in this area in order to interview them, with their consent. If, for any reason, you believe a person might be involved in any illegal activities, it would be best for you to contact them directly and then have them contact me if they are interested in participating, in order to preserve their confidentiality. If you have participants you are willing to contact for me, in order to preserve their confidentiality, I would greatly appreciate it.

Who are the experts in your field?
Who are the informal leaders?
Most experienced/knowledgeable members?
Who else do you work with?
Would any of the above be willing to talk to me?
Should I contact them directly or would you rather contact them for me?
Are there other organizations I should contact?
Can you recommend specific individuals within them who might be willing to talk to me?
Do you have access to prostitutes?
Would you be willing to talk to them about my study and ask them to contact me if they're interested?

Final Questions
Are there additional things I should be considering in my research? What am I leaving out?
Do you have any additional questions about my research?
Anything you'd like to add?

Notes

NOTES TO THE PREFACE

1. I have taken the liberty of editing my participants' language for readability, but I have not changed any of the key words or phrases.
2. All geographic locations and names, as well as the names and identifying information of my participants, have been changed, following general ethnographic practice to protect the identities of my participants. Other publications based on this research refer to the research site, Jemez. I chose to change this name to Nemez after learning there is an actual town in the southwest named Jemez Springs, and although this town is very different from my research site, I did not want to inadvertently mislead readers.
3. Appendix B: Research Process and Layers of Data outlines the research questions related to each site.
4. For the sake of consistency and readability, unless the language is my own, I use the terms *sex work/ers*, *prostitute*, and *prostitution* in the context in which they are used by the source or speaker.
5. In an attempt to gain my participants' insights as well as their contribution to a more complete understanding of street-based sex work, I asked most of them if they would be interested in reading and responding to drafts of this manuscript. But because that can be an onerous task, and many said they were not interested in participating at that level, I was not able to incorporate their perspectives after the initial interviews. Given the reading and writing involved at this level is labor intensive, and I did not have funding to pay them for their time, I did not want to impose upon them in this capacity. I include the stories they told about their lives as well as lengthy excerpts from our interviews to create space for my participants to speak for themselves as much as possible within this context.
6. In order to maintain anonymity of my research site, the name of this organization has been changed. See Appendix B: Research Process and Layers of Data for a more detailed description of my roles within and time spent at *Casa Segura*.
7. See Britt 2001; Cintron 1997; Kulick 1998.
8. As this second definition is vague, state law and individual courts must be relied upon to define specific situations. For example, providing domination for the purpose of titillation in exchange for money is illegal in many states, yet penetration of any orifice is not required. To compare, exotic dancing is legal, yet involves face-to-face and mental stimulation, which demonstrates that an overarching definition is difficult to determine. Sociologist Ronald Weitzer (2012) defines the sex industry as "the workers, managers,

owners, marketers, agencies, clubs, and trade associations involved in sexual commerce, both legal and illegal varieties" (p. 3).

9. The term *cisgender* was coined by Carl Buijs and means "on this side of the behavioral, cultural, or psychological traits typically associated with one sex. Stated simply, it means that one's identity and presentation matches their physical morphology" (Matthews 1999).

10. The term *transgender* was adeptly explained by one of my participants, Dr. Julie Everett, a 36-year-old, white, lesbian woman who works as a medical doctor in the HIV/STI division at the county health department:

    Jill: How do you define transgender?
    Dr. Julie Everett: Mmm hmm. That's an excellent question because, you know, it's so widely . . .People self-identify in a whole variety of ways. When I'm talking with medical providers just for some clarity. And when it's a bunch of trans folks talking and we're all talking, there's all kinds of excitement and discussion.But when I'm talking with providers, I specifically mean that someone who feels that their physical self doesn't match who they feel they are and who they would like to live their life as. So we specifically talk about trans-sexuality with respect to individuals who want medical intervention, whether that's hormones, whether that's laser for hair removal, whether that's surgery.You know, the assumption is that everyone goes to surgery; that's certainly not true. But transgender, I think, is just sort of a broad umbrella for something . . . . for the physical body not matching who people really are.

11. See Appendix B: Research Process and Layers of Data for more detailed information about my methodologies with participants.

12. See Bernstein 2007b; Dewey and Kelly 2011; Epele 2002; Romero-Daza, Weeks, and Singer 2003; and Wahab 2004 for some examples.

13. See Lerum et al. 2012, p. 93; and Koyama 2011.

14. I want to thank Susan Dewey and Penelope Saunders for their help in thinking through this complex issue.

15. I borrow from Sociologist Wendy Chapkis's (2000) categories in her article "Power and Control in the Commercial Sex Trade," expanding on her categories based on my own analysis of the central issues that emerged.

16. In this statement I am not claiming that they are more victimized than people who are involved in labor or sex trafficking, which is explored more fully in Chapter 2.

17. According to Officer Eugene Matthews, the vice unit includes the adult entertainment industry, escort services, street prostitution, alcohol-related investigations, and illegal gambling.

18. I limit the statistics to these years (2003-2006) because it is the time period of my ethnographic research.

19. Commercialized sex crimes are divided amongst the categories: prostitution, pandering, house of ill fame, and other.

20. In order to maintain anonymity, all reported figures are approximate.

21. See Romero-Daza, Weeks, and Singer 2005; Shannon, Strathdee, Shoveller, Rusch, et al. 2009; and Surratt, Kurtz, Weaver, and Inciardi 2005.

22. All names of counties, organizations, and individuals have been changed to protect the anonymity of the participants involved in the research.

23. In order to maintain anonymity, the sources that include geographic locations have been omitted.

24. *Emergent* cases are defined as the sum of new HIV cases and new AIDS cases not diagnosed as HIV infections in any prior calendar year. These cases are used as an estimate of incidence, as every case of HIV/AIDS may only be counted as *emergent* once—in the year in which it was first reported.

25. See Dalla, Xia, and Kennedy 2003; Epele 2002; Porter and Bonilla 2010; Raphael and Shapiro 2004; Romero-Daza, Weeks, and Singer 2003.
26. The word *pimp* is contested and stereotypically understood to be a person who exploits women who exchange sex. See McCracken 2006; and Pheterson 1989, for a more thorough explanation of this term.
27. See Norton-Hawk 2004; Pheterson 1989; and Porter and Bonilla 2010
28. Documentation of this violence is extensive. For examples, see Dalla, Xia, and Kennedy 2003; Epele 2002; Kurtz, Surratt, Indiardi, and Kiley 2004; Monto 2004; and Quinet 2011.
29. Systems include legal, economic, political, and governmental, among others.

NOTES TO CHAPTER 1

1. Brummett borrowed the term *mosaic* from Samuel Becker in his 1971 essay in the landmark volume of rhetorical studies *The Prospect of Rhetoric*, which aimed "to provide a way to account for the ways in which people, going about their daily business, process the sources of information available to them in meaningful (and meaning-managing) ways" (p. 63).
2. Personal correspondence with E. Koyama September 2012.
3. See also Shannon et al. 2008 who argue "the complex vulnerabilities of Aboriginal women stem from a legacy of oppression and colonization and the multigenerational effects of social isolation, discrimination, entrenched poverty, and the residential school system" (p. 912).
4. Cooper draws on Glen A. Mazis's term *surround* "to suggest that natural environments cannot be distinguished from social ones" (p. 444).

NOTES TO CHAPTER 2

1. Portions of this section have been previously published in McCracken (2006b).
2. Because there were numerous articles within the Nemez newspapers that touched on a wide variety of themes, I examined the articles by using the word list, collacates, and clusters features of *Antconc* 3.2.0 (See Appendix B for a more detailed explanation of methods). This software enabled me to easily search for particular words, as well as words frequently clustered together, and find out how frequently each word and cluster was used within the entire corpus.
3. A more detailed analysis of the word *drug* in this corpus and its relationship to prostitution is included in Chapter 3.
4. These occurrences do not relate directly to sex work in every case—and it is not my intent to argue that case—as it would require I examine the context of every use of every word and how it is used within the article as a whole. More important here is how often specific terms and phrases are used contextually in articles that discuss or are about sex work, and therefore, what types of general associations are likely to be made when street-based sex work is present.
5. See Appendix C: Number of Times Terms Included in Newspaper and Participant Interviews for a complete listing of the terms and numbers found in the corpus.
6. See McArdle and Erzen 2001; and Sausa, Keatley, and Operario 2007.
7. These occurrences do not relate directly to sex work in every case—and it is not my intent to argue that as the case, as it would require that I examine the

context of every use of every word and how it is used within the article as a whole. More important here is how often specific terms and phrases are used contextually in articles that discuss or are about sex work, and therefore, what types of general associations are likely to be made when street-based sex work is present.
8. In making this statement, I do not mean to imply that people who exchange sex are more prone to experiencing physical or sexual abuse. See Potterat, Rothenberg, Muth, et. al. (1998) for an examination of the relationship between sexual and drug abuse and participation in prostitution. Critiques are raised that this same attention to historical physical and sexual abuse is not paid to those people who participate in other occupations, for instance police officers or school teachers. It is irresponsible to make this connection unless extensive data is also collected based on other occupations.
9. Because there were numerous articles within the Nemez newspapers that touched on a wide variety of themes, I examined the articles by using the Key Word in Concordance (KWIC) feature of *Antconc* 3.2.0 (See Appendix B for a more detailed explanation of methods). This software enabled me to easily search for particular words, as well as words frequently clustered together, to discern how frequently each word and cluster was used within the entire corpus.
10. Because clusters are found based on the number of times they occur within the corpus, which therefore did not require that I know every possible word potentially clustered with a key word, many words were clustered with forms of the word *prostitute* I had not previously considered, such as, *addicts, dealers, junkies,* and *pushers*. Because these words are also associated with drugs and drug use, I included them in my overall count.
11. See McCracken (2010) for a more extensive coverage of the newspaper analysis and findings.
12. See also Ratner 1993.
13. See also Shannon et al. 2008; Shannon et al. 2007; Shannon et al. 2009; and Spittal et al. 2003.
14. Multiple sources document this cyclical nature of street-based sex work, drug use, and violence. See Dalla, Xia, and Kennedy 2003; El-Bassel et al. 1997; Erickson, Butters, McGillicudy, and Hallgren 2000; Kurtz et al. 2004; Maxwell and Maxwell 2000; Phoenix 2000; Young, Boyd, and Hubbell 2000;

NOTES TO CHAPTER 3

1. Portions of this and other chapters were published in McCracken 2011.
2. Trafficking is also a contested term. As Anthropologist Laura Agustín (2005d) argues, the migrants who are characterized as victims of trafficking are defined by only one side of the contemporary debate because the migrant women's own descriptions of what they are doing contrasts drastically from that of outsiders. Agustín also contests the problem of defining some women as "victims" and others as "helpers" within this same debate.
3. For extensive coverage of this history, see, for example, Agustín 2007; Bernstein 2007a; Chapkis 2005; Chuang 2010; Doezema 2004; Lerum et al. 2012; Soderlund 2005; and Weitzer 2007.
4. See also Chuang 2010 and Weitzer 2007.
5. Susanne Thorbek (2002) argues that it is difficult to distinguish between people who have been trafficked and those who have not:
   A woman may decide to go abroad, knowing she will work as a prostitute, and then find the conditions under which she has to work and the payment of the debt and the interest rates charged unacceptable;

in this sense she may be considered a victim of trafficking. Another woman may be lured or cheated into the trade but decide that, in the circumstances, her best option is to go on. Has she been trafficked if she does not want to be liberated? (5)

This stance is controversial and complicated, especially as it relates to transnational issues. Like Thorbek, Anthropologist Laura Agustín (2002) complicates these distinctions when she discusses five Latin American women who are connected with the sex industry. She writes:

> Given the very different stories these women have to tell, labeling them *either* "migrant sex workers" or "victims of trafficking" is incorrect and unhelpful to an understanding of why and how they have arrived at their present situations. The placing of labels is largely a subjective judgement dependent on the researcher of the moment and is not the way women talk about themselves, something like the attempt to make complicated subjects fit into a pre-printed form. (30)

Agustín argues for a framework of migration studies in order to think about those who work in sex, domestic, and "caring" services and advocates locating these women as migrants, which then "allows consideration of all conceivable aspects of people's lives and travels, locates them in periods of personal growth and risk-taking and does not force them to identify as sex workers (or as maids, or 'carers', for that matter)" (31). Her point about identification underscores my own, because it is in this identification that certain acts and attributes are emphasized while others are ignored or erased completely.

6. See also Saunders 2004.
7. See also Alliance for a Safe and Diverse DC 2008.
8. See McCracken 2006a; Phoenix 1999, 2000; for further discussion of the problematic nature of this term and its application to individuals. See also sources that provide a detailed description of "pimps" and their relationships to street-based sex work: Curtis et al. 2008; Norton-Hawk 2004; Sterks 2000; Weidner 2001; Weinkauf 2011; and Williamson and Schwartz 2002. See Vorenberg and Vorenberg's (1977) examination of criminal enforcement as the "biggest pimp of all" because women working on the street were often paying fines to the courts due to its criminal status.
9. According to this source, the number of arrests appears to be steadily decreasing. During the years 1994-1997 the number of arrests were approximately 99,000 per year. They have steadily decreased to the lowest number of arrests recorded during this time frame occurring in 2009 at 71,400.
10. See also Alexander 1987; Bernstein 2007; Porter and Bonilla 2010.
11. See Agustín 2004 for an analysis and critique of researching marginalized communities and their responsibility to tell the "truth" to researchers.
12. See also Ritchie and Mogul 2007.

NOTES TO CHAPTER 4

1. A subset of twelve articles includes those whose stated purpose is to provide an in-depth exploration of street prostitution, including its causes, consequences, and possible solutions, within the ten-year period examined.
2. Rather than continuing to use my language of choice, at this point I use the actual language included in the articles in order to provide the reader with a more seamless picture of the language and context found in the corpus.
3. While I am drawing on a limited corpus and cannot make generalizations about how johns and prostitutes are discussed in the mass media on a large scale, this analysis is quite sound within the regional context from which

my data was derived. As such, I believe it fairly and accurately represents an ordinary reader's understanding of prostitution as derived from the newspapers she or he consumes in the Nemez region.
4. This and other quotations are paraphrased in order to maintain anonymity, but the key terms such as *comfort* and *loneliness* are those actually used in the articles.
5. Within these articles all of the people who exchange sex are women and all of the people who purchase sex are men. There is no mention of men who exchange sex or women who purchase sex. Although men also exchange sex on the street for both male and female clients, there is no mention of these transactions in this corpus.
6. A subset of twelve articles within the Nemez newspaper corpus includes those whose stated purpose is to provide an in-depth exploration of street prostitution, including its causes, consequences, and possible solutions, within the ten-year period examined.
7. In order to maintain anonymity of the people I interviewed for other parts of my research, I am not at liberty to reveal the names of the organizations mentioned in these articles.
8. See online site "Community Resources for Sex Work and Public Policy" for additional resources (http://www.stpt.usf.edu/mccracken/research/sexwork/community_resources).

NOTES TO CHAPTER 5

1. See Bernstein 2007b; Dewey and Kelly 2011; Doezema 2006; Jeffreys 2008; and Weitzer 2012 for more detailed and historical accounts of the debates surrounding the terms *sex work* and *prostitution* in particular.
2. See Farley 2003; Jeffreys 2009; and Sullivan 2007.
3. Personal conversation with sex worker rights activist Susan Lopez.
4. In the interview transcripts with public figures the word "victim" was used 61 times. The interview transcripts with the women who exchanged sex did not include this word.
5. See The PROS Network 2012; San Francisco Task Force 1996, and Sex Workers Project 2011.
6. For more studies about violence specific to street-based sex work see Epele 2002; Kurtz, Surratt, Inciardi, and Kiley 2004; Romero-Daza, Weeks, and Singer 2003.
7. See also Bao, Whitbeck, and Hoyt 2000; Kurtz, Surratt, Kiley, and Inciardi 2005.
8. See McCracken 2011 for a more thorough exploration of "help" and street-based sex work.

NOTES TO CHAPTER 6

1. See West Coast LEAF's mission statement.
2. See also Flaherty 2010a; 2010b; 2011a; 2011b.
3. See also Lerum et al. 2012 for a description of the Universal Periodic Review Process and the US State Department's acceptance of recommendation #86, which the authors argue "is an indication of the ability for organised sex workers and their allies to press for change" (p. 99).
4. See Vance 2010 for a more thorough analysis of the proscribed roles of women and heteronormative behavior within marriage.

5. Run by RainCity Housing in Ontario, British Columbia and is funded by the Mental Health Commission of Canada.
6. See Mansson and Hedin 1999; and Williamson and Folaron 2003.
7. See also Segrave, Milivojevic, and Pickering 2009.
8. See Sex Workers Project 2009.

NOTES TO THE APPENDICES

1. I began volunteering at *Casa Segura* in January 2005, and during this time, I spent between five and ten hours each week at the center. I then became a paid employee in June 2005, where I was allowed to work only ten hours per month due to budgetary constraints. In addition to these ten working hours, I spent several hours per week volunteering and working in the office on my own research. I worked as both a volunteer and employee throughout the remainder of my time on this study. During the two years of my research study, there were weeks when I did not spend time at the center and other periods when I was there every day.
2. My work at HealthWise from January through July of 2007 required that I be present at the organization on a daily basis, which further educated me about both personal and systemic issues related to homelessness and my research population in particular.
3. Being identified as an employee at *Casa Segura* necessarily complicated my research in numerous ways. I realized as I started my position as a volunteer that I would be less of an outsider to this community, or at least to the women who partook of the center's services. Although my status as volunteer and later as employee necessarily complicated my perspective as a researcher, it also enabled me to learn a tremendous amount about the system from the perspective of a social service organization and gain access to many public figures and women who exchange sex for money or drugs that I wouldn't have had access to without working in this position. I explain the problems and benefits of volunteering/working/researching within a site later in this appendix when I discuss *Casa Segura* in more detail.
4. I refer to communicative interactions as any kind of communicative event, which includes verbal language, body language, laughs, silences, grunts, etc. It also includes literature that may have been handed out, signs, and/or assaults that I witnessed, along with the communicative interactions that occurred between these women and those with whom they interacted (other women, public figures, children, etc.).
5. See Appendix D for a copy of the flier distributed.
6. See Appendix D for copies of the interview questions.
7. *Antconc* is freeware concordance software developed by Applied Linguist Laurence Anthony, a Ph.D. in applied linguistics. Anthony developed the software in 2002, and it was initially designed for use in the Scientific and Technical Writing Program at the Graduate School of Engineering at Osaka University in Japan. It was initially developed using the PERL 5.8 programming language and is distributed as freeware for Windows and Linux. The software offers an extensive set of text analysis tools including KWIC concordance (a corpus analytical tool for creating word frequency lists, concordances, and collocation tables using electronic files), a search term distribution plot (a tool that plots the occurrence of the search term based on where and with what frequency it appears in the document), file view/file search (enables one to move back and forth quickly from search terms to the context in which the terms are embedded), word clusters (enables one to search for groups of word), and keyword lists (Anthony).

8. It is important to note that in this analysis, I am not making claims about the number of times these words are mentioned as related to newspaper articles in general. I make term-frequency claims about how many times certain words are used in *this* corpus, in articles about prostitution or sex work, and how this proximity might influence the interpretation of the lexical items that are the focus of my research. This analysis seeks to show that there are certain words and phrases used and omitted that serve to highlight the material conditions related to street-based sex work that ultimately influence the reader's perspective of sex work as a whole.
9. Initially, I did searches that were larger and found that the results did not vary significantly, as the key terms showed up within five words of the target word.
10. In order to maintain anonymity of the people I interviewed, I am not able to reveal the location of my research site. Therefore, any indicators of personal identities or geographic locales—including the titles of local newspapers—have been changed.
11. I selected *The Nemez Daily* and *The State's Daily News* due to their wide circulation in the local community. *The State's Daily News* is distributed in the morning and has a circulation of approximately 110,000 copies. *The Nemez Daily* is distributed in the afternoon and averages approximately 30,000 copies. The two daily papers contain largely the same information, although *The State's Daily News* is marketed as more liberal, containing more local Nemez information, and is more expensive than *The Nemez Daily*, which contains more national information (personal correspondence with editors of both papers). *The Nemez Weekly* was selected as a news source because of its circulation. It is a weekly paper that is free and available in places of business to be "picked up" by the reader. *The Nemez Weekly* markets itself as an alternative news source whose median reader is 43 years of age. This age is approximately fifteen years younger than the median age of the two other daily papers (personal correspondence with the *Weekly* editor). Their circulation averages approximately 50,000 copies.
12. In order to compile a body of texts that would allow for both a broad and in-depth analysis of the local media that was also practical in terms of accessing the archives (see below for more information about my archival research), I chose to examine the articles included in the decade prior to and including the time period of my research study. I included articles that covered the past ten years for two of the three periodicals (*The Nemez Weekly* and *The State's Daily News*). Because *The Nemez Daily* did not have their daily editions archived prior to 1999, making only the past eight years accessible through electronic searches, I chose to include and analyze the articles from the past eight years. Including articles from ten years would have required that I scan every daily newspaper in its entirety through microfiche/film for the two years prior to their archive date. Because this search would have probably only added a few articles to my corpus, I decided to omit these past two years and only include eight years from this periodical. Of the two daily periodicals circulated in Nemez, *The State's Daily News* is archived through 1950 and is considered the more important newspaper because it is circulated and covers information throughout the state (per conversation via e-mail with university librarian). The three periodicals include two daily newspapers and one weekly paper. By examining the articles, I provide a picture that reflects the environment while also incorporating the immediate history of sex work in Nemez.
13. During the initial phases of my analysis, I had intended to include news stories from both newspapers and televised news broadcasts. Pictures are

an excellent source of persuasive rhetoric, and these texts would have been fascinating to include in my analysis. One of the limitations of my study was locating archived copies of these televised news broadcasts in order to analyze both their verbal and visual aspects. The time and energy needed to locate and transcribe these stories was prohibitive, and therefore I focused only on print news media. As I moved into my analysis of print media, I again confronted issues related to the images included with the news stories. The archived versions of the print media do not include the images associated with each news story, and the only way to locate these images and include them with the news stories is to physically scan every daily and weekly paper through microfiche/film. Again, the time and energy required to scan every article was prohibitive, and therefore, I focused on the language alone. This decision supported my choice to exclude televised media because of their heavy reliance on images. Including only the language of the televised media stories without subsequent analysis of the visual images would not offer a balanced depiction of their representations of sex work.

14. I began by initially including words like *whore*, *hooker*, and *'ho*, but soon found that when these terms were included in an article, the terms *prostitute* and/or *sex work* were also mentioned. There were cases when the words *hooker* and *'ho* were included in articles that were not about sex work/prostitution.

15. The process of choosing which articles to include in the body of text for analysis quickly became complicated because these articles spanned a variety of areas related to sex work, such as arrests for prostitution, local community issues, and crime in general. In some cases I had to search the article for the specific word in order to find out how it was used because the words were often buried in long articles that were generally unrelated. For instance, there were numerous authors who used the concepts of *prostitution* and *whore* as metaphors for other activities, particularly in editorials and in relationship to political figures and issues. When a word was used in this context, I did not include the article in my corpus, as it was not directly related to sex work in Nemez. There were also many articles and notices that focused on books and films that included sex work. Because the goal of my research was to examine how local sex work, specifically street-based sex work, is represented and discussed in the community, throughout my searches and subsequent analysis I included only the articles that specifically mentioned local sex work and issues related to sex work in the community.

16. This average was taken from the past eight years because articles in *The Nemez Daily* from years one and two were not included in the overall count and analysis. As I explained, *The Nemez Daily* did not have their daily editions archived prior to 1999, making only 1999-2006 accessible through electronic searches. In order to show a representative average, I used only the years where all three circulations were represented.

17. See Chapkis 1997; Leigh 1994; Nagle 1997; Porter and Bonilla 2010; and Weitzer 2000a.

18. This process of searching and narrowing was a circular one, as I searched on numerous dates throughout the two years of my research. The above decisions were ones I came to in the process of my searching for, reading, and categorizing articles. I struggled over which ones to include because every article creates a different picture that ultimately influenced the corpus I would be analyzing. As I continued searching and analyzing my previous categorizations, I revisited these decisions about the inclusion of particular articles. Therefore, I did not come to these decisions quickly, but questioned both the names and the categorizations of the articles throughout my searches.

226 Notes

The number of articles alone helped me to further articulate my research goals and how this body related to my research as a whole because the inclusion of every article, even those tangentially related, would change what was revealed in my analysis. Therefore, I was forced to think through what the inclusion and exclusion of particular articles would mean for my analysis as a whole. As a result, my research captures how local sex work was framed and represented in print journalism during this time period.

19. The articles are not categorized according to whether the women/prostitutes or men/johns were discussed. Rather, they are categorized according to the primary focus of the article.
20. The words were counted in terms of how many times they appear in the corpus whether or not they were directly related to sex work/prostitution.

References

Adair, V. C. (2002). Branded with infamy: Inscriptions of poverty and class in the United States. *Signs*, 27 (2), 451–71.
Agustín, L. M. (2002). The (crying) need for different kinds of research. *Research for Sex Work*, 5 (June), 30–32.
———. (2004). Alternate ethics or: Telling lies to researchers. *Research for Sex Work*, (June), 6–7.
———. (2005a). At home in the street: Questioning the desire to help and save. In E. Bernstein and L. Schaffner (Eds.) *Regulating sex: The politics of intimacy and identity*. New York: Routledge, 67–82.
———. (2005b). The cultural study of commercial sex. *Sexualities*, 8 (5), 618–31.
———. (2005c). Helping women who sell sex: The construction of benevolent identities. *Rhizomes Neo-Liberal Governmentality: Technologies of the Self and Governmental Conduct*, 10. <http://www.rhizomes.net/issue10/agustin.htm>. Accessed December 2012.
———. (2005d). Migrants in the mistress's house: Other voices in the "trafficking" debate. *Social Politics*, 12 (1), 96–117.
———. (2007). *Sex at the margins: Migration, labour markets and the rescue industry*. London: Zed Books.
Alexander, P. (1987). Prostitution: A difficult issue for feminists. In F. Delecoste and P. Alexander (Eds.) *Sex work: Writings by women in the sex industry*. Pittsburgh: Cleis Press, pp. 184–215.
Alliance for a Safe and Diverse DC. (2008). Move along: Policing sex work in Washington D.C. Different Avenues. <http://dctranscoalition.files.wordpress.com/2010/05/movealongreport.pdf>. Accessed September 2012.
Althusser, L. (1971). Ideology and ideological state apparatuses. Lenin and philosophy and other essays. *Monthly Review Press*. http://www.marxists.org/reference/archive/althusser/1970/ideology.htm. Accessed November 2012.
Anthony, Laurence. (2005). "A Freeware Multi-platform Corpus Analysis Toolkit for the Classroom." IPCC Conference. Limerick, Ireland. Presentation. 13 July 2005. <http://www.antlab.sci.waseda.ac.jp/abstracts/ipcc05_pres_20050713/IPCC_05_Anthony_fin_handouts.pdf>. Accessed March 2006.
Bao, W., Whitbeck, L. B., and Hoyt, D. R. (2000). Abuse, support, and depression among homeless and runaway adolescents. *Journal of Health and Social Behavior*, 41, 408–20.
Bennett, D. (21 Sept. 2012). Supreme court decision in SWUAV—the short version. PIVOT Equality Lifts Everyone. <http://www.pivotlegal.org/scc_decision_in_swuav_a_triumph_for_access_to_justice>. Accessed September 2012.
Bernstein, E. (2007a). The sexual politics of the "new abolitionism." *Differences: Journal of Feminist Cultural Studies*, 18 (3), 128–151.

228 References

———. (2007b). *Temporarily yours: Intimacy, authenticity, and the commerce of sex.* Chicago: The University of Chicago Press.
Britt, E. (2001). *Conceiving normalcy: Rhetoric, law, and the double binds of infertility.* Tuscaloosa: University of Alabama Press.
Brown, B. (2010). *The gifts of imperfection: Let go of who you think you're supposed to be and embrace who you are.* Center City, MN: Hazelden.
Brown, L., Ed. (1993). Prostitute. *The new shorter Oxford English dictionary on historical principles.* New York: Oxford University Press, p. 2386.
Brummett, B. (1991). *Rhetorical dimensions of popular culture.* Tuscaloosa: University of Alabama Press.
Butler, J. (2011). *Bodies that matter: On the discursive limits of "sex."* New York: Routledge.
Campbell, R., and H. Kinnell (2000). "We shouldn't have to put up with this": Street sex work and violence. *Criminal Justice Matters,* 42 (1): 12–13.
Center for Constitutional Rights. Louisiana's crime against nature law: A modern-day scarlet letter. <http://www.ccrjustice.org/files/CCR_ScarletLetter_Factsheet.pdf>. Accessed September 2012.
Chapkis, W. (1997). *Live sex acts: Women performing erotic labor.* New York: Routledge.
———. (2000). Power and control in the commercial sex trade. In R. Weitzer (Ed.), *Sex for sale: Prostitution, pornography, and the sex industry* (181–202). New York: Routledge.
———. (2005). Soft glove, punishing fist: The trafficking victims protection act. In E. Bernstein and L. Shaffner, (Eds.), *Regulating sex.* New York: Routledge.
Chuang, J. (2010). Rescuing trafficking from ideological capture: Prostitution reform and anti-trafficking law and policy. *University of Pennsylvania Law Review,* 158 (1655), 1655–1728.
Cintron, R. (1997). *Angels' town: Chero ways, gang life, and rhetorics of the everyday.* Boston: Beacon Press.
City of Toronto. (2010). Public health champion awards. *Toronto.* March 2010. <http://www.toronto.ca/health/awards/pastwinners.htm>. Accessed August 2012.
Clark, C. S. (1993). Will neighborhood crackdowns curb the sex trade?" *The CQ Researcher Online* 3 (22). 11 June 1993. <http://library.cqpress.com.ezproxy.library.arizona.edu/cqresearcher/cqresrre1993061100>. Accessed December 2005.
Cohen, J., P. Alexander, and C. Wofsy. (1988). Prostitutes and AIDS: Public policy issues. *AIDS and Public Policy* 3: 16–22.
Cooper, M. M. (2011). Rhetorical agency as emergent and enacted. *College Composition and Communication* 62 (3), 420–49.
Crane, G. R. Prostituto. *The Perseus Digital Library.* Ed. Gregory R. Crane. Medford, MA: Tufts University. <http://www.perseus.tufts.edu/cgi-bin/ptext?doc=Perseus%3Atext%3A1999.04.0059%3Aentry%3D%2339094>. Accessed May 13, 2007.
———. Statuo. *The Perseus Digital Library.* Tufts University. <http://www.perseus.tufts.edu/cgi-bin/ptext?doc=Perseus%3Atext%3A1999.04.0059%3Aentry%3D%2345295>. Accessed May 13, 2007.
Curtis, R., K. Terry, M. Dank, K. Dombrowski, and B. Khan (2008). The commercial sexual exploitation of children in New York City. Vol. 1. The CSEC Population in New York City: Size, Characteristics, and Needs. Report submitted to the National Institute of Justice, United States Department of Justice. <http://www.courtinnovation.org/sites/default/files/CSEC_NYC_Volume1.pdf>. Accessed September 2012.
Dalla, R. L. (2001). Et tu brute?: A qualitative analysis of streetwalking prostitutes' interpersonal support networks. *Journal Family Issues,* 22: 1066–85.

———. (2006). 'You can't hustle all your life': An exploratory investigation of the exit process among street-level prostituted women. *Psychology of Women Quarterly*, 30: 276–90.
Dalla, R. L., Xia, Y., and Kennedy, H. (2003). "You just give them what they want and pray they don't kill you": Street-level sex workers' reports of victimization, personal resources, and coping strategies. *Violence Against Women*, 9 (11), 1367–94.
Dewey, S. (2011). *Neon wasteland: On love, motherhood, and sex work in a rust belt town.* Berkeley: University of California Press.
Dewey, S. and P. Kelly (2011). *Policing pleasure: Sex work, policy, and the state in global perspective.* New York: New York University Press.
Ditmore, M. (2008). Sex work, trafficking: Understanding the difference. *RH: Reality check. Reproductive & sexual health and justice news, analysis, and commentary.* <http://www.rhrealitycheck.org/blog/2008/05/05/sex-work-trafficking-understanding-difference>. Accessed May 2009.
Ditmore, M. (2011). Prostitution. In P. J. Quirk and W. Cunion (Eds.), *Governing America, 3-volume set: Major decisions of federal, state, and local governments from 1789 to the present.* New York: Facts on File, 2011, 794–798.
Doezema, J. (2006). Abolitionism. In M. H. Ditmore (Ed.), *Encyclopedia of prostitution and sex work.* Vol 1. Westport, CT: Greenwood Press, 4–7.
———. (2010). *Sex slaves and discourse masters: The construction of trafficking.* London: Zed Books.
Donovan, B. *White slave crusades: Race, gender, and anti-vice activism, 1887–1917.* Urbana: University of Illinois Press.
Duff, P., K. Deering, K. Gibson, M. Tyndall, and K. Shannon. (2011). Homelessness among a cohort of women in street-based sex work: The need for safer environment interventions. *BioMed Central Public Health*, 11 (643), 1–7.
El-Bassel, N., Schilling, R. F., Irwin, K. L., Faruque, S., Gilbert, L., Von Bargen, J., et al. (1997). Sex trading and psychological distress among women recruited from the streets of Harlem. *American Journal of Public Health*, 87, 66–70.
Emerson, R. M., Fretz, R. I., and Shaw, L. L. (1995). *Writing ethnographic fieldnotes.* Chicago Guides to Writing, Editing, and Publishing. Chicago, IL: University of Chicago Press.
Epele, M. E (2002). Gender, violence and HIV: Women's survival in the streets. *Culture, Medicine and Psychiatry* 26: 33–54.
Erickson, P. G., Butters, J., McGillicuddy, P., and Hallgren, A. (2000). Crack and prostitution: Gender, myths, and experiences. *Journal of Drug Issues*, 30, 767–788.
Farley, M., (Ed.). (2003). *Prostitution, trafficking, and traumatic stress.* Binghamton, NY: Haworth Press.
Federal Bureau of Investigation. Easy access to FBI arrest statistics: 1994–2009. <http://www.ojjdp.gov/ojstatbb/ezaucr/asp/ucr_display.asp.> April 25, 2012.
Flaherty, J. (15 January 2010a). Her crime: sex work in New Orleans. *Huffington Post.* The blog. <http://www.huffingtonpost.com/jordan-flaherty/her-crime-sex-work-in-new_b_424774.html>. Accessed September 2012.
———. (20 April 2010b). New complaints of police violence in New Orleans. Huffington Post. The Blog. <http://www.huffingtonpost.com/jordan-flaherty/new-complaints-of-police_b_544335.html.> Accessed September 2012.
———. (17 March 2011a). Federal civil rights suit challenges Louisiana's felony sex work law. ColorLines for Action. <http://colorlines.com/archives/2011/03/federal_civil_rights_suit_challenges_louisianas_felony_sex_work_law.html>. Accessed September 2012.
———. (29 June 2011b). Sex offender registration for sex workers ends in Louisiana. *The Louisiana Justice Institute.* <http://louisianajusticeinstitute.blogspot.

com/2011/06/sex-offender-registration-for-sex.html>. Accessed September 2012.
Frye, M. (1983). *The politics of reality: Essays in feminist theory*. Freedom, CA: The Crossing Press.
Gordon, A. F. (2008). *Ghostly matters: Haunting and the sociological imagination*. Minneapolis, MN: University of Minnesota Press.
Gulliver, Tonya. (2011). Mourning the passing of Wendy Babcock. *Rabble.Ca*. August 16, 2011. <http://rabble.ca/news/2011/08/mourning-passing-wendy-babcock>. Accessed August 5, 2012.
Haraway, D. (1988). Situated knowledges: The science question in feminism and the privilege of partial perspective. *Feminist Studies*, 14 (3), 575–600.
Harding, R. and P. Hamilton. (2009). Working girls: Abuse or choice in street-level sex work? A study of homeless women in Nottingham. *British Journal of Social Work*, 39, 1118–1137.
Harper, D. Prostitute. *Online Etymology Dictionary*. Douglas Harper. <http://www.etymonline.com/index.php?search=prostitute&searchmode=none>. Accessed 4 April 2007.
INCITE! Women of Color Against Violence. (22 April 2011). No simple solutions: State violence and the sex trades. < http://inciteblog.wordpress.com/2011/04/22/no-simple-solutions-state-violence-and-the-sex-trades/>. Accessed September 2012.
Jeffreys, S. (2008). *The idea of prostitution*. North Melbourne, Victoria: Spinifex Press.
———. (2009). *The industrial vagina: The political economy of the global sex trade*. New York: Routledge.
Jewell, E. J. and F. Abate. (2001). Prostitute. *The new Oxford American dictionary*. Oxford University Press, New York. p. 1369.
'Juliet.' (2006). Prostitution shake-up: One sex worker's view, *British Medical Journal*, 332, 245.
Kail, B. L., Watson, D. D., and Ray, S. (1995). Needle-using practices within the sex industry. *American Journal of Drug and Alcohol Abuse*, 21 (2), 241–56.
Kempadoo, K. and Doezema, J. (1998). *Global sex workers: Rights, resistance, and redefinition*. London: Routledge.
Koyama, E. (2012). Anti-criminalization: Criminalization happens on the ground, not in the legislature. Eminism.org. <http://eminism.org/blog/entry/362>. Accessed December 2012.
Krishnamurti, J. (1968). *Talks and dialogues: Saanen, 1967*. Servire/Wassenaar, The Netherlands.
Kulick, D. (1998). *Travestí: Sex, gender, and culture among Brazilian transgendered prostitutes*. Chicago: University of Chicago Press.
Kuo, L. (2002). *Prostitution policy: Revolutionizing practice through a gendered perspective*. New York: New York University Press.
Kurtz, S. P., Surratt, H. L., Inciardi, J. A., and Kiley, M. C. (2004). Sex work and "date" violence. *Violence Against Women*, 10 (4), 357–85.
Kurtz, S. P., Surratt, H. L., Kiley, M. C., and Inciardi, J. A. (2005). Barriers to health and social services for street-based sex workers. *Journal of Health Care for the Poor and Underserved*, 16, p. 345–361.
Lazarus, L. J. Chettiar, K. Deering, R. Nabess, and K. Shannon. (2011). Risky health environments: Women sex workers' struggles to find safe, secure, and non-exploitative housing in Canada's poorest postal code. *Social Science & Medicine*, 73 (11), 1600–07.
Leigh, C. (1994). Prostitution in the United States: The statistics. *Gauntlet*, 1 (7), p. 17–18.
———. (1997). Inventing sex work. In J. Nagle (Ed.), *Whores and other feminists*. New York: Routledge, 225–31.

Lerum, K., K. McCurtis, P. Saunders, and S. Wahab. (2012). Using human rights to hold the US accountable for its anti-sex trafficking agenda: The universal periodic review and new directions for US policy. *Anti-Trafficking Review*, 1, 80–103.
Lutnick, A., and D. Cohan. (2009). Criminalization, legalization or decriminalization of sex work: What female sex workers say in San Francisco, USA. *Reproductive Health Matters*, 17 (34), 38–46.
M°ansson, S. A., and U. C. Hedin. (1999). Breaking the Matthew effect on women leaving prostitution. *International Journal of Social Welfare*, 8, 67–77.
Marcus, G. E. (1995). Ethnography in/of the world system: The emergence of multi-sited thnography. *Annual Review of Anthropology*, 24, 95–117.
———. (1999). *Critical anthropology now: Unexpected contexts, shifting constituencies, changing agendas*. Santa Fe, New Mexico: School of American Research Press.
Marshall, C. (2004). "Bid to decriminalize prostitution in Berkeley." *The New York Times* September 14 2004, Late ed., sec. A: 16, Column 4.
Martin, E. (1992). *The woman in the body: A cultural analysis of reproduction*. Boston: Beacon Press.
Matthews, D. L. (1999). "Definitions." <http://cydathria.com/ms_donna/tg_def.html#cisgender>. Accessed June 30, 2012.
Maxwell, S. R., and Maxwell, C. D. (2000). Examining the "criminal careers" of prostitutes within the nexus of drug use, drug selling, and other illicit activities. *Criminology*, 38, 787–809.
McArdle, A. L. and T. Erzen, Eds. (2001). *Zero tolerance: Quality of life and the new police brutality in New York City*. New York: New York University Press.
McClintock, A. (1993). Sex workers and sex work: Introduction. *Social Text*, 37 (Winter), 1–10.
McCracken, J. (2006a). Pimp. In M. H. Ditmore (Ed.), *Encyclopedia of prostitution and sex work*. Vol 2. Westport, CT: Greenwood Press, 359.
McCracken, J. (2006b). Resident activism. In M. H. Ditmore (Ed.), *Encyclopedia of prostitution and sex work*. Vol 2. Westport, CT: Greenwood Press, 398–400.
McCracken, J. (2010). "Street sex work: Re/Constructing discourse from margin to center." *Community Literacy Journal*, 4 (2), 1–18.
McCracken, J. (2011). "Some of them they do right; Some of them they do wrong": Moral ambiguity and the criteria for help among street sex workers. *Wagadu*, 9 (Spring), 189–216.
McCracken, J., J. Thukral, and E. C. Savino. (2006). Street-based prostitution. In M. H. Ditmore (Ed.), *Encyclopedia of prostitution and sex work*. Vol. 2. Westport, CT: Greenwood Press, 465–66.
Monto, M. A. (2004). Female prostitution, customers, and violence. *Violence Against Women*, 10 (2), 160–188.
Moss, B. (2011). Literate activity and behavior. *Community Literacy Journal*, 5 (1), 1–24.
Nagle, J., Ed. (1997). *Whores and other feminists*. New York: Routledge.
Norton-Hawk, M. (2004). A comparison of pimp- and non-pimp-controlled women. *Violence Against Women*, 10 (2), 189–94.
Pheterson, G. (1989). Not repeating history. In G. Pheterson (Ed.), *A Vindication of the rights of whores*, Seattle: Seal Press, 3–30.
———. (1990). The category 'prostitute' in scientific inquiry. *The Journal of Sex Research*, 27 (3), 397–407.
———. (1999). Prostitutes, ponces and poncing: Making sense of violence. In J. Seymour and P. Bagguley, (Eds.), *Relating intimacies: Power and resistance*. London: Macmillan.
Phoenix, J. (2000). Prostitute identities: Men, money and violence. *British Journal of Criminology*, 40, 37–55.

Piano, D. (2011). Working the streets of post-Katrina New Orleans: An interview with Deon Haywood, Executive Director, Women with a Vision, Inc. *Women's Studies Quarterly*, 39 (3/4), 201–18.
Porter, J. and Bonilla, L. (2010). The ecology of street prostitution. In R. J. Weitzer (Ed.), *Sex for sale: Prostitution, pornography, and the sex industry*, 2nd ed. (163–185). New York: Routledge.
Potterat, J. J., R. B. Rothenberg, S. Q. Muth, W. W. Darrow, and L. Phillips-Plummer (1998). Pathways to prostitution: The chronology of sexual and drug abuse milestones. *The Journal of Sex Research*, 35 (4), 333–340.
PROS Network. (2012). Public health crisis: The impact of using condoms as evidence of prostitution in New York City. Report published April 2012. <http://sexworkersproject.org/downloads/2012/20120417-public-health-crisis.pdf>. Accessed September 2012.
Quinet, K. (2011). Prostitutes as victims of serial homicide: Trends and case characteristics, 1970–2009. *Homicide Studies*, 15 (1), 74–100.
Ramage, J. D. (2006). *Rhetoric: A user's guide*. New York: Pearson Education.
Raphael, J. and Shapiro, D. L. (2004). Violence in indoor and outdoor prostitution venues. *Violence Against Women*, 10 (2), p. 126–139.
Rapp, R. (1999). *Testing women, testing the fetus: The social impact of amniocentesis in America*. New York: Routledge.
Ratner, M. S. (1993). *Crack pipe as pimp: An ethnographic investigation of sex-for-crack exchanges*. New York: Lexington Books.
Raymond, J. (2003). Ten reasons for not legalizing prostitution and a legal response to the demand for prostitution. *Journal of Trauma Practice*, 2, p. 315–332.
Ritchie, A. and J. L. Mogul. (2007). In the shadows of the war on terror: Persistent police brutality and abuse of people of color in the United States. <http://www2.ohchr.org/english/bodies/cerd/docs/ngos/usa/USHRN15.pdf>. Accessed September 2012.
Roche, B., Neaigus, A., and Miller, M. (2005). Street smarts and urban myths: Women, sex work, and the role of storytelling in risk reduction and rationalization. *Medical Anthropology Quarterly*. 19 (2), 149–70.
Romero-Daza, N., Weeks, M., and Singer, M. (2003). "Nobody give a damn if I live or die": Violence, drugs, and street-level prostitution in inner-city Hartford, Connecticut. *Medical Anthropology*, 22, 233–59.
———. (2005). Conceptualizing the impact of indirect violence on HIV risk among women involved in street-level prostitution. *Aggression and Violent Behavior*, 10, 153–170.
Royster, J. J. (2000). *Traces of a stream: Literacy and social change among African American women*. Pittsburgh: University of Pittsburgh Press.
Sanders, T. (2005). *Sex work: A risky business*. Portland, Oregon: Willan Publishing.
San Francisco Task Force on Prostitution. (1996). Documents: Condoms as evidence. Final report March 1996. <http://bayswan.org/CondomsAsEvidenceS-FTFP.pdf.>. Accessed September 2012.
Saunders, P. (2004). Prohibiting sex work projects, restricting women's rights: The international impact of the 2003 U.S. Global AIDS Act. *Health and Human Rights*, 7 (2), 179–92.
Sausa, L.A., J. Keatley, and D. Operario. (2007). Perceived risks and benefits of sex work among transgender women of color in San Francisco. *Archives of Sexual Behavior*, 36 (6), 768–77.
Segrave, M., S. Milivojevic, and S. Pickering. (2009). *Sex trafficking: International context and response*. Devon, UK: Willan Publishing.
Sex Industry Worker Safety Action Group (SISWAG). (2009, July 30). SISWAG-Outline. http://vancouver.ca/police/diversity/2009/SISWAG-outline.pdf. Accessed August 2009.

References 233

Sex Workers Outreach Project (SWOP) USA. International Day to End Violence Against Sex Workers. <http://www.swopusa.org/dec17/>. Accessed September 2012.

———. (2004). Why You Should Vote Yes on Measure Q. 23 October 2004. <http://www.swop-usa.org/>. Accessed September 8, 2006.

Sex Workers Project. (2009). Use of raids to fight trafficking in persons. SWP. <http://www.urbanjustice.org/pdf/publications/Kicking_Down_The Door_Exec_Sum.pdf>. Accessed September 2012.

———. (2011). New York State Assembly Bill A1008/S323. Sex Workers Project. <http://sexworkersproject.org/campaigns/2011/new-york-condom-bill/>. Accessed September 2012.

Shannon, K., V. Bright, S. Allinott, D. Alexson, K. Gibson, and M. W. Tyndall. (2007). Community-based HIV prevention research among substance using women in survival sex work: The Maka Project Partnership. *Harm Reduction Journal*, 4 (20), 20–26.

Shannon, K., T. Kerr, S. Allinott, J. Chettiar, J. Shoveller, and M. W. Tyndall. (2008). Social and structural violence and power relations in mitigating HIV risk of drug-using women in survival sex work. *Social Science & Medicine*, 66, 911–21.

Shannon, K., T. Kerr, S. A. Strathdee, J. Shoveller, J. S. Montaner, and M. W. Tyndall. (2009a). Prevalence and structural correlates of gender based violence among a prospective cohort of female sex workers. *BMJ*, 339, 2939.

Shannon, K., S. A. Strathdee, J. Shoveller, M. Rusch, T. Kerr, and M. W. Tyndall (2009b). Structural and environmental barriers to condom use negotiation with clients among female sex workers: Implications for HIV-prevention strategies and policy. *American Journal of Public Health*, 99 (4), 659–65.

Sherlock, T. (2011). A new home leads to new lease on life. *Vancouver Sun*. 16 Aug 2011. West Coast News, p. A4.

Smart Voter. (2009, Jan 24). Proposition K: Changing the enforcement of laws related to prostitution and sex workers. City of San Francisco. <http://www.smartvoter.org/2008/11/04/ca/sf/prop/K/>. Accessed September 7, 2012.

Soderlund, G. (2005). Running from the rescuers: New U.S. crusades against sex trafficking and the rhetoric of abolition. *National Women's Studies Association Journal*, 17 (3), 54–87.

Spittal, P. M., J. Bruneau, K. J. P. Craib, C. Miller, F. Lamothe, A. E. Weber, K. Li, M. W. Tyndall, M. V. O'Shaughnessy, and M. T. Schechter. (2003). Surviving the sex trade: a comparison of HIV risk behaviors among street-involved women in two Canadian cities who inject drugs. *AIDS Care*, 15 (2), 187–95.

Starhawk (1990). *Truth or dare: Encounters with power, authority, and mystery*. San Francisco: Harper San Francisco.

Starr, P. (2011, June 28). Clinton: Meeting with 'sex workers' is 'people-to-people diplomacy at its best'. *CNS News*. Retrieved from <http://www.cnsnews.com/news/article/hillary-state-dept-officers-meeting-sex>. Accessed July 14, 2011.

State of Texas. (2003, Sept 1). Penal Code. Title 9. Offenses against public order and decency. Chapter 43. Public indecency. Subchapter A. Prostitution. <http://www.statutes.legis.state.tx.us/docs/PE/htm/PE.43.htm>. Accessed September 2012.

Sterks, C. (2000). *Tricking and tripping: Prostitution in the era of AIDS*. New York: Social Change Press.

Sullivan, M. L. (2007). *Making sex work: A failed experiment with legalised prostitution*. North Melbourne, Victoria: Spinifex Press.

Surratt, H. L., Kurtz, S. P., Weaver, J. C., and Inciardi, J. A. (2005). The connections of mental health problems, violent life experiences, and the social milieu of the "stroll" with the HIV risk behaviors of female street sex workers. *Journal of Psychology and Human Sexuality*, 17 (1/2), 23–44.

Thorbek, S. (2002). Introduction: Prostitution in a global context: Changing patterns. In S. Thorbek and B. Pattanaik (Eds). *Transnational prostitution: Changing global patterns*. New York: Zed Books, 1–9.

Thukral, J. (2006) Prohibition. In M. H. Ditmore (Ed.), *Encyclopedia of prostitution and sex work*. Vol. 2. Westport, CT: Greenwood Press, 369.

United States Government. (2010, January 20). Victims of Trafficking and Violence Protection Act of 2000. http://www.state.gov/documents/organization/10492.pdf. Accessed September 2012.

Valera, J., R. G. Sawyer, and G. R. Schiraldi. (2001). Perceived health needs of inner-city street prostitutes: A preliminary study. *American Journal of Health Behavior*, 25 (1), 50.

Vance, C. (2010). Thinking trafficking, thinking sex. *Gay & Lesbian Quarterly*, 17 (1), 135–43.

Vorenberg, E. and J. Vorenberg. (1977). The biggest pimp of all: Prostitution and some facts of life. *Atlantic Monthly*, January, 27–38.

Wahab, S. (2004). Tricks of the trade: What social workers can learn about female sex worker through dialogue. *Qualitative Sex Work*, 3 (2), 139–60.

———. (2006). Evaluating the usefulness of a prostitution diversion project. *Qualitative Social Work*. 5, 67–92.

Wallace, J. I., Porter, J., Weiner, A., and Steinberg, A. (1997). Oral sex, crack smoking, and HIV infection among female sex workers who do not inject drugs. *American Journal of Public Health*, 87 (3), 470.

Ward, M. (2012, August 25). Texas rethinks law making repeat prostitution a felony. *Austin American Statesman*. <http://www.statesman.com/news/texas-politics/texas-rethinks-law-making-repeat-prostitution-a-felony-2442512.html>. Accessed September 7, 2012.

Weidner, R. R. (2001). *I won't do Manhattan: Causes and consequences of a decline in street prostitution*. New York: LFB Scholarly Publishing.

Weiner, A. (1996). Understanding the social needs of streetwalking prostitutes. *Social Work*, 41 (1), 97–105.

Weinkauf, K. (2011). 'Yeah, he's my daddy': Linguistic constructions of fictive kinships in a street-level sex work community. *Wagadu*, 9 (Spring), 14–33.

Weitzer, R. J. (1994). Community groups vs. prostitutes. *Gauntlet* 1, 121–24.

———. (2000a). The politics of prostitution in America. In R. J. Weitzer (Ed.), *Sex for sale: Prostitution, pornography, and the sex industry*. New York: Routledge, 159–80.

———. (2000b). Why we need more research on sex work. In R. J. Weitzer (Ed.), *Sex for sale: Prostitution, pornography, and the sex industry* (1–13). New York, NY: Routledge.

———. (2007). The social construction of sex trafficking: Ideology and institutionalization of a moral crusade. *Politics & Society* 35 (3), 447–75.

———. (2009). Sociology of sex work. *Annual Review of Sociology*, 35, 213–34.

———. (2010). *Sex for sale: Prostitution, pornography, and the sex industry*, 2nd edition. New York: Routledge.

———. (2012). *Legalizing prostitution: From illicit vice to lawful business*. New York: New York University Press.

West Coast LEAF. Mission Statement. <http://www.westcoastleaf.org/index.php?pageID=224&parentid=6>. Accessed September 2013.

———. (26 Sept. 2012). SCC decision affirms equal access to justice for marginalized groups. <http://www.westcoastleaf.org/index.php?newsid=222&pageID=1>. Accessed September 2012.

Williamson, C. and T. Cluse-Tolar. (2002). Pimp-controlled prostitution: Still an integral part of street life. *Violence Against Women*, 8, 1074–92.

Williamson, C. and G. Folaron. (2003). Understanding the experiences of street level prostitutes. *Qualitative Social Work*, 2, 271–87.
Wolcott, H. F. (1999). *Ethnography: A way of seeing*. Walnut Creek, CA: Altamira Press.
────── (2005). *The art of fieldwork*. 2nd ed. Walnut Creek, CA: Altamira Press.
Women With A Vision. (29 June 2011). New Orleans groups applaud change in "Scarlet Letter" law. <http://wwav-no.org/new-orleans-groups-applaud-change-in-%E2%80%9Cscarlet-letter%E2%80%9D-law>. Accessed September 2012.
Young, A. M., C. Boyd, and A. Hubbell. (2000). Prostitution, drug use, and coping with psychological distress. *Journal of Drug Issues*, 30, 789–800.

Index

A
abuse, childhood, 36–37, 88, 95, 102–103, 177; origins of, 125; physical, 73, 90–91, 97, 108,147; by police, 10; sexual, 35–36, 37, 96, 136–139, 220n8; substance, *see* drug abuse; *see also* trauma, abuse and neglect
Adair, Vivian, 90
Adele Weiner, xxv, 115
agency, and language, 161–162; and representation, 89
agential choice, xxix, xxxii–xxxiii,12, 45, 76, 82, 129, 132–166; and choosing sex work, 147–150; and decriminalization, 139–145; opportunities for, 150–151; as process, 157–158
Agustín, Laura, xvii, 100, 103–104, 164, 191, 220n2, 221n5n11
analysis, contextual, xvii, 14, 134, 142, 147, 157, 201, 203, 219n4, 220n7
anti-criminalization, 162
arrests, as access to services, 70–77, 83, 104; alternatives to, 78–83; criminalization and, xxii–xxiii, 16; criminal status and, 56–59; effect on negotiations, 58, 69, 70; fear of, 53, 58, 69ills, 78, 132; impact on lives, 65–66, 90, 172–173, 175; as material condition, xxii, 3; Nemez penalties, xxiii; as solution, xxxii, 22–23, 78,104; as solution and problem, 59; statistics, 58, 91, 221n9, 225n15; as viewed by sex worker, 61–62

authentic choice, xxix, xxxii, 132–134, 147

B
birdcage, 24–25, 114, 118; as cage of oppression, 132–166
Bonilla, Louis, 40, 58, 115, 119,
Brown, Brené, 158,
Brummett, Barry, xxxi, 1–2, 5, 135, 219
Butler, Judith, xxxi, 7–13

C
Casa Segura, xvii, 51, 75, 88, 111, 120–121, 167, 174, 192, 198, 223n1n3
Center for Constitutional Rights, 143–144
change, impediments to, xxxii, 119–125; opportunity to, 83–97
Chapkis, Wendy, xv, 16, 40, 55, 102, 115, 141, 159, 218n15
choice, agential, *see* agential choice
co-constructs, 8, 130, 133
co-creation, xxvii, xxx, xxxiii, 2,13, 105, 134, 166; of solutions, xx; of values, xix;
collages, ideological, xxix–xxxi, 1–13, 82, 128, 150
condoms (health control and safety), 15, 40, 65, 110–114, 153
control, lack of, xxvi, 31, 40, 56, 58, 70, 85–86, 99, 106, 108–109, 117, 132, 147–148; drug use and, 108–109; one's health and, 155–156, 181
Cooper, Marilyn, xxxii, 11–12, 132, 133, 135, 150, 219n4

238 Index

Council on Prostitution, The, 130
COYOTE, 58, 100
Crime Against Nature law, 143–145
criminalization, general, xxii, xxvii, xxix, xxxi, 55–82, 150, 162; as agent of violence, 9–10, 59, 106–107, 131, 139, 141, 161–166; as door to services, 70–72; as problem, xxxii, 69ills, 135, 140, 148, 162; as solution, 15–16, 24, 59, 100; solution or problem, 65–70; *see also* arrests

D
Dalla, Rochelle, 36, 157
decriminalization, xxxii–xxxiii, 139–145, 162
Ditmore, Melissa, 56–57
diversion program/project, 74–75, 88, 91, 103, 187
Donovan, Brian, 56
Dover Project, xxiii
drugs, abuse xxvii–xxxi, 12, 14, 25, 28, 31, 38–54, 89, 93–94, 104, 111, 127–128; exchanging sex for, xvi–xxiii, xxv, xxvii, xxviii, xxix, xxx, 8, 11–13, 14, 16, 35, 40, 45, 47–49, 53–54, 55, 58, 60, 63–67, 73, 78, 81–91, 96, 98, 100–109, 113–119, 123, 126, 128, 131–136, 140–141, 147–149, 164, 169, 182, 185, 188, 191–198, 199–201, 205, 207, 219n25, 220n8, 222n5; treatment, 62, 72, 76–78, 81, 127–128, 161; reasons for using, 34–49; reasons for not using, 49–54; relationship with prostitution, 42–49; and systemic responsibility 41ills, 54

E
ethnography, xvii–xviii, xxxi, 72, 191–192

F
feminism, *see* prostitution, feminism and
Freeman, Walter J., 135
Frye, Marilyn, 25, 114, 118

G
Gordon, Avery, xxii, 71
Grant, Emily, 156

Gulliver, Tonya, 139

H
amilton, Paul, 100, 139, 149–150
Harding, Rachel, 100, 138–139, 149–150
harm reduction, 101, 157, 165, 190
Haywood, Deon, 144, 157

I
identity, prostitution as, xix, 5
ideology, as agent, xxix, xxxii, 5, 54, 90, 95, 104, 125, 135, 150, 154, 157, 164–166; embedded, xviii–xix, 2, 129, 132, 192, 223
INCITE! 9, 57, 165
International Day to End Violence Against Sex Workers, 131
interviewees: *see* public figures; women; police

J
Jeffreys, Sheila, 55

K
kaleidoscope, as framework, xxxi, 6–7, 12–14, 135, 139. 150, 201
Karras, 5, 100
Kempadoo, Kamala, 57, 73, 100, 101
Kuo, Lenore, 11

L
language, as problem, 117; awareness of, xix; as condition, xxxi; as related to stigma, 118; as related to street-based sex work, xvi–xviii, xx–xxi, xxvii–xxviii, xxx, xxxii
Leigh, Carol, 58–51, 100–101
Lerner, 5, 100

M
mainstream, xxvii, 8–9, 78, 96, 103, 201
Mann Act, 56
marginalization, i, xxii, xxvii, xxxi, 9–10, 56–57, 70–97
material bodies, 7–8, 163
material conditions, i, xvi–xxxiii, 1–13, 26–31, 34, 46, 57, 70, 78, 104–106, 118, 127, 130, 135–135, 145, 157, 162–163, 166, 192–193, 201–202, 207, 224n8; fixed, 2–5, 13, 70, 106;

Index 239

influential, 2–5, 12–13, 25, 70, 106
McClintock, Anne, 97, 134, 140
molestation, 34–37, 102, 171, 176, 185
morality, xxviii, xxxii, 7–9, 55–56, 59–66, 127, 133, 164, 166
mosaics, 5–6, 12, 135, 201, 219n1; as entity, 6
Moss, Beverly, 5

N
neighborhood, broken window theory, 21–23; as victim, 14–54, 66, 79–84, 91–93; response to prostitution, 72, 104, 116, 141, 162
neighborhood associations, xvi-xxv, 16–23, 72, 83, 91–92, 116
Nemez, attitude toward sex industry, xxiv; as material condition of street based sex work xxi-xxix
newspaper, as site of analysis, xvi-xvii, 15–16, 24–25, 34, 38, 46, 53, 83, 88–96, 128, 144, 193–194, 200–208; frequency of terminology, 209–210;
normative regime, 8–9, 11, 13

O
opportunities, for change, xviii-xix, 7, 55, 74, 103–105, 127, 135, 142, 150–153, 159
oppression, 104, 219n; cages of, 132–167; of sex workers, xxii, xxvii-xxviii, 25, 73, 130

P
pattern, 5–6, 53, 135; of discrimination, 142
performativity, 11
personhood, 137, 161–162, 166; complex, xxii, 71–72
Pheterson, Gail, 97, 101–102, 115
pimps, xxvi-xxvii, 17–18, 22, 58, 104, 109,140, 215, 219n26, 221n8
police, interviewed: Matthews, Ofc. Eugene, 18, 67–68, 73, 74–75, 78, 80, 87, 110–111, 114, 120–121, 188; Castillo, Ofc. Jennifer, 21–22, 40, 67, 87–88, 121, 186–187; Johnson, Ofc. Eric, 17–18, 21, 75, 79, 120, 187; Hixson, Ofc. Tom, xxiii, 19, 20–21, 37–38, 74, 187
polymorphous paradigm, 104

Porter, Judith, xxv, 40, 58,115, 119, 219,
poverty, as defined by public figures, 34; as systemic problem xxvii-xxviii, xxx, 14, 20–26 55, 65, 73, 78, 90, 93–96, 125–128, 146; surviving, 31–34, 37, 51, 102–106, 114, 134, 140
power: over, with, within, 132–135, 166; and status, 163
prostitutes, material reality of, 7–11; news treatment of (see newspaper); as entity, 5
prostitution (see criminalization); legalization of, 64–65,139,150; morality of, 59–64; as non-victimless crime, 16–18 and STDs, xxv-xxvi, 18–21, 111, 205
public figures interviewed: Adele, 83, 186; Alvarez, Dr. Veronica, 34,73–74, 112, 122, 146, 151–154, 186; Chelley, 22–23, 33, 110, 116, 145–146, 187; Evelyn, 85–86, 157–158, 187; Everett, Dr. Julie, 154–155, 187, 218n10; Kristina, 77, 121–122, 188; Lily, 37, 96–97, 103, 107, 111–112, 116, 118, 149, 156, 188; Linda, 188; Joan, xxiv-xxv, 20, 22–23, 33, 55, 65, 68, 80, 107–108, 116, 146, 188; Rosalie, 33–34, 108, 188; Russell, 19, 21, 76, 79–80, 189; Sarah, 105, 189; Shepherd, Dr. Annie, 34–35, 46, 98, 112–113, 189; Sue, 16–17, 21, 23, 79, 83, 189; Sylvia, 32–33, 45–46, 72, 87, 88, 102–103, 106–107, 114, 116–117, 119, 122, 125–126, 189;

Q
Quinet, Kenna, 10
quotidian rhetoric, xxxi, 1–13, 166

R
Ramage, John, 161
research directions, 164
responsibility, and choice, 83–97; moving from victim to, 85–88; personal (ideology), xxix, xxxii, 2, 12, 54, 56, 78, 82, 88–89, 93–95, 104, 111–114, 120–121, 125–127, 132–136, 153,

161–163, 166; systemic, xxvii, xxxii, 54, 96, 125–129, 136, 143, 145, 153, 158
resource availability, xxiii, 56, 75, 79, 126–128, 140–145, 153, 156, 188; exchange sex for, 49; lack of, xxvi-xxviii, 34, 36–37, 49, 65, 78, 119, 121–122, 150
rhetorical agency, xxxii, 11–13, 134–136, 145–150, 165–166
rhetorical analysis, xviii-xix, xxviii, 201–202
Roche, Neaigus & Miller, 66
Romero-Daza, 130
Royster, Jacqueline Jones, xxvii, 6

S
Sanders, Teela, 55, 73
SCAN, see Crimes Against Nature
sex industry, xix-xxi
sex trafficking, 9–10, 162–163, 218n16, 220n2n5; definition, 57
sex work, definition, xix; and society: systemic opportunities, 159–161
sex worker, as entity, xxi, 106; importance in solution, 162; victim or criminal, 72–78
Sherlock, Tracy, 156
Sprinkle, Annie, 131
Starhawk, power, xxxii, 132–133
St. James, Margo, 9
stigma, of sex work, xxiv, xxvii, xxxii, 25, 31, 42, 73, 97, 100, 114–119, 131, 134, 141, 148–149, 161, 164, 189; problems related to, 119; perpetuating the victim, 114–119
SWUAV (Sex Workers United Against Violence Society), 142
systemic violence, 98–131; and responsibility, 125–129; and justice, 162–166

T
Thukral, Juhu, xx, 100

trauma, 123, 136, 141, 151; abuse and neglect, 14, 25, 31, 34–54, 106, 114, 136; coping with, 34–42
TVPA (Trafficking Victims Protection Act), 57

V
victim, definition, 99–100; status, 10, 14–15, 25, 61, 73, 74, 84–86, 93–94, 98–131, 166; rethinking, 151–159; replacing with agential choice, 136–139; vulnerable to, 69; systemic, 98–131; see also criminalization
violence, safety and health, 106–114

W
Wahab, Stéphanie, xvii, 103
White Slave Traffic Act, 56
Weitzer, Ronald, 15, 36, 58, 73, 117, 140–141, 217–218n8
women, interviewed: Anna, 27, 32–33, 63, 167; Ava, 30–31, 39–40, 82, 126, 167–168; Brenda, 31–32, 42–43, 45, 47–50, 84, 109, 132, 168–169; Denise, 27–28, 32, 60–61, 64, 169–170; Donna, 29–30, 33–34, 50–51, 66, 98, 109, 114–115, 170–173; Eve, 173; Julie, 30, 35–36, 48, 52, 63, 65, 78, 84, 95, 115, 173–174, 198; Karen, 126, 136, 149, 174–176; Laura, 61, 109–110, 114, 176–177; Linda, 177–178; Lisa, 28–29, 45, 62–63, 68–69, 77, 127, 178–179; Lourdes, 179–180; Olivia, 49, 60, 70–71, 98 126, 180; Sandy, 39, 43–44, 45, 52–53, 108, 110, 180–182; Tess, 63–64, 182; Tiffany, 26–27, 109, 182–184; Vicki, 64–65, 184–185
WWAV, Women with a Vision, 143–145

CPSIA information can be obtained
at www.ICGtesting.com
Printed in the USA
BVHW062139031218
534694BV00014B/176/P